TRACING YOUR SERVICE WOMEN ANCESTORS

FAMILY HISTORY FROM PEN & SWORD

TRACING YOUR SERVICE WOMEN ANCESTORS

A Guide for Family Historians

Mary Ingham

Pen & Sword
FAMILY HISTORY

First published in Great Britain in 2012 by
PEN & SWORD FAMILY HISTORY
an imprint of
Pen & Sword Books Ltd
47 Church Street
Barnsley
South Yorkshire
S70 2AS

ISBN 978 1 84884 173 4

A CIP catalogue record for this book is
available from the British Library.

Typeset in Palatino and Optima by
Phoenix Typesetting, Auldgirth, Dumfriesshire

Printed and bound by
CPI Group (UK) Ltd., Croydon, CR0 4YY

Pen & Sword Books Ltd incorporates the imprints of
Pen & Sword Aviation, Pen & Sword Family History, Pen & Sword Maritime,
Pen & Sword Military, Pen & Sword Discovery, Wharncliffe Local History,
Wharncliffe True Crime, Wharncliffe Transport, Pen & Sword Select, Pen &
Sword Military Classics, Leo Cooper, The Praetorian Press, Remember When,
Seaforth Publishing and Frontline Publishing

For a complete list of Pen & Sword titles please contact
PEN & SWORD BOOKS LIMITED
47 Church Street, Barnsley, South Yorkshire, S70 2AS, England
E-mail: enquiries@pen-and-sword.co.uk
Website: www.pen-and-sword.co.uk

CONTENTS

ACKNOWLEDGEMENTS

I am most grateful to the staff of the archives, libraries and museums mentioned in this book. They kindly gave their time and took trouble to answer my questions, source photographs, etc. I am particularly indebted to Sarah Paterson at the Imperial War Museum and Julia Massey at the Queen Alexandra's Royal Naval Nursing Service archive. Any errors and omissions are my own.

As well as giving encouragement and support, Peter White most generously granted access to his impressive photographic postcard collection, bringing to life the women described in these pages. Paul White's continued interest, Debbie Beavis's valuable input and Alison Miles's careful attention to detail were much appreciated.

I am grateful to Simon Fowler and Rupert Harding at Pen & Sword for their patient encouragement, and to David Lister for his stoic support.

Illustrations that are not otherwise credited are part of my own collection.

PREFACE

Military service records open a fascinating window on the lives of our ancestors through documentary sources that would otherwise never have been preserved.

Since the nineteenth century, women have increasingly worked alongside the armed services. Tens of thousands served in the First World War, pioneering new roles and overturning prejudices about women's physical and mental capacities.

Most guides to tracing service ancestors offer only a brief section on the women. This book attempts, within the space constraints of covering so many different services, to remedy that. It is dedicated to my Great Aunt Lizzie (Betsy Elizabeth), in search of whom I began exploring nursing service records nearly twenty years ago. Sadly, she still eludes me, but my search for her uncovered many other people's great aunts, grandmothers and great-grandmothers who engaged my interest, enthusiasm and admiration. Without her, and certainly without them, this book wouldn't have been written.

I hope it will help you find the woman you are researching, whether she is a blood or a spiritual ancestor. It should help you to learn more about the part women have played in recent history; I have certainly learnt a lot researching it.

If this is your first foray into family history research, it may be useful to read the section of the Introduction headed 'Getting Started'.

INTRODUCTION

This guide aims to help you research women who worked alongside the armed forces from the 1850s to the 1920s, the main period for which records are currently in the public domain. Some earlier naval nursing records are mentioned. Crimea nurses are included and the Boer War is covered. The main focus, however, is on the First World War, when tens of thousands of ordinary women pioneered the women's auxiliary services, driving lorries and taking on men's semi-skilled technical jobs, as well as the more traditional women's work of catering, cleaning and nursing the sick and wounded.

Structure of the Book

It seemed only right to begin with the first official body of women employed by the armed services – army schoolmistresses. The chapters are otherwise divided into two main sections, the first covering medical services of the army, navy and air force. This section begins with army nursing, arranged chronologically. An explanation of the organization of army hospital care precedes the chapters on the First World War, which include army nurses, Voluntary Aid Detachment (VAD) members, masseuses, the First Aid Nursing Yeomanry (FANY), women doctors employed by the armed forces and the Royal Air Force nursing service, followed by a short section on Queen Alexandra's Military Families Nursing Service (QAMFNS). The final chapters in this section cover the naval and Indian army nursing services.

The second section includes the women's auxiliary services set up in the First World War, and their precursors, the Army Pay Department (APD) and the Women's Legion (WL). The Women's Forage Corps (WFC) and the Women's Land Army (WLA) are covered more briefly. The latter was purely an army in name, only linked with the armed services through its association with the Women's Forage Corps, but it seemed wrong to leave it out.

Encompassing so many services has inevitably limited what I have been able to include, but I have offered suggestions for further reading on most services. A key to abbreviations will be found at the end of the book. The history and organization of each service are described, together with what life was like, uniforms worn, casualties suffered and a section titled 'recognition of service'. Research sources are listed under headings according to where they are held, with some examples of what may be found.

Recognition of Service

This section of each chapter briefly mentions service medals, decorations and awards as well as other instances of women named in recognition of outstanding service.

The Royal Red Cross (RRC) was created in 1883 by Queen Victoria, as an award to nursing sisters or ladies for outstanding service in the care of the sick or wounded of the armed services. Worn suspended from a blue bow edged in red, this decoration had two classes: first class (members), given the post nominal letters RRC, and second class (associates), ARRC. Those promoted from second to first class returned the ARRC. Bars to the RRC were first awarded in the First World War.

Army nurses were awarded medals for service in a few nineteenth-century campaigns and in the Boer and the First World wars.

Those who served on the establishment of a unit in one of seven accepted theatres of war between 4 August 1914 and 11 November 1918 qualified for the Allied Victory Medal and also the British War Medal. The latter, for service abroad, could be issued alone. The 1914 Star was awarded for service in France or Belgium between 5 August and 22 November 1914. The 1914–1915 Star was awarded to those serving on the establishment of a unit in a theatre of war before the end of 1915.

Army nurses were among those awarded the Florence Nightingale Medal for exceptionally meritorious nursing services in connection with the sick and wounded.

Several women were awarded the Albert Medal for acts of gallantry. From June 1916, women became eligible for the Military Medal and by December 1918, 115 awards had been made to women.

In 1917, the Order of the British Empire was instituted for services at home or abroad, in civil and military divisions, with five classes (women were eligible for all of these), from GBE (Dame Grand Cross) to MBE (Member), most receiving OBEs (Officers) and MBEs. Women also received the Medal of the Order of the British Empire (renamed British Empire Medal in 1922), mentions in despatches (MiD), as well as foreign decorations. These orders, awards and mentions were published in the *London Gazette* (LG).

The Silver War Badge (SWB) was awarded for discharge due to sickness or wounds caused by war service at home or abroad after 4 August 1914.

Further detail on service and gallantry medals may be found in The National Archives (TNA) catalogue research guides. Your local library should have reference books on medals, including the *Medal Yearbook*. Information on specific awards may also be found online.

Casualties

Rolls of honour and memorials to women of a particular service are mentioned in the chapter on that service.

The Imperial War Museum's Women's Work Collection (digitized as *Women, War & Society 1914–1918 (WW&S)*) contains many rolls of honour for First World War service women. However, the most comprehensive records appear in *Femina Patriae Defensor: woman in the service of her country (FPD)*, published by the Women's Auxiliary of the Interallied Veterans Federation (*Fédération Interalliée des Anciens Combattants* (FIDAC)) in 1934, and available to consult at the Imperial War Museum (IWM) and the British Library (BL).

Many – but not all – women casualties appear on the Commonwealth War Graves Commission Debt of Honour register, which may be searched at www.cwgc.org/debt_of_honour.asp.

A number of First World War memorials include rolls of honour to women, notably the screen at York Minster which records the names of many women casualties inscribed behind decorated oak panels. The Scottish National War Memorial commemorates casualties of both world wars, including Scottish service women who died in the First World War. Their website at www.snwm.org includes a searchable database.

Part of the Scottish National War Memorial commemorating service women in the First World War.

Types of Records and Where to Find Them

Prior to the First World War, most records of individual service were recorded briefly in handwritten ledgers. Use of typewriters in the early part of the twentieth century led to individual service files for women with officer-equivalent status. The extent and detail of records that have survived vary accordingly. You may find yourself downloading a treasure trove of 200 pages including letters your ancestor wrote, or having to content yourself with one-line confirmation of what she did.

Women's service records have tended to survive only partially and are also somewhat scattered. Many are held at TNA, either as original documents or on microfilm, or available to search and download digitally online via DocumentsOnline. This service is accessible free at TNA, and for a small fee from your home computer. (Individual service records of women born post-1900 are generally still held by the armed service with which they served. Application forms for copies may be obtained from the Service Personnel and Veterans Agency.)

Important sources of individual service are also held elsewhere, notably in *WW&S* which is available to consult free of charge at the Imperial War Museum. This collection, painstakingly assembled during and immediately after the war itself, is an Aladdin's cave on First World War service women. Its treasures are mentioned throughout this book and can now be easily accessed by searching the database.

Online databases are a very useful resource. TNA's DocumentsOnline includes First World War campaign medal index cards and surviving women's auxiliary service records. The *LG* online archive holds back copies that published ('gazetted') many women's auxiliary service appointments as well as awards to nurses and other service women. Historical nursing journals (searchable online on the Royal College of Nursing website) give individual nursing appointments as well as informative articles on the services themselves. Passenger lists (searchable among migration records at Findmypast.co.uk and Ancestry.co.uk) may be helpful in respect of army schoolmistresses or nurses serving in India. *The Times* online archive (accessible through some public libraries and institutions) is another useful resource.

London Metropolitan Archives (LMA) and other more specialist museums and archives also contain important sources for service women. (Some smaller archives do not allow public access, but will undertake research for a small fee.)

Archives and online databases are listed with their addresses (and the abbreviations I have used for them in the text) at the end of the book. If you exhaust given sources to no avail, it is always worth trying local record offices or local history centres.

I have also listed published books, either as sources of individual service or for more detail of a particular service. Many are likely to be out of print, but may be available online as ebooks, or obtainable through secondhand bookshops at www.abebooks.co.uk. The BL or the IWM also usually hold copies.

Getting Started

Your starting point may depend on what has triggered your interest. This could be an old family photograph of a woman wearing a badge or a uniform, a story recounted when you were a child and not really paying attention or something you have stumbled across in the course of other family history research – a census entry showing an army nursing sister or schoolmistress, for example.

Before going any further, it will help to collect as much information as you can about the person you are researching, including birth, marriage and death certificates and census returns. These may give clues, including family connection with a particular armed service. Vera Laughton's family naval connection, for example, led to her distinguished career in the Wrens rather than the Women's Army Auxiliary Corps (WAAC).

Marriage certificates are particularly important. Your great-grandmother might have had a brief first marriage you know nothing about. Agnes Mudie married during her service as an army nurse in the First World War, was widowed two months later, then remarried after the end of the war. She has two files in TNA series WO 399, one under her maiden name and another under her first married surname of Parker, but not the subsequent married surname by which her grandchildren knew her. Occasionally, the files of women who married after leaving the service

One of Staff Nurse Agnes Jack Rowe's three First World War service medal index cards. It mentions the British Lahore General Hospital but does not show medal roll references, which appear on the card in her maiden name, Mudie. (Courtesy of IWM)

have been re-opened and re-titled at a later date, if, for example, they queried their pension or needed a reference.

The file of another army nurse, Agnes Angus, is titled under the familiar name the family knew her by – Nan – rather than the name on her birth certificate. Ask older relatives and do not overlook the possibility of another branch of the family knowing more than you do. Even if a story is not entirely accurate, there is usually a kernel of truth.

Study carefully any photograph of the woman in question wearing uniform and/or a badge. I have given descriptions of uniforms, with illustrations. A magnifying glass (or magnifying a scanned image) may help identify the shape of a badge. Length of skirt or type of headdress can help date a photograph.

If you believe she served abroad during the First World War, the campaign medals index cards are available online at TNA website, via DocumentsOnline, but not through Ancestry.co.uk, as the originals of the women's cards are held at the IWM and were not re-filmed with the men's. If a woman applied herself (as army nursing sisters did), the reverse of the original card should show date of application and home address. Application for a photocopy of the original card may be made to the IWM Collections department.

The First World War campaign medal index can be very helpful. To ensure duplicate medals were not issued to the same person, the index cards were cross-referenced by married and maiden surnames. They should show her rank and the service she served with – possibly several, as women didn't necessarily spend the whole war doing the same thing. The actual medal roll (in TNA series WO 329, identifiable on the catalogue by entering the roll reference on the card, for example, NURSES/3, in the search box) may offer a little more detail, but is currently only available to consult in the reading room at TNA.

Many women served at home or were posted abroad after the Armistice and did not qualify for a medal, but it may still be worth looking, as index cards were made out for many women who applied in ignorance. (Medal index cards are among the very few sources of individual service with the Women's Land Army.)

When planning a visit to an archive, it's best to prepare as much as you can before you go, to maximize your research time there. This may include an online catalogue search beforehand and ordering your documents in advance, or contacting the archive for their advice or to book a seat. The archive website will usually tell you what to do. Websites can be a bit overwhelming and off-putting. Just take a bit of time to find your way around them.

TNA's website gives access to catalogues of other archives, for example, Access to Archives (A2A). If you select the A2A advanced search, you will find a drop-down box that lists all the archive catalogues included, so you can restrict your search, for example, to the BL APAC catalogue if you are

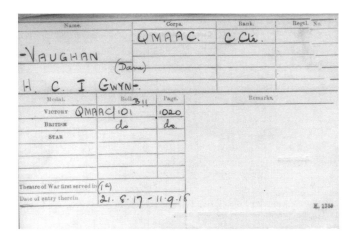

Helen Gwynne-Vaughan's misspelled First World War medal index card, showing references to the medal roll page with her entry.

researching an Indian Army Nursing Service (IANS) nurse. TNA's catalogue includes a number of helpful research guides.

Don't assume that because records are online they will fall into your lap. They may do, but fallible human beings were involved in creating the record of your ancestor's service, as well as more recently filming or entering it in an online index. QMAAC BEF Chief Controller Dame Helen Gwynne-Vaughan set up and ran the service in France, but her name was misspelled as Gwyn-Vaughan on her campaign medal card, and the card was missed out (the postcard-size index cards are difficult to separate when handled) when the cards were filmed.

Some searchable databases use software that recognizes characters in a text, but this process is not always accurate. Others involve creating an index – entered by a keyboard operative who may have misread or mis-keyed something, or used an abbreviation. Read the help section on the website, try different or fewer search terms or another source (the *LG* is held at Kew, with its index) before you give up.

Good luck.

TRACING YOUR SERVICE WOMEN ANCESTORS

Chapter 1

ARMY SCHOOLMISTRESSES AND QAS

Army Schoolmistresses (AS) pre-date the Army Nursing Service (ANS) as the first official body of women employed by the British Army. They taught soldiers' children all over the world. In 1926 they became the Queen's Army Schoolmistresses (QAS), but never achieved corps status.

Origins

Queen Victoria's Royal Warrant of October 1840 authorized a schoolmistress in every regiment, battalion and depot 'qualified to instruct the Female Children of Our Soldiers as well in reading, writing and the rudiments of arithmetic, as in needlework and other parts of housewifery, and to train them in habits of diligence, honesty and piety'.

From 1792, when barracks were first built, six wives per hundred troops below the rank of sergeant were permitted to live within camp, with their children. These women cooked, washed and mended for the men of their barrack. Gradually, more women were allowed, and numbers of children increased accordingly.

Sergeant-schoolmasters were employed mainly to school the illiterate recruits, but were also expected to teach the regiment's offspring, to produce 'loyal subjects, brave soldiers and good Christians' and a useful workforce. Boys learnt tailoring and cobbling, while 'the best qualified and best behaved women of each regiment' taught the girls laundering, plain needlework and knitting.

By the late 1830s, schools were set up wherever regiments were stationed, with a second schoolmaster where numbers justified it. In 1839, Lieutenant Colonel Henry Somerset commanding the South African Cape Mounted Rifle Corps asked for a schoolmistress instead of a second schoolmaster, to teach the Corps' 213 female children. This suggestion came at a time when the civilizing benefits of education were increasingly recognized.

It prompted the new Secretary at War, T B Macaulay, to raise in Parliament a proposal for a schoolmistress for every regiment. He cut short the inevitable sniggering by adding that there were at least 10,000 female children in the army, constantly uprooted, following their fathers' regiments to all corners of the empire. Their education could only be achieved by employing women teachers, probably sergeants' wives.

Army Schoolmistresses in the Nineteenth Century

Regimental schools soon included infant schools, which both sexes attended as soon as they could walk. They were taught by a schoolmistress until they could read two-syllable words and then transferred to the schoolmaster. The schoolmistress held 'industrial school' every afternoon, where the girls and younger boys learned to knit, mark laundry, etc.

From 1858, unqualified AS candidates were funded to attend civil teacher-training institutions for six or twelve months, in London, Dublin, Edinburgh and Glasgow. Candidates had to be aged 18–35, with a character reference from a clergyman. They needed to read well, have good, clear handwriting, be proficient at spelling, basic arithmetic, an ear for music, a good singing voice and basic knowledge of the Bible and world geography. They were also expected to cut out and make a child's dress, teach knitting and marking and preparing linen.

Unsurprisingly, such paragons among NCOs' wives and daughters proved thin on the ground. As an added complication, NCOs' wives had to follow their husbands, who might be transferred to a station that already had a schoolmistress. (This remained a very real problem for married AS.)

After 1863, AS applicants aged 21–30 were accepted either with teaching certificates or uncertificated, with previous experience in army schools, and appointed or promoted as third, second or first-class schoolmistresses, according to merit, qualifications and length of service. Monitresses aged 14–16 (recruited from the abler pupils) helped in larger classes and pupil teachers (appointed from 17, after sitting an examination) were employed in schools with more than fifty children. Assistant schoolmistresses, selected from NCOs' wives, could train or be appointed as third-class schoolmistresses.

Children attended regimental schools at Gibraltar, Malta, Corfu and in China, Africa, the West Indies, Australia, New Zealand and Canada. By the 1870s, the army school population worldwide had reached 20,000, with 238 AS in 172 schools, helped by 66 pupil teachers and 336 monitresses. Infants were taught spelling, reading and singing and industrial school was still held in the afternoons. Pay was increased after complaints from unmarried AS that they earned less than infantry drummers, and went without food in order to dress respectably.

The Model School, Chelsea, with 500 pupils, was set up to give probationers practical training. When Eliza Woodman, a sergeant's wife, found herself widowed at the age of 24 with three children to support her husband's commanding officer encouraged her to train as an AS. She

Army school class. (RAEC collection, courtesy of AGC Museum)

began at the Model School in 1874, embarking on a twenty-three-year career, which took her to India (where she re-married in 1883) and Gibraltar, before becoming head mistress of the Royal Army School, Aldershot.

By 1887, AS could retire at 50 on a pension of roughly half their salary. By 1893, AS were teaching older girls at single-sex schools at Chatham, Woolwich and Gibraltar. New kindergarten methods of education were included in training at the Model School. Surprisingly, corporal punishment was forbidden in army schools and army children left school better educated than their peers in the civil system. Monitresses could pursue a good career in teaching, trained at government expense.

Army Schoolmistresses in the Early Twentieth Century

Advances in civil education in the early part of the twentieth century, however, led the army to decide to abolish its home infant schools. Nearly fifty closed, until the Board of Education stepped in, objecting to army pupils swamping civil schools. The closure policy ceased and a few schools re-opened.

In the early 1900s, army schoolmasters could marry after three years' enlisted service or after reaching the age of 23. Their social position was awkward – officers tended to regard them as over-educated upstarts. Many married an AS, a kindred spirit similarly awkwardly socially placed.

3

An AS was not allowed to marry a soldier below the rank of sergeant, or a commissioned officer. Dismissal followed marriage without permission. Retirement on marriage was not enforced if a vacancy existed for a schoolmistress where her husband was stationed.

The army offered foreign travel, but under orders. Schoolmistresses were no longer employed within a particular regiment, with relatives and friends. They could be posted anywhere and, if they refused a posting, asked to resign.

AS candidates were now accepted aged 20–22, having spent a probationary year at the Model School. Application forms from this period show the continuing importance of a good singing voice, family association with the army, a morally unimpeachable character and pure, 'unmixed' European blood – this last question also appeared on the medical examination sheet.

Training included 'criticism lessons' where probationers judged one another's teaching abilities and methods. And an AS in the early 1900s

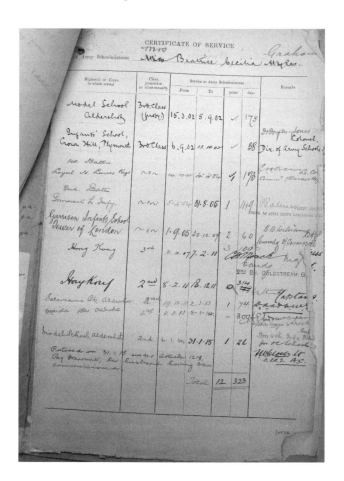

Beatrice Graham (née Myles)'s Certificate of Service, showing her career from probationer at the Model School in 1902 to forced retirement in 1915, via Hong Kong, where she married in 1910. (TNA WO 374/28405)

could expect the schoolroom door to open suddenly without warning for the daily visit of the orderly officer, complete with sash and white gloves, on his round of inspection. The Command's inspector of army schools could also visit at any time, to assess children's progress and submit a confidential report on each schoolmistress.

First World War

Throughout the First World War, AS continued to serve abroad, in Gibraltar, Malta, Egypt, South Africa, the West Indies, India, Hong Kong, Ceylon and Tientsin (now Tianjin).

At home, many army schools were requisitioned as soldiers' billets. Some AS took civil posts vacated by enlisted schoolmasters, or joined the women's services. Those who remained found themselves in makeshift premises, teaching much larger classes including older boys, as many army schoolmasters had taken a more combatant role.

Retired AS returned to the fold, including those retired on marriage. They could find themselves once more relegated to retirement when their NCO husbands were given commissions, an increasing occurrence with the high casualty rate among junior officers. AS Beatrice Graham had married an Army Ordnance Corps staff sergeant in Hong Kong, but was obliged to retire in 1915, when he was granted a commission.

The strain borne by AS during the First World War, working long hours with larger classes, left its mark on their health. Although army schoolmasters and schoolmistresses were often remembered individually with affection by several generations of the same family, both groups lacked the status and recognition they deserved. However, when army schoolmasters' pay was raised, AS pay was left unchanged. This left nearly 300 serving AS at the end of 1919 on a level with a lance corporal, earning less than civil teachers or army nurses.

Post-war

In 1920 the Corps of Army Schoolmasters became the Army Educational Corps (AEC, later Royal Army Educational Corps (RAEC)) which now administered the AS, with yearly inspections conducted by an AEC officer. Revised regulations barred uncertificated mistresses from higher pay or status.

But their camaraderie compensated for what these women lacked remuneratively. Friendships formed during training were cemented through yearly reunions and their newsletter, the *Army Schoolmistress* (nicknamed the *Link*), which kept AS throughout the world in touch with one another.

After the Armistice, 190 army schools continued, one-third at home mostly around garrison towns and the rest overseas with the BAOR and in China, the West Indies, Gibraltar, Malta, Egypt, Palestine and India, mostly educating ORs' children. (Officers sent their children to UK boarding schools.)

Service Abroad

AS letters to the *Link,* warning about or warmly endorsing different postings, convey both the feel of the army family and the excitement of foreign travel in an era when only leisured classes ventured abroad. A posting to Tientsin offered a Japanese tea house, Russian food and an annual ball thrown by the Italians.

One woman embarked for India, regaled by tales of the glittering social life ahead of her. At the end of the voyage, when the 'male escort' promised in the pamphlet failed to turn up – not an uncommon occurrence – she had to make the three-day train journey alone. At her new station on the North West Frontier she found five children in a barn schoolroom and instead of the house she had been led to expect for herself, four rooms in the same block as the guardroom, the nearest woman 200yd away. 'Two years later my worries ended by my committing matrimony.'

In India, AS frequently taught 6–14-year-olds, assisted by a warrant officer or regimental sergeant instructor. The school year was organized to allow schools to move to the hills during the hot season. With the BAOR, AS were stationed in Cologne, Mulheim or Solingen. Malta was a pleasant, sociable posting, where eighteen AS shared housekeeping expenses and a maid. The eighty army schools at home allowed schoolmistresses respite from foreign service.

Interwar Years

In 1926 the Army Schoolmistresses Association was formed, with a motto: 'The Link that Binds'. In 1927, Queen Mary became patron of the newly titled Queen's Army Schoolmistresses.

Candidates over 19 with a teacher's certificate were appointed as certificated AS. Preference for appointment as uncertificated AS was given to army pupil teachers (aged 19–21) or other candidates with army connections. Pupil teachers had to pass an examination and complete at least two years' satisfactory service.

First posting orders arrived shortly after training ended. No one knew in advance where they would be going. Orders could arrive on Friday to report for duty the following Monday morning.

Candidates had to be single and serve five years after one year's probation. Marriage without permission still meant compulsory retirement. A husband below the rank of sergeant was still not permitted, nor one whose character or status was not satisfactory. Schoolmistresses could be transferred at home or abroad as required, and asked to resign if they refused a posting.

Having become a probationer in 1917 at the age of 20, Hilda Battle was posted three years later to the garrison school on Alderney, in the Channel Islands. Still young and inexperienced, she found the isolation too daunting and failed to return from leave with her parents in Gibraltar. Her request for transfer or placement on the unemployed list was refused and she was obliged to resign.

Army routine still involved regular invasions of the classroom by Royal Engineers officers inspecting buildings and equipment, or quartermasters checking inventories. Woe betide the schoolmistress borrowing a table or broom.

The badge issued to AS in the First World War. (Courtesy of AGC Museum)

In 1930, eighty QAS were serving in India, with seventeen acting QAS on loan from local education authorities, a sign of things to come. Army schools at home were closing. Separate civil primary and secondary education required re-organization into infants, junior and senior schools – often too small to be sustainable. Barrosa Elder Girls School took over as the Centre for QAS on probation.

Uniform

AS were never issued a uniform. During the First World War, with more and more women in uniform, AS found themselves unfairly branded as 'slackers'. Badgering the War Office for a uniform, they were finally offered a small round black and red cloth badge. Many were apparently too disgusted to wear it.

Researching Army Schoolmistresses

The National Archives

If you know which regiment an AS served with in the late nineteenth century, you should find her in the regimental pay ledgers. Series WO 16 contains heavy leather-bound muster rolls and pay lists covering the period 1878 to 1898. The pay lists include printed pages headed 'Regimental Schools' or 'Regimental and Garrison Schools' recording schoolmistresses' and monitresses' names, class and pay.

PMG 34/1-5 comprise ledgers recording pension payments to AS (1909 to 1928). PMG 34/1 lists 1909 pension recipients including those granted a pension from 1879 onwards. Entries only give name, address, with sometimes date of death. (A pension was granted after twenty-one years' service; pro rata if retired after ten years due to ill health, with a gratuity for less than ten years or if retired on marriage after at least six years.)

Some individual service records for AS serving in the early part of the twentieth century are currently still held by the Ministry of Defence. Others (due to be made available online) have been released to TNA, in series WO 374, with a larger number in WO 339, catalogued by surname and name or initials. Contents vary, and may include original application form (with personal details and work experience), references, medical board sheets, army marriage certificate, confidential reports, original correspondence and certificate of service showing postings and reason for retirement.

WO 374/9737 shows AS Mrs Gertrude Brown having been a civil school-teacher prior to marriage in 1905. Her army form W5129 lists her four children, born between 1907 and 1912. She returned to civil teaching in 1917. A qualified and experienced teacher and the wife of the bandmaster of the 2nd Battalion Gloucestershire Regiment stationed in Ahmednegar, India, she was well placed to be employed, when the vacancy arose in 1920, as a certificated army schoolmistress, aided by the character reference – 'a lady of unimpeachable moral character' – offered by her husband's commanding officer. The army, however, put her on probation and appointed her as uncertificated. Her request for promotion was supported by the commander-in-chief in Simla, but – she was after all only teaching infants and sewing – the army kicked this ball into the long grass by responding that promotion would be considered in due course. Two years later, when her husband transferred to 6 Gurkha Rifles, Abbottabad, where there was no army school, she was obliged to resign. Her promotion never materialized.

The physical cost of the burden on AS during the First World War is shown in WO 374/14007, the file of Frances Clarke, a quiet, gifted infant teacher, among those whose health broke down after six months teaching elder boys.

The First World War campaign medal roll index (at DocumentsOnline) includes cards for AS serving abroad who qualified for the British War Medal. WO 329/2134 (the relevant medal roll) lists over seventy, giving full name, marital status, dates and country of service abroad.

National Army Museum

The RAEC collection includes a few items relating to AS, including a run of copies of *the Army Schoolmistress* (incomplete) from 1923 to 1981. These are an important source of information on the postings and service of individual AS, and paint a colourful picture of their lives.

The newsletter kept working and retired AS/QAS in touch through a regular 'Where is She?' column, with names and places of posting. It listed probationers at the Model School; members of the Army Schoolmistresses' Association; examination results; birth, marriage, death notices and detailed obituaries; with subscriber lists, reminiscences of foreign postings, QAS seniority list, resignations and retirements. The life and career of Eliza Pinkerton (formerly Woodman), for example, is described shortly before and after her death in 1927.

Adjutant General's Corps Museum

A small collection relating to AS includes (mostly unidentified) photographs, correspondence, badges and a run of 1980s QAS newsletters.

British Library

Many AS served in India. The India Office Records (IOR) in the British Library Asia, Pacific & Africa (APAC) collections represent a rich family history source for the British Army in India, including many birth, marriage and burial records. The latter are increasingly being transcribed on to its online Family History Search database at indiafamily.bl.uk/UI/Home.aspx, including a small number of marriages and deaths of AS. If the record you are seeking does not appear on the database, transcribed returns of baptisms, marriages and burials (up to 1969) may be consulted on microfilm in the Asian and African Studies reading room. (Army returns of marriages in India may also be searched online at www.findmypast.co.uk. Eliza Woodman's re-marriage in 1883 to John Pinkerton appears in the GRO Index to Army Marriages, 1881–1955.)

Military Collection IOR/L/MIL/7 covering c. 1850–1950 includes files on AS pay and conditions, with occasional surnames. Collection 210 Army Schools in India 1878–1939 includes AS pay, funeral allowances, hardships, etc.

India Office private papers collections holds a diary kept in the early 1880s by Kate Georgina Fry, an AS in India and Egypt.

Other Documentary Sources

Westminster College Archives (Westminster Institute of Education, Oxford Brookes University) holds student records of the first Wesleyan Methodist training college for teachers founded in Westminster in 1851, where, from 1858, unqualified AS candidates could be sent for training. Brief details of holdings may be found online at www.brookes.ac.uk/schools/education/wco/library.html.

Census and BMD Records

Your first realization of an AS ancestor may come from a census entry or marriage certificate. Conversely, parts of the jigsaw of the career of an AS may be pieced together through such records. Census entries for AS sometimes give the regiment with which they worked.

The marriage certificate of Clara Neely (whose former fiancé, a sapper with the Royal Engineers at Aldershot, committed suicide shortly before her posting to India in 1888) shows her as a schoolmistress at Rawalpindi with the 2nd Seaforth Highlanders, marrying the colour sergeant.

Other Online Sources

Passenger lists may include AS not travelling by troop ships. Miss Dorothy M Bottle, for example, appears on the *Patuca* returning from Jamaica in 1924.

The Times, Hansard and *London Gazette* online archives contain references to AS. They may be mentioned in online histories of army schools.

Printed Sources

Colonel N T St John Williams, *Tommy Atkins' Children: the story of the education of the Army's children* (1971) and *Judy O'Grady and the Colonel's Lady: the army wife and camp follower since 1660* (1988)

Colonel A C T White, *The Story of Army Education 1643–1963* (1963)

Myna Trustram, *Women of the Regiment: marriage and the Victorian Army* (available online at books.google.com) describes service families and early regimental schoolmistresses

Dorothy Mabel Bottle, *Reminiscences of an Army Schoolmistress* (1936), transcribed online at www.john_bottle.talktalk.net. Born in 1886, Dorothy Bottle's service record is currently still with the MoD. However, census entries show her as ideal AS material – daughter of a Grenadier Guards band sergeant. The First World War campaign medal roll (WO 329/2134) records her service in Jamaica, 1913–1917. *The Army Schoolmistress* 'Where is She?' column lists her in 1925 as teaching at the Garrison Elder Children's School, Greenhill. By 1930, the seniority roll shows her serving in Cairo.

NURSING
AND MEDICAL SERVICES

Chapter 2

CRIMEA NURSES

Florence Nightingale famously pioneered military nursing as a respectable occupation for a woman by leading a group to nurse at Scutari, in 1854. The women who went out to nurse Crimean sick and wounded were not the first army nurses, however.

Early Army Nurses

From the late sixteenth century onwards, small numbers of women nurses were employed in military garrison hospitals at home, on campaigns and in the West Indies and the Far East. In 1798, one 'decent, sober woman nurse' was allowed for every ten patients. During the Napoleonic Wars, nurses were employed in regimental hospitals, often chosen from among the wives or widows of sergeants or soldiers.

Although small regimental hospitals in the colonies continued to employ local female nurses, in 1845 new regulations stipulated that women could only be employed in special circumstances. This policy may have been introduced to protect male army personnel at a time of stringent cuts, or could have reflected concern about the standard of available nurses or the propriety of women caring for male patients.

In the first half of the nineteenth century, nuns ministered to the sick, but the popular image of the paid nurse was that of Dickens' disreputable Mrs Gamp. Nursing was certainly a grim occupation: low-paid, heavy domestic work, doing unpleasant tasks without rubber gloves or modern conveniences, witnessing patients suffering without painkillers. Medical care was crude and basic, with little awareness of sanitation, other than the belief that bad smells spread diseases. In such squalid circumstances, sobriety must have been a challenge, for nurses of both sexes.

Crimea Nurses

At the beginning of the Crimea campaign in 1854, 300 Chelsea pensioners were sent out to serve as stretcher bearers and nursing orderlies. Those who survived the journey reached the base hospital in Constantinople barely able to look after themselves. They were then faced with the arrival of hundreds of wounded. It seems hardly surprising that many apparently turned to drink while the suffering soldiers struggled to help one another.

Improved postal and telegraphic communications brought news of the appallingly inadequate care of the wounded to English breakfast tables faster and more graphically than in any previous war. One young upper-class woman burned to help. Florence Nightingale was no mere well-meaning society lady. She had fixed on nursing as a vocation, briefly studied nursing methods, visited hospitals and volunteered at the Middlesex Hospital during a cholera epidemic, shortly before reading the Crimea report in *The Times*.

Nightingale's letter to the wife of Sidney Herbert, Secretary at War, reputedly crossed with one from him, asking her to take a group of nurses to the military hospital set up in army barracks at Scutari in Turkey, across the Black Sea from the Crimea.

Nightingale selected thirty-eight suitable women, including fourteen professional lay nurses, ten Roman Catholic nuns, six Anglican sisters and eight Sellonites. The Sellonites, an Anglican working sisterhood based in Plymouth, had valuable experience nursing cholera patients. Their presence also reduced the proportion of Roman Catholics, allaying what turned out to be justifiable fears of attempted deathbed conversions of the mostly Protestant soldiers. Nightingale made it clear her orders were to be obeyed without question. Any nurse found misbehaving with the troops would be instantly dismissed.

Florence Nightingale (centre behind patient) at Scutari, 1854. This depiction shows a nun standing to the left of Nightingale and a nurse kneeling beside the patient, offering a drink.

The party left London in late October 1854. After a nightmare voyage from Marseilles, they reached Scutari shortly after the Battle of Balaclava. Conscious of likely resistance to women nurses, Florence insisted they should only work on the wards when requested by the medical staff. Frustrated, they passed the time sewing shirts, pillows and slings and bailing rainwater from their leaky quarters in a tower at one corner of the Barrack Hospital. They had brought supplies, but equipment was very sparse and rudimentary.

At first they were only asked to feed patients, but their chance to wash and dress wounds came soon enough. A few days after the Battle of Inkerman, on 5 November, over 2,000 casualties began pouring into the Barrack Hospital. They lay in an estimated 4 miles of closely packed low wooden trestles in wards with broken windows stuffed with rags.

A party of nurses was also sent to the smaller General Hospital. A few nurses were sent home, including five nuns from Norwood described as 'more fit for heaven than a hospital' and Elizabeth Wheeler, who fell into disfavour after her letter home describing shortages of supplies and food ended up in the newspapers. Those who remained coped with the spartan conditions, the horribly wounded men crawling with fleas and lice and a chaotically inflexible system of issuing stores that meant they often did not reach the men. The women made a difference – mainly by administering sustenance – and the nursing experiment was reported as a success, prompting many more women to write offering their services.

From these, Sidney Herbert selected another party of forty-six, comprising nine ladies, fifteen nuns and twenty-two hired nurses of varying calibre, under the charge of the Herberts' friend, Mary Stanley. They arrived in December 1854, after an exhausting journey during which they spent all their funds, to find they were not expected, not welcome and there was no accommodation for them. They were temporarily housed in Therapia (now Terabya, Turkey) on the Bosphorus. They offered their services to the nearby British naval hospital, but nurses were already on their way from the Admiralty. Stanley's nurses marked time mending piles of linen, doing laundry, visiting the men and writing letters for them.

The situation created and exacerbated clashes inside and between the different religious factions. Eventually, the new party dispersed. A total of eleven nurses, led by Elizabeth Davis, a capable older nurse from Stanley's party, decamped to the General Hospital at Balaclava (where Nightingale's authority did not extend). Five of the best hired nurses stayed at the Barrack Hospital, and five nuns went to the smaller General Hospital at Scutari.

Mary Stanley and the remaining nuns chose to go to Koulali, where Turkish cavalry barracks were to be turned into a hospital, but there were no beds and no food when the first 300 patients suddenly arrived. The nuns did little hands-on nursing, death rates soared and Mary Stanley broke down and eventually went home.

In February 1855, the mortality rate at Scutari Hospital rose to 52 per cent of admissions. The Barrack Hospital latrines were prone to flood into the wards after heavy rain and water tanks at the General Hospital were contaminated by sewage seeping from blocked sewers, eventually cleared out by a special Sanitary Commission.

The Koulali Hospital slowly improved. The lady nurses contrived, by altering their uniform, to distance themselves from the hired nurses, out of whom, within a few weeks, there remained only eleven, the rest having been sent home. In April 1855 three more ladies and seven nurses arrived. Jane Shaw Stewart led the group nursing at the newly opened Castle Hospital near Balaclava. Civil hospitals with some women nurses were opened at Smyrna and Renkioi.

A total of 229 women are recorded as having been sent between 1854 and 1856 to nurse the Crimean sick and wounded. Of these, eleven died and were buried at Scutari, Balaclava and Smyrna, seventeen (including Nightingale) served until the end of the war, forty-nine are recorded as

Artist's impression of Charlotte Wilsdon wearing the Scutari Hospital sash. (By kind permission of Marjorie Stephen)

having been dismissed (eighteen for intoxication) and forty resigned. Nightingale's verdict on the nurses was 'careful, efficient, often decorous, and always kind, sometimes drunken, sometimes unchaste'.

Uniform

The Bermondsey nuns and Sellonites wore black habits, the Norwood nuns white – as impractical as they themselves turned out to be. Nightingale devised a uniform for the other nurses: a grey tweed (or black woollen) dress with white collar, unbleached linen apron, grey worsted jacket, short woollen cloak and white frilled bonnet. Each nurse wore a diagonal coarse linen sash with 'Scutari Hospital' embroidered in red. (Charlotte Wilsdon's surviving Scutari Hospital sash apparently has 'CW' faintly marked on it.)

Researching Crimea Nurses

Florence Nightingale Museum

The Museum holds Florence Nightingale memorabilia and papers, including her *Register of Nurses sent to Military Hospitals in the East, 1854–55*, listing over 200 names with some personal details. The list appears to include those who nursed in civil as well as army hospitals and is available to consult at the Museum in a digitized form.

London Metropolitan Archives

Florence Nightingale's remaining papers are held here, including an index and summary of her register (H01/ST/NC Appendix 1), correspondence regarding St John's House nurses who served in Crimea hospitals (H01/ST/NC/03/SU/A) and correspondence from nurses' relatives and nurses after their return home (H01/ST/NC/02 Box XII–Box XVII). These boxes contain Nightingale's correspondence organized chronologically. Their contents are available on microfilm. A list of the letters (H01/ST/NC/APPENDIX/001) and card index to correspondents and subjects (H01/ST/INDEX/005) should be consulted first.

An indexed register of nurses sent to private houses includes some who nursed in the Crimea, H01/ST/SJ/C/03/001 1849 April–1855 Jan.

List of letters from and regarding Crimea nurses, H01/ST/K/02/016/002.

The National Archives

WO 25/264 is a large box crammed with small bundles of folded letters, some with printed forms, relating to applications, both successful and unsuccessful, to nurse in Crimea. Some include testimonials. The bundles are arranged by letter of the alphabet (with some strays). Some of the applicants are difficult to identify and much of the correspondence is undated. Some are annotated 'declined' or 'answered', 'engaged and compensated' or 'shown to be undesirable'.

Some applications include printed character reference forms that state that 'Nurses sent out to Hospitals in the East should be persons of experience and exceptional character', ask whether sober, honest, 'cleanly' active, intelligent, and that the form should be filled out 'to prevent imposition'. Testimonials describing a 35-year-old widow, Mrs Willesden (Charlotte Wilsdon, later Cox), as 'another excellent person . . . strong, active, most respectable', are dated March 1855, and marked 'Gone to Scutari'. Ann Clarke, aged 33, who had been nursing at the Middlesex Hospital, appears not to have been engaged initially, but is recorded as sent as a housekeeper to Scutari.

WO 43/991 contains correspondence and a list of officers and general staff (mainly male) attached to the civil hospital at Renkioi dated 1855, with correspondence and reports about this hospital. The list includes 'upper' and 'under' nurses, laundresses and sempstresses with a footnote '30

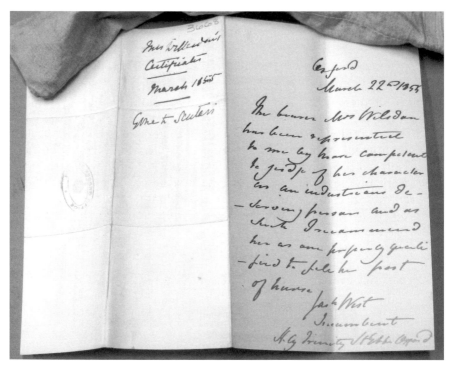

Character reference for Charlotte Wilsdon, marked 'Mrs Willesden's certificates' and 'Gone to Scutari'. (TNA WO 25/264)

second class passages provided in the *Bacchante* for nurses and orderlies' – presumably the ship they returned on.

Other lists name ladies and female nurses at Inkerman and Renkioi.

WO 43/963 holds original letters bound between cloth covers, mostly regarding expenditure and expenses claims, with few references to individual Crimea nurses, although it does include the amount of port, brandy and stout consumed by Mary Clarke and four nurses on their return voyage from Scutari in 1855 and a leaflet of *Rules and Regulations for the Nurses Attached to the Military Hospitals in the East.*

Online Sources

Lists of women who nursed Crimea sick and wounded may be found at www.dorsetbay.plus.com/hist/crimea.

Some nurses' accounts of their work during the Crimean War are available to read online, including A Lady (Martha Nicol), *Ismeer, or Smyrna and its British Hospital in 1855* (1856). She appears to have supervised a hired nurse who did the actual nursing.

Printed Sources

Nightingale apparently dreaded the idea of nurses writing about their experiences in the Crimea. Fortunately, several did.

Robert G Richardson (ed.), *Nurse Sarah Anne: with Florence Nightingale at Scutari* (1977), the journal of Sarah Anne Tebbot, one of the Sellonites who accompanied Florence Nightingale to Scutari in 1854. A comprehensive introduction describes the nurses and the medical services

Jane Williams (ed.), *Betsy Cadwaladyr: A Balaclava Nurse: an autobiography of Elizabeth Davies* (1987). Davies, a former ladies' maid and critical of Nightingale, led a group from Stanley's party to serve in the field hospital at Balaclava

Frances (Fanny) Margaret Taylor, *Eastern Hospitals and English Nurses, The Narrative of Twelve Months Experience in the Hospitals of Koulali and Scoutari, by a Lady Volunteer, Vol. II* (1856), available as a facsimile reprint or an ebook

Sister Mary Aloysius, *Memories of the Crimea*, 1897, by Catherine Doyle, an Irish nun in Mary Stanley's party

Margaret Goodman, *Experiences of an English Sister of Mercy* (1862), written by one of the Sellonites, mentioning individuals by name (other accounts, though fascinatingly detailed, avoid naming individuals).

More information on individual nurses may be found in:
Cecil Woodham Smith, *Florence Nightingale* (1950)
Mark Bostridge, *Florence Nightingale: the woman and her legend* (2008).

Chapter 3

ARMY NURSING SERVICE

Despite its difficulties and personality clashes, the Crimea experiment fostered a more positive image of women nurses. This did not lead to immediate adoption of female nursing staff in military hospitals at home, however. For one thing, there were hardly any properly trained nurses. In 1860 the Nightingale School of Nursing was founded at St Thomas's Hospital, London, from which future army nursing sisters would be drawn.

In 1859 new army regulations created female superintendents of nursing, responsible for supervising and allocating nurses to wards. Nurse applicants had to be aged 30–40, literate and possessing certificates of good conduct. They retired at 60 and received a pension, depending on years of service. However, regimental hospital orderlies, or men of the Medical Staff Corps (later Army Hospital Corps), usually retired soldiers or pensioners, continued to do most of the nursing of their sick comrades.

The vast new Royal Military Hospital at Netley on Southampton Water opened in 1863. (This grand building allowed easy disembarkation from hospital ships, but was badly designed for patient care.) A total of six nurses from St Thomas's Hospital were employed there, with Jane Shaw Stewart (who had nursed at Balaclava) as superintendent.

An 1866 royal warrant provided for female nurses to be appointed at any military general hospital. Over the next twenty years several new military hospitals opened. Mrs Jane Cecilia Deeble, an officer's widow, succeeded Shaw Stewart as Lady Superintendent at Netley in 1869. Shaw Stewart took eight nurses to the airy, modern Herbert (later Royal Herbert) Military Hospital, Woolwich, lodging at the female infirmary there. They were not appreciated – most patients preferred male nurses. Lady nurses were 'an innovation from which no benefit can possibly be derived'. Nevertheless, small numbers remained at Chatham, Woolwich and Netley.

In 1880, the National Society for Aid to the Sick and Wounded in War (NSASW, forerunner of the Red Cross) announced an annual grant for the training of nurses at Netley, to be sent out to other military hospitals. Nurses were taken on a month's trial before a year's probation then two years in a military hospital, funded by the NSASW. Preference was given to army or navy officers' widows and daughters.

They learned to prepare invalid food, apply dressings and leeches, give injections, medicines and enemas and observe sick patients. In 1884, two served in Egypt and three transferred to the new ANS. However, the scheme was hampered by a problem that was to dog all women pioneering work with the armed forces – lack of suitable living accommodation. In the end, only Chatham could accommodate them and only twelve nurses were trained before the scheme fizzled out.

In 1881 an ANS had been formally established, its HQ at Netley. Trained nurses were to be employed in army hospitals of 100 beds or more, including Malta and Gibraltar. Mrs Deeble preferred ladies, but conceded, given the shortage of suitable applicants, that social position might be overlooked in the case of a really good nurse. There was moral safety in numbers – nurses were sent to military hospitals in groups of not less than four or five, especially if they were to go on night duty.

The Director General of the Army Medical Services (DGAMS) had overall charge of the appointment or dismissal of female nursing staff. Each hospital had a head sister, whose role was more practical than managerial, as there were so few nursing sisters.

Nursing sisters supervised two male orderlies in each ward who were supposed to do the basic nursing, but the nursing sisters had no real authority over orderlies, who could suddenly be ordered elsewhere.

Nursing was becoming more respectable, with army nurses gradually establishing themselves in military hospitals and small numbers accompanying military campaigns. In 1879, Mrs Deeble and fourteen nurses were sent out to tend casualties in the Zulu wars. In 1882, army nurses accompanied British troops sent to Egypt. They also served in the 1883–1884 Sudan war (one nurse died falling out of a carriage in Cairo) and 1889 Nile campaign. Sir Alexander Ogston, eminent army surgeon and campaigner for better military medical care, described the Netley nurses' arrival in Egypt as 'a revolution' in nursing care. By 1888, there were sixty ANS sisters, with about a dozen at Netley.

However, during the 1890s, a period of relative peace, the ANS shrank. Helen Campbell Norman, who had succeeded Mrs Deeble at Netley, became the only lady superintendent, with nineteen superintendent nurses under her. The

MRS DEEBLE,
LADY SUPERINTENDENT OF NETLEY HOSPITAL.

Portrait of Mrs Deeble wearing the RRC. (Courtesy of AMS Museum)

Army Medical Department was re-organized and the Royal Army Medical Corps (RAMC) set up in 1898.

Army Nursing Service Reserve

In 1894, Princess Christian proposed a reserve of trained nurses for military service in time of war, and the Army Nursing Service Reserve (ANSR) with herself as president came into being in 1897. Candidates had to be aged 25–35, with at least three years' experience in a general civil hospital including one year nursing adult males, and provide written references confirming their social status, character and nursing abilities. Members signed an undertaking to serve in a military hospital in time of war. On reaching 50, their membership ceased.

The ANSR played an important part in the South African (Boer) War, with over 800 members serving there, 33 at other stations abroad and 538 at home, replacing regular ANS on active service. The ANS was based on a matron and 8 nursing sisters or staff nurses for every 100 beds in military hospitals of over a hundred beds. While the ANS remained under strength, ANSR continued serving at home and abroad.

Following re-organization, Queen Alexandra's Imperial Military Nursing Service (QAIMNS) replaced the ANS in 1903. The ANSR was allowed to continue without any connection with the QAIMNS, which would, however, in the event of war, give preference to members of the ANSR.

As the regular QAIMNS increased, ANSR numbers in military hospitals decreased, although Reserve nurses continued to be employed at home and abroad until 1908, when the QAIMNS Reserve was formed. In 1913, there were still 469 ANSR nurses, with members categorized as suitable for the new reserve; suitable to supplement the reserve, should their services be required; or unsuitable. In this way, the ANSR was gradually absorbed into the QAIMNSR, although in September 1914, 337 names still remained on the ANSR roll.

The South African War

The Boer War of 1899–1901 became the first campaign to which female army nurses were sent in significant numbers, although complaints were voiced in nursing circles that army nurses had only been 'dribbled into South Africa'.

In October 1899, Boer armies invaded Natal and the Cape Province, and British army garrisons at Ladysmith, Kimberley and Mafeking found themselves under siege. There were twelve female army nurses serving in Natal and Cape Town. Several were trapped in the siege of Ladysmith, where typhoid broke out.

Of the 250,000 British troops sent out, casualties were high. A war zone spread out over a vast expanse of the veldt created difficulties of supply.

In the blistering heat, many troops – teenage volunteers rather than seasoned soldiers – drank contaminated water. Disease became a more daunting adversary than the Boers. Poor sanitation, inadequate rations and contaminated water contributed to 74,000 being treated for dysentery alone, against 22,000 wounded. By May 1900, over 14,000 troops were hospitalized, mostly from sickness.

On the outbreak of war, 100 ANSR nurses were called up for home service, replacing regular army nurses sent abroad. Over the first winter, 800 more Reserves enrolled, to serve both at home and abroad. Ultimately, over 1,000 nurses were sent out, mostly Reserves. Army nurses served on hospital ships and in hospital trains transporting the wounded, as well as in field hospitals. Nurses were also taken on locally, giving rise to complaints about the frivolous behaviour of 'lady amateurs' bringing real nurses into disrepute.

The wounded were evacuated by stretcher and ox-cart to tented field hospitals. Those able to be moved were transferred to so-called stationary hospitals, and ultimately by train to larger, more permanently established base hospitals. Army nurses were only intended to serve at base hospitals, well away from the action. Transport difficulties and overwhelming numbers soon overturned that cautious restriction, and they were moved forward into the thick of the chaos in makeshift field hospitals. Edith Hancock described working half the night as well as all day in Kroonstadt, where the town hall and schools were filled with patients, many lying on the floor: 'There are 4 to 5 thousand sick at Bloemfontein & it is called a death trap. Two Sisters died here last week and more are down . . . The medical work to be done here is tremendous, but they are all sick.'

The army nurses shared the men's discomfort, sleeping on bare floors in deserted houses, eating the same rations and drinking the same muddy water. They worked parched with thirst, in hot, dusty conditions. Hospitals were often tented camps with patients housed in double-walled marquees which offered some insulation, whereas the nurses slept in single-skin bell tents, stiflingly hot or freezing cold, which flooded in torrential thunderstorms. Newspaper reports praised the nurses' work and devotion to duty, mentioned in official despatches from the front. The troops now voiced their appreciation of the comfort of a woman's care.

Army nursing sisters at Rondebosche, during the Boer War. (Courtesy of AMS Museum)

Casualties

A total of twenty-three out of the twenty-four nurse casualties died from disease.

Uniform

The earliest Netley nurses wore a brown dress with a starched apron. In 1888, ANS uniform was formalized as a grey serge dress with linen collar and cuffs, an apron, shoulder cape, a muslin cap and a bonnet with a veil, plus a summer and a winter cloak.

The ANS nurses' kit was impractical for the South African climate. They wore long, grey, long-sleeved dresses with white bib aprons, white veils and starched collar and cuffs, a scarlet shoulder cape, a straw boater with a scarlet ribbon when off duty, and carried white scarlet-lined parasols. A black leather pouch hung from their belt containing forceps, scissors and a probe. The discomfort of working in 100 °F temperatures may be easily imagined.

Rudyard Kipling wrote of their uniform that at home it was 'hideous, but out here one sees the use of the square-cut vermilion cape. Everything else is dust-coloured, so a man does not ask where a Sister may be. She leaps to the eye across all the camp.'

ANSR members had a blue cloak with red-lined hood and wore a large circular silver brooch embossed with the Geneva cross and 'Princess Christian's Army Nursing Reserve', pinned on the right side of their civil hospital uniform or cape.

Queen Alexandra's Imperial Military Nursing Service

Having proved its worth, the ANS was to be put on a more prestigious footing. Previously it had consisted of one lady superintendent, nineteen superintendents and sixty-eight sisters, all of whose powers, an advisory committee had concluded, were too limited.

In 1902, Queen Alexandra's Imperial Military Nursing Service came into being. The new nursing service was administered by a Nursing Board, comprising the DGAMS, the QAIMNS matron-in-chief and the matrons of two prestigious London civil hospitals. Their badge was finalized three years later: the cross of the order of Dannebrog, in recognition of the Queen's Danish origins, with A for Alexandra at its centre, surmounted by a crown, enclosed in the name of the service in the shape of an oval over its motto: '*sub cruce candida*', meaning 'under the white cross'.

QAIMNS candidates were required to have at least three years' training in a recognized civil hospital. Class and military connection continued to feature in the selection of applicants. The matron-in-chief worked with an assistant principal matron at the War Office and a principal matron was based in South Africa. The new QAIMNS had 27 matrons, 50 sisters and 150 staff nurses.

Army nurses now served at twenty-seven hospitals at home and in Hong Kong, Malta, Egypt and West Africa. Matrons were now responsible for training male RAMC nursing orderlies and in complete charge of hospital wards. (Some RAMC nursing orderlies were permitted to join the QAIMNS.)

The abbreviation QAIMNS was such a mouthful that the new service members became known simply as 'QAs'.

Queen Alexandra's Imperial Military Nursing Service Reserve

The QAIMNSR was formed in 1908, to supplement the QAIMNS in the event of war. Some (but not all) ANSR members joined the new Reserve.

Candidates as matrons, sisters and staff nurses were invited, single or widowed, aged 26–45 with three years' training in a recognized hospital or nursing school. Birth certificates were required as proof of age. Members signed an agreement to serve at home or abroad if called upon in time of war and were paid a small annual retaining fee. Enrolment was for three years, renewable for further periods and reviewed yearly. Members reported in writing annually to the matron-in-chief to confirm they continued to be currently employed in nursing. They were normally retired at 50.

Recognition of Service

In 1883, Queen Victoria instituted the Royal Red Cross (RRC), a decoration specifically for nurses or ladies who had given outstanding service in the care of the sick or wounded of the fighting services.

Army nurses who served in South Africa during the Boer War qualified for campaign medals, although their names were apparently omitted from lists published in newspapers.

Researching Mid- to Late-nineteenth-century Army Nurses

The National Archives

WO 25/3955 contains much information relating to army nurses in the late nineteenth century. It includes nominal rolls of female nurses, with nurses who served with the Egyptian campaign in 1882 and a roll *c.* 1885 of twenty-four ANS members showing where they were then serving. Detail on the National Aid Society training scheme is also included, plus nominal rolls for larger army hospitals, and brief service details of *c.* 150 ANS members between the 1860s and the 1890s, indexed at the rear.

Individual service details show, for example, Mrs Deeble's maiden name, her date of birth, her date of entry into the ANS, mention of her service during the Zulu War, her RRC decoration and the date of her retirement.

Emma Gough Bayley, born in 1856, was stationed at Netley in 1887, rejected after the probationary period, then given a further four months' grace. Her appointment was confirmed, and she had a very satisfactory report at Woolwich and Devonport. Her service ended, however, in 1891, when 'Having become a mother, she is to be dismissed the service when convalescent.'

Series WO 100 (now digitized at DocumentsOnline) comprises medal rolls for various campaigns for which nurses received medals, including WO 100/61 (Egypt) and WO 100/67 (Nile, 1889).

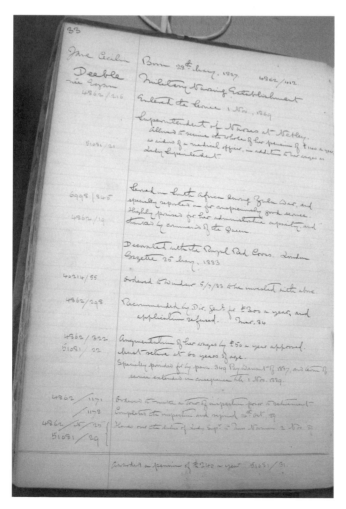

Service record of Jane Cecilia Deeble. (TNA WO 25/3955)

Army Medical Services Museum

Copies are held here of medal rolls for army nurses relating to the Nile Campaign (1889), Egyptian Campaign (1882–1889), Ashanti, First South African War (1895–1896 and 1900) and Second South African (Boer) War (1899–1901).

Online Sources

An index to WO 25/3955, with transcribed brief details, may be found at Findmypast.co.uk. Early army nursing sisters' careers may be followed on the censuses, which show nursing sisters in military hospitals. The *British Journal of Nursing* is another very useful source on early army nurses. Annie Ellen Caulfeild's obituary, in February 1937, for example, details her career at Netley and the Herbert Hospital, before serving in the 1881 South African War and the 1882 Egyptian uprising.

Researching Boer War Army Nurses

The National Archives

Series WO 100 (digitized at DocumentsOnline) includes WO 100/229, the Queen's South Africa Medal roll. This shows all specially appointed nurses and nursing sisters who served in South Africa for a certain period from 11 October 1899 and were eligible for this medal. The returns were originally made by the hospitals to which the nurses were posted, and then brought together in one roll. Some names (nurses who served at more than one hospital) appear several times. Spelling variations, similar names or initials make it difficult to identify the unit some served with, and parts of the roll appear to be missing. Some hospital names are abbreviated. Some casualties and nurses who refused medals are included.

WO 100/353 holds the nurses' roll for the King's South Africa Medal, for service on or after 1 January 1902, having completed eighteen months' war service before 1 June 1902. Nurses were not eligible for clasps for either medal.

WO 25/3462 details mainly male Army Hospital Corps members but also about eleven nursing sisters, mostly ANSR, who died on active service mostly during the Boer War, giving name and date of death, occasionally with manner of death.

Army Medical Services Museum

The Army Medical Services Museum holds letters from army nurses who served in the Boer War, lists of ANSR nurses and where they served, copies (incomplete) of South Africa Medal rolls and the South African War casualty roll (vol. II), giving rank, name, initial, date, cause and place of death for ANSR casualties.

AMS also has the full printed nominal roll of members of the ANSR at November 1900, showing those serving with the Field Force in South Africa. These lists are alphabetical, with each nurse's number, date of appointment to the Reserve (from 1897, but mostly 1900), where trained and where presently employed. Resigned members appear in italics.

Online Sources

The *BJN* includes reports from nurses serving in South Africa during the Boer War, lists of those being posted out (with dates and sometimes the ship on which they travelled), names of Reserve nurses appointed to home hospitals in their place, recipients of the Royal Red Cross and nurses mentioned in Lord Roberts' despatches.

The Times includes reports on the role of army nurses during the war and mention of individual army nursing sisters. E J Wood and A A S Hill (both ANSR) are reported in *The Times* of 2 August 1901 among the sick onboard the *Orcana*, due to dock at Southampton.

The *LG* carries lists of RRC recipients, and regular and Reserve army nursing sisters mentioned in despatches during the Boer War (for the largest list, see issue 27353, 10 September 1901, pp. 5958–5959).

Researching Early Twentieth-century Army Nurses

The National Archives

WO 25/3956 is an indexed register of candidates to be appointed to the newly formed QAIMNS including the earliest appointed members, showing previous service, including with the ANSR during the Boer War. Other details include full name and marital status, father's occupation, education and training details, previous experience, references and where posted.

Emma Maud McCarthy, who served in the ANSR in South Africa (and became BEF matron-in-chief in the First World War), is described in glowing terms and selected as a matron. Dates of appointment only appear partway through; dates of earlier entries may be inferred from candidates' dates of previous experience.

Army Medical Services Museum

The AMS holds a 1905 ANSR alphabetical roll showing number, date of appointment, where trained and present employment, with asterisks against those who served in the South Africa War.

Online Sources

An index to WO 25/3956, with transcribed brief details on each nurse, may be searched at Findmypast.co.uk.For a summary of the early history of the ANS and transcribed detailed reports on army hospitals relating to the early years of the QAIMNS, consult www.scarletfinders.co.uk.

The *BJN* carries information on the re-organization of the army nursing service.

Printed Sources

Anne Summers, *Angels and Citizens, British women as military nurses 1854–1914* (1988)

Colonel Eric Gruber von Arni and Major Gary Searle (compilers), *Sub Cruce Candida, a celebration of one hundred years of Army Nursing 1902–2002* (2002).

Chapter 4

CARE OF THE WOUNDED IN THE FIRST WORLD WAR

From the battlefield or front line, the wounded were carried by regimental stretcher bearers to the regimental aid post for basic first aid, then possibly several miles over rough ground to advance dressing stations or a main dressing station set up by the field ambulance in tents or available buildings. Those needing further attention were taken to the casualty clearing stations (CCS), and from there to stationary hospitals (SH), and finally by hospital train to general hospitals (GH), from which some were shipped home to 'Blighty'.

CCS were about halfway between the front line and the base area (possibly 40km behind the front line), and usually close to a main railway line or waterway. They held beds and stretchers to treat at least 200 sick or wounded. Army Service Corps (ASC) ambulance convoys collected casualties from the main dressing stations. After four weeks, those who hadn't died or recovered sufficiently to return to their unit would be transferred by ambulance train or barge to a hospital.

Stationary hospitals, despite their name, were more mobile than CCS. Every division had two SH, often requisitioned civilian hospitals holding up to 400 casualties. A GH would be on or near a railway line, to facilitate transfer of casualties. Some were in large hotels, others were camps with huts and tents.

Hospitals in the UK

By 1914, the UK had 6 major military hospitals, and 6 others with more than 200 beds. On the eve of the war, there were 150 military hospitals (mostly small units of less than 10 beds) totalling about 7,000 beds. At the Armistice, capacity had increased to over 350,000 beds.

This was achieved by enlarging existing military hospitals with huts and marquees and opening annexes in nearby buildings, mobilizing and enlarging the civil hospitals chosen as territorial force general hospitals, building or taking over buildings for new military hospitals and establishing special war hospitals in asylums, Poor Law institutions and other public buildings. (The civilian staff of asylums and Poor Law infirmaries continued working after they were taken over.) In addition, civil hospitals allotted some wards to military patients, and a large number of auxiliary hospitals (organized through the Voluntary Aid Association) opened all over the country.

The twenty-three territorial force general hospitals were expanded by taking over schools and other public buildings, often miles apart. By 1917,

Nursing staff of a First World War home hospital, showing one regular and a number of Reserve QAIMNS of differing ranks, with VADs. (Peter White collection)

2 Western General, in Manchester, for example, was spread over thirty-four different premises, mostly schools.

The voluntary hospitals (some of which were private homes, offered by individuals) were mainly accepted through the Joint War Committee of the BRCS and Order of St John, and mostly staffed by Voluntary Aid Detachments (VAD) including trained nurses. These hospitals were described as auxiliary hospitals and included convalescent hospitals.

Command depots were set up towards the end of 1915, to accommodate increasing numbers of convalescent military patients. Treatment mainly involved exercise and massage, to improve men's mobility sufficiently for them to rejoin reserve units. By April 1918, 20 command depots with a capacity for 75,500 men had been established.

A CCS opened at Eastleigh near Southampton in 1915, to process patients from hospital ships not needing in-patient hospital care. They would be discharged after two or three weeks, or sent to other hospitals. This unit expanded to fill several buildings and huts, accommodating over 1,000 patients, changing its name temporarily to the Military Hospital, Eastleigh in 1917 and taking slightly wounded and non-seriously ill cases, before reverting to CCS, Eastleigh in January 1918.

Military hospitals abroad and at home were staffed by varying combinations of regular and Reserve army nurses, nursing and general service (GS) VADs, and in the later stages of the war, Assistant Nurses (AN) and Special Military Probationers (SMP) on six-month contracts. In 1918, the German spring offensive put great pressure on the nursing services, as did the Allies' autumn push and the influenza epidemic. ANs with two years' minimum experience in fever nursing were sent to France from February 1918. SMPs were selected from promising territorial civil hospital probationers or VADs, and attached to the Territorial Force Nursing Service (TFNS) or QAIMNSR.

In surgical wards, much of the daily work involved changing dressings. Medical wards with specialist fever nurses had patients with pneumonia, malaria, trench fever, enteric fever and influenza, often needing longer hospitalization and careful nursing.

By the end of the war, about 10,000 had served with QAIMNS and QAIMNSR. Over 8,000 had served with the TFNS, including 2,280 abroad.

Territorial Force Nursing Service

The TFNS was created in 1908, in the wake of the newly formed Territorial Force. (The Territorial Force comprised volunteers raised in counties and large towns, prepared to defend the country in case of invasion.) The TFNS was planned as a reserve of trained civilian nurses to be called up to serve in home hospitals for the treatment of casualties of invasion.

The territorial force medical service was planned to include 12,000 hospital beds in 23 GH spread around the UK, centred around large civil hospitals in 19 towns and cities, from Aberdeen to Plymouth. The nursing staff of each hospital would comprise 1 matron, 22 sisters and 68 staff nurses, with names of 120 nurses (to allow for resignations, etc.) kept on a roll, updated yearly.

Local committees consisting of prominent ladies from each hospital's catchment area organized public meetings to encourage enrolment, which was slow, as few people anticipated war. Candidates had to be aged over 23, with at least three years' training in a recognized hospital and the consent of the matron where they were currently employed. Those accepted signed a declaration of willingness to serve if called up to their allocated hospital. They were required on 1 January each year to confirm their employment status and notify any change of address, to maintain their names on the roll. Retirement was at 55 for matrons, 50 for nurses.

Enrolled members received a badge. Uniform was to be issued on call-up. Some nurses on the TFNS roll volunteered for active service in the Balkan wars in 1912 and 1913. New regulations were then issued, limiting TFNS volunteering for active service in any war to twelve from each hospital.

Civil Hospital Reserve

Reference to the Civil Hospital Reserve (CHR) may be found when researching a First World War army nurse. Just to confuse matters, the CHR existed separately from the ANSR, the QAIMNS Reserve or the TFNS. It was set up in 1911, as an extra reserve of nurses in civil hospitals to replace army nurses sent to a theatre of war and supplement home hospitals.

In 1914, the CHR had 800 civil nurses on its roll. Over 400 were sent abroad. Many appear to have joined the QAIMNSR (possibly a requirement for foreign service). A nursing sister mobilized from a civil hospital may have CHR on her service medal index card, appear on the CHR medal roll and be referred to in official statements of her service as having served with the CHR, yet have signed a QAIMNSR agreement and have QAIMNSR on her B103 form.

Army Nursing in the First World War

On the outbreak of war, there were 290 QAIMNS on the active list and 173 in the Reserve, but over 500 were estimated to be needed for British Expeditionary Force (BEF) hospital units in France. The shortfall was made up from the remaining ANSR members and the CHR.

TFNS members were notified to be ready for duty at very short notice and mobilization of the London general hospitals (LGH) began in early August.

Civil hospital posts left vacant by the mobilization of TFNS were often filled by nurses coming out of retirement. About 100 had been Queen's Nurses (similar to district nurses).

Meanwhile, army nurses already in France were hearing about heavy losses and wondering where the wounded were. Kate Luard (a QA Reserve and Boer War ANSR veteran) wrote from Le Havre that they had been mobilized two weeks and still had no work. It was all a bit like a wet camping holiday. Skirts had to be shortened and gumboots issued, the site got so muddy. She learned to sleep under a rug – 'You don't miss sheets after a day or two'– on a mattress on the ground, washing underclothes overnight as her luggage hadn't arrived. (The sisters were notorious for their extensive luggage – each had a holdall, kitbag and trunk.)

Finally in mid-September she was sent to Le Mans, where over 500 cases arrived in cattle trucks which she struggled round with a tray of dressings and a pail of water, dealing with wounds full of straw and dirt, with gangrene already setting in. (The well-manured farmland being fought over was to contaminate many wounds, creating a fatal condition known as 'gas gangrene'.) Now working day and night, Luard realized the Mauser rifle wounds of the Boer War had been mere pinpricks in comparison to these shrapnel injuries caused by hot, jagged shards of metal flung out in shell explosions. Dirt, lack of water to drink or wash in and sleeping in boots, mackintoshes and aprons was all still 'thrilling'.

At home, by September 1914, most of the territorial GH were up and running. Many TFNS members were still in civilian uniform, the material for their TFNS uniforms having been held up by the chaos in France. Those with uniforms complained of the impracticality of wearing the grey and red shoulder cape while working, especially in theatre.

By November, all twenty-three territorial GH were at full capacity, treating evacuated sick and wounded. TFNS members were feeling the strain of working at full stretch while having to supervise untrained ward orderlies. By spring 1915, TFNS members had increased to 4,000, and 2 more GH opened.

As sick and wounded continued to flood into the UK, the territorial hospitals were enlarged as much as possible. Hutted annexes were built in the grounds of some, while others took over nearby buildings. Principal matrons wilted under the responsibilities of their unpaid TFNS role, on top of their civil work. Hospital matrons, paid less than in civilian life and taken on to run 500-bed hospitals, found themselves in charge of 4 times that many beds, their staff supplemented by nursing VADs, 2 replacing 1 trained nurse.

Service in France

On mobilization, each principal matron had submitted to the TFNS matron-in-chief the names of nurses wishing to work abroad and some TFNS had already been sent to France. Arriving at the end of September

1914, Frances Maud Rice described the frightening sight of hoards of army sisters – 'I think most of them think us intruders.' Many TFNS members felt intimidated by the regular QAs in their red tippets, who seemed – at least at first – to look down on them.

Army nurses were only supposed to serve in base hospitals, but were rapidly also routinely posted to ambulance trains, barges and CCS.

Ambulance Trains

Nursing sisters were assigned to ambulance trains from September 1914. Before this, they were posted to railway stations, dressing wounds and handing out hot drinks while the train was in the station. Early trains were simply cattle trucks with straw bedding. French passenger trains were then refitted to take lying and walking cases. Having nursing sisters on board dressing wounds and relieving some of the discomfort of the journey worked well and nursing staff were appointed to the first seven ambulance trains.

Many early trains had no communicating corridor between carriages. Each carried about 500 patients, often in a critical condition. On all journeys at least half a dozen men died, so it was vital to get round them all. The sister – strictly against regulations – clambered from one coach to another, carrying a knapsack of dressings and medicines, and at night a swaying hurricane lamp. One recalled an amazed stationmaster seeing her clinging to the side of the train as it flew through a small station.

Casualty Clearing Stations

Army nurses on station duty and ambulance train sisters waiting at railheads began offering their services at the nearest CCS. At the end of October 1914, QAIMNS were formally posted for the first time to a CCS.

Each CCS occupied about half a square mile of marquees and wooden huts, with operating theatres, X-ray unit, wards, kitchens, dispensary, stores, incinerator, latrines and mortuary, plus sleeping accommodation for the staff. This comprised seven medical officers, a dentist, a pathologist, a quartermaster, seventy-seven other ranks and seven QAIMNS.

About 1,500 patients a day might be admitted, but only urgent cases operated on. Initially, patients simply lay on stretchers. In 1915, trestles for the stretchers were provided, which were more comfortable for patients and easier for the nurses.

From May 1915 a permanent reserve of seven nurses was stationed at Malassise, near St Omer, to be sent in an emergency to any CCS. This arrangement continued for the duration of the war, and five other reserve pools were set up. Selection was based on physical fitness, service record and confidential reports.

Nursing at a CCS was harrowing, demanding and sometimes dangerous, especially during the spring 1918 German offensive, when CCS often had to decamp at short notice. Postings were officially restricted to three months, later extended to six, but even this rule wasn't always kept. Nurses suffering from exhaustion might be sent on leave or to convalescent homes to recuperate.

Pressure of work in makeshift CCS operating theatres led to theatre sisters standing in as anaesthetists and eventually training was organized. Principal matrons held lists of nurses trained in anaesthetics, ready to work with a surgical team if required.

Hospital Barges

Barges to transport the wounded via waterways in northern France were first used by the French Red Cross and British Red Cross Society (BRCS), especially for transferring patients to hospital ships. This proved so successful in not jolting badly wounded patients that in early 1915 the RAMC took over four former coal barges. The barges were large – about 40m long, 5m wide and 3m high. They were painted grey with large red crosses and striped red and green awnings. Soon several flotillas of ambulance barges were carrying the worst head, chest and compound fracture cases. Each flotilla consisted of six barges, travelling in pairs, towed by steam tugs. Each barge, with a nursing sister and staff nurse in addition to RAMC MO and staff, had thirty beds, two bathrooms, a kitchen, a stove and even electric lighting and electric fans for summer.

The barges suffered condensation and occasional leaks, and gumboots were needed on canal banks at times ankle-deep in mud, but nursing sisters loved the cosy, calm, comfort as the barge slid along. Patients often didn't realize they were actually moving. A trip to the coast could take two or three days, travelling at walking pace.

Nursing Abroad

From January 1915 an embarkation sister met army nurses off the boats at Boulogne, interviewed them at the Hôtel du Louvre and organized their accommodation and postings.

Emily MacManus, a sister at Guy's Hospital, joined the CHR and was posted as a staff nurse to France in 1915. She describes her group of 'mere reserves' being met by the embarkation sister who sorted them into smaller groups. On hearing that Emily was from Guy's and had a sister working at Le Touquet, she sent her to 18 GH (initially an all-Guy's unit) at Etaples. Emily spent her first night sleeping in the open with a mackintosh to hand in case it started raining. She had to learn army hospital routine, and found herself working under a young sister who had been one of her probationers at Guy's.

At that stage there was nowhere to go and relax when off duty – no YWCA hut or sisters' rest house, although sometimes a bus took a few of them into Etaples where there was a YMCA canteen and a small cafe.

Nurses certainly needed respite. A small nurses' club opened in Wimereux in 1914, taking over a villa with a garden. This led to Princess Victoria's Rest Clubs opening in huts in hospital camps or houses in small towns, staffed by VADs. The clubs were homely and attractive and very popular 'for rest, writing and meeting friends for a quiet tea. It was such a relief to throw off the strain of the wards, and feel at home.'

One month you could be working in clean, dry wards in a solid building with running water and a comfortable billet with nice food in a small town; a couple of months later, surrounded by utter devastation, miles from anywhere, stumbling through old dugouts and stray barbed wire; a few weeks after that, in pretty woods; then back among shell holes.

'Trying' was the understatement most used by army nursing sisters, when overwhelmed, or working in difficult or dangerous conditions. Mustard gas, used later in the war, was 'trying'. It not only caused a very painful death but clung to clothing, affecting those treating the sufferers. Handling the uniforms of gassed men burnt Emily MacManus's arms and neck and permanently affected her vocal chords.

As the war progressed, landmines, tanks and flamethrowers brought other dreadful kinds of injury and terrible head or stomach wounds. QA Reserve Lily Petter knew which she dreaded most – she slept with her tin hat over her stomach, not her head.

Rats invaded tents, making nests in nurses' mattresses. Aside from illness brought on by exhaustion and working or sleeping in damp conditions, the nursing sisters also caught lice from their patients, which carried trench and typhoid fever.

Sick nurses were admitted to special sections of hospitals called the sick sisters hospital, or ward. The BRCS ran several convalescent homes for nurses near the coast. In the south of France, Villa Rocquebrune, near Cap Martin, was run as a convalescent home for nurses of all services. The Hôtel de l'Esterel at Cannes had fifty beds for military nurses.

Army nurses also served in Italy, Egypt and Malta, where a large number of hospitals received sick and wounded from the Mediterranean area. During the Gallipoli Campaign, QAs were based at a hospital at Mudros on the island of Lemnos and worked on the hospital ships that ferried the wounded to Mudros. When the army went to Salonika, 1,000 trained nurses followed and two hospitals also opened in East Africa. The nurses coped with wild dogs and large spiders, sand flies and mosquitoes.

In October 1918, fourteen QAs accompanied the Russian Expeditionary Force to Archangel in north Russia, in a specially converted passenger liner, the *Kalyan*. This became a floating wharfside hospital for eight months until the Allies withdrew and icebreakers released the ship, enabling the force to return. The sisters were issued sheepskin coats and fur caps with ear flaps, but otherwise wore normal uniform. Patients arrived by sleigh in fur-lined sleeping bags, but the front was over 200 miles away and the sisters encountered a new medical complication: frostbite.

Home Service

QAs and Reserves as well as TFNS nurses worked in 250 military hospitals, in the 25 territorial hospitals and also in some auxiliary war hospitals, dealing with the longer-term care of a large number of the nearly 3 million sick and wounded brought back to the UK and dispersed to hospitals all over the country during the course of the war.

Army nurses serving at home included those not fit enough for service abroad. Nurses might also be posted for home service as respite from a theatre of war, although this could be a mixed blessing. No longer entrusted with more specialized work, nor with the acting higher rank they had had in France, where they had been part of a highly motivated team intent on getting the job done, it was hard to adjust to the petty, rule-bound life of the home hospital, under a matron who was not always benevolent or reasonable.

Casualties

Nurses themselves inevitably became casualties, some killed in bombing raids, or drowned when hospital ships were torpedoed or struck mines, while others died accidentally. Most, however, died from sickness contracted from contact (without rubber gloves) with infection, prolonged exposure to cold, wet, or extreme heat, the strain of working long hours and the added stress of confronting mutilation, death and suffering on a daily basis. Nurses suffered malaria and dysentery and in 1918 many succumbed in the influenza epidemic.

Almost 150 QAs (mostly Reserves, but including a few SMPs and one AN attached to the QAIMNS) died either during or shortly after the war. Nearly sixty TFNS appear to have died, including several ANs and SMPs attached to the TFNS.

A special memorial service for nurses was held during the war, in April 1918, at St Paul's Cathedral. Army nurses are commemorated on Scottish and Irish national war memorials, in York Minster and six UK cathedrals, in St George's Church, Ypres, and the Monument des Infirmières at Reims. A bronze memorial tablet set in green marble was unveiled at St Giles Cathedral, Edinburgh, in 1921, commemorating Scottish nurses who died in the First World War, including seventeen TFNS sisters, staff nurses and ANs.

In addition, five QAIMNS, two QAIMNSR and three TFNS nurses were named on a teak memorial panel (now lost) to deceased members of the nursing services in St George's Church, Baghdad.

Recognition of First World War Service

Over 1,700 army nurses were mentioned in despatches. Over 1,000 received the ARRC and RRC and 17 bars to this decoration were given for the first time. The Military Medal was awarded to fifty-one army nurses. Army nurses were also awarded the Albert Medal, Florence Nightingale Medal and various foreign decorations.

From December 1917, chevrons worn on the lower right sleeve denoted service overseas since 4 August 1914. These were red if earned in 1914, blue from 1915 onwards, one for each year's service.

From mid-1917 onwards, gold braid wound stripes were awarded to military nurses wounded by the enemy while serving the country. Many nurses qualified for SWB.

Nearly 280 TFNS nurses qualified for the Territorial Force Medal, awarded to those who volunteered for overseas service before 30 September 1914 and rendered such service before 11 November 1918.

Uniform

QAIMNS uniform comprised a long grey dress (soon shortened to just above the ankle), long white bib apron, tippet or shoulder cape (scarlet for regulars, grey with scarlet border for Reserves), starched white belt, collar and cuffs, softly folded white muslin veil with the QAIMNS badge embroidered in the bottom corner, and oval QAIMNS or circular QAIMNSR badge on a ribbon at the right side of the tippet.

Matrons had scarlet cuffs and a scarlet coat collar, edged with grey. Sisters-in-charge had three scarlet bands 1in apart on both sleeves, above linen cuffs. Sisters wore two scarlet bands 1in apart, 6in above the wrist on each sleeve, above linen cuffs. On overalls, the red bands were worn lengthwise, on the shoulder strap. Sisters and staff nurses had grey-beige collars edged with scarlet on their coats.

From 1919, retired regular QAIMNS when permitted to wear uniform wore an 'R' on the right-hand corner of the tippet.

One silver 'T' on her tippet (denoting she is a TFNS member) is visible in this photograph of Staff Nurse Agnes Jack Parker, MM. (By kind permission of Charlotte Rowe)

TFNS wore a grey dress with sleeves buttoned to the elbow and a skirt straight at the front and gathered into the waistband at the back, with two tucks near the bottom and a hem 2in from the ground. The belt was of the same material as the dress. Sisters wore a band of the same material as the dress edged with scarlet on their right sleeve, 6in above the wrist. Each wore a grey tippet with a red border, a small oval badge on a ribbon and two (optional) silver-plated 'T's, one on each front point of the tippet.

They also had outdoor cloaks, bonnets, waterproofs and gloves. Those sent on active service took gumboots, plus a camp bed, waterproof sheet, bucket and canvas washbasin on a tripod.

Their silver badge had Queen Alexandra's crossed double 'A' motif, inside an oval containing the words Territorial Force Nursing Service, surmounted by a crown.

Sleeve stripes denoted years of war service.

Researching First World War Army Nurses

The National Archives

Series WO 399 (now digitized on DocumentsOnline) contains the service papers of most regular and Reserve QAIMNS and over 6,000 TFNS members who served in the First World War and the immediate post-war period. (The series includes a few files for ANs, SMPs and VADs.) These fascinating documents usually contain some detail on service and postings, although the contents do vary. They generally comprise official documents and correspondence, but some original letters from the nurse herself may also be included. Such letters, and annual confidential reports, bring the subject to life, and sometimes a story may be pieced together. Several files may exist for the same person.

Hopefully, the record will include the original application form, with personal details, and army B103 Casualty/Active Service form on which postings, sickness and leave dates are recorded. Millicent Eva 'Millie' Brown's service record (WO 399/10065) shows that she completed three years' training at Croydon Infirmary in 1915, joined the TFNS in 1916 and was posted to 3 LGH, Wandsworth. In 1917, she passed a medical to serve abroad and was posted to 46 SH (WO 95/4088) at Etaples. After a year, she was sent to the Portuguese Hospital at Ambleteuse, near Boulogne. Here a QAIMNS matron and TFNS nurses looked after sick and wounded of the Portuguese Expeditionary Force. After the Armistice, Millie joined 11 CCS (WO 95/343) at Steenwercke, near the Belgian border.

Service details before 1915 are often missing from B103 forms, although clues about early postings may be found in minutes and other documents in the file.

TFNS member Frances Maud Rice kept an illicit detailed diary following her mobilization in September 1914, substituting letters for names. The

Staff of 11 CCS Steenwercke, with Millicent Brown, TFNS far right. (By kind permission of Mary Snowden)

ship she crossed to France on is simply called the 'A'. She writes that she is posted to Angers, without giving the name of the hospital. Lists of military hospitals, CCS, etc. and their locations in MH 106/2389 suggest that this was 5 GH. Her army B103 form in WO 399/6979 does not record her postings before October 1915. However, other items in her service record give clues and her name appears in various documents in WO 95/3982, the diary of the Deputy Director Medical Services. This covers the period of the arrival of army nurses in France in the early weeks of the war and includes orders from St Nazaire, 28 September 1914, listing disembarkation from the hospital ship *Asturias* of a number of TFNS, Reserve and CHR nurses, including Sister F M Rice. Another document dated 30 September gives a list of postings, including that of Miss F M Rice to 5 GH at Angers.

Series WO 95 contains war diaries of units abroad, including hospitals, CCS, hospital ships, ambulance trains and barge flotillas to which army nurses were posted, offering the opportunity of further research on army nurses who served abroad. Their contents vary, depending on the person responsible for keeping them. They should (but do not always) name individual QA or TFNS postings in and out, and give a feel of the conditions that the nurse you are researching was working in.

The identity of Kate Luard as the author of *Diary of a Nursing Sister on the Western Front* may be confirmed by consulting the war diaries of early ambulance trains. The author described being sent to Villeneuve to join an ambulance train on 13 October 1914. One army sister and two Reserves

Frances Maud Rice's army B103 form, showing her many postings. (TNA WO 399/6979) were already on the train. On the evening of 14 October they set off for Braisne, arriving next day. WO 95/4131 the war diary of 5 Ambulance Train has an entry for 13 October 1914 at Villeneuve: 'A fourth nursing sister (Sister Luard QAIMNSR) was put on the train for duty.' The war diary records the train leaving Villeneuve Triage at 9pm and loading cases at Braisne the following morning. Fascinatingly, it also includes a diagram of how the train was laid out, showing the sleeping compartments and dining area for the nursing sisters and medical staff. Luard's nursing colleagues are identified as Staff Nurse Adler, Sister Woodhouse and Staff Nurse Cathels.

Luard's file includes her signed agreement dated 6 August 1914, with confidential reports extolling her as clever, capable, a good disciplinarian, a very good influence on her staff, with 'the gift of getting on well with all under whom she serves'. The officer commanding 41 CCS described her as having 'tact, sound judgment, patience and marked administrative prowess'.

Other files in WO 399 may not always contain such glowing reports, but hopefully will convey something about the character and skills of the nurse you are researching.

Medal index cards and medal rolls may be searched for army nurses who served abroad and qualified for campaign medals and/or were awarded a SWB or Territorial Force Medal.

Series MH 106 contains specimen hospital and CCS admission and discharge registers or medical sheets, including QAIMNS and/or TFNS patients, for example: MH 106/1010, MH 106/1030, MH 106/1055, MH 106/1061, MH 106/1280, MH 106/1281, MH 106/1284, MH 106/1287 and MH 106/1391. The hospital unit name is given at piece level in the catalogue. MH 106/2386 lists military hospitals at home and abroad.

PMG 42/1-12 comprises payment ledgers for nurses' gratuities and pensions, including those awarded in respect of disabilities through war service. They give name, address, rank, service and age and occasionally other brief information, for example, maiden name, date of death. Names of recipients of gratuities are listed at the back. Series PMG 44 includes pension payments to relatives of deceased nurses.

WO 222/2135 has an incomplete roll of army nurses killed or who died on active service, with some detail of a few casualties and of official war memorials to army nurses.

Army Medical Services Museum

The Queen Alexandra's Royal Army Nursing Corps archive is held here. It has army nursing uniforms, pamphlets, brochures, autograph and photograph albums, scrapbooks and diaries covering the First World War (including Malta and home hospitals), Nursing Board minutes, papers of Dame Sidney Browne and Dame Maud McCarthy with her diaries, material relating to service in the Middle East, badges, a large collection of First World War photographs, newspaper cuttings, lists of recipients of honours and awards, including alphabetical nominal rolls of the RRC and MM (with some citations) awarded to QAIMNS, QAIMNSR, TFNS, CHR, SMP, some photocopies of 1914 and 1914–1915 Star campaign medal roll pages and nominal rolls of MiD.

Imperial War Museum

Although lists of those eligible for campaign medals were forwarded by the matron-in-chief, army nursing sisters, like officers, had to apply for their own medals. Their addresses and date of application generally appear on the reverse of the index card. The IWM holds the originals of the women's First World War medal index cards.

The Department of Documents holds firsthand accounts of army nursing service, mostly abroad, but one or two documenting home service.

The *WW&S* database includes nominal rolls and some details of army nurses who died in the First World War, including some dates and cause of death, with next of kin details. *WW&S* also includes lists and photographs of some army nursing Military Medal recipients, TFNS standing orders and a summary of TFNS work during the war.

London Metropolitan Archives

Among the records of St Thomas's Hospital (5 LGH), H01/ST/C/04/001 is an indexed register of TFNS members serving between 1915 and 1919 with entries giving name, age, address, date of enrolment, position held, hospital, institution or district, name and address of matron, training school and date of demobilization.

H01/ST/C/06/001, a marbled ledger with TFNS marked on the spine, is indexed (including what appear to be cross-referenced married surnames). It covers 1915–1918, with over 100 entries, one page per entry, with reports, holidays, sickness and dates of service, later entries including age and address. H01/ST/C/05/001 contains an undated typed list of names and address of TFNS members and the unit they are to be transferred to.

Online Sources

In addition to awards and mentions in despatches to army nurses, the *LG* includes TFNS matrons' appointments and promotions.

BJN holds sources of information on individual QAIMNS and Reserve nurses including RRC awards, MiD, casualties, obituaries and some appointments. TFNS matrons' appointments and promotions also appear in the *BJN*. The issue of 13 March 1915 lists the nursing staff of 5 Northern GH, Leicester.

The website www.scarletfinders.co.uk is a mine of information on QAIMNS and army nurses in general, including transcriptions of BEF Matron-in-Chief Maud McCarthy's official war diaries, 1914–1919 (TNA ref. WO 95/3988-91).

Printed Sources

The half-yearly *Army List* of October 1918 includes MiD of army nurses with *LG* dates. Monthly *Army Lists* covering the First World War show TFNS appointments by seniority of the rank of matron and above

R R and J M Walsh, *Queen Alexandra's Imperial Military Nursing Service: roll of honour: 1914–1918 and 1939–1945* (1999), a nominal roll arranged by place of death/burial, with indication for some entries of cause of death

J H Leslie, *The Historical Roll (with portraits) of those Women of the British Empire to whom the Military Medal has been Awarded During the Great War, 1914–1918* (1919–1920) includes personal and service details relating to some army nursing recipients, as well as more specific information than appears in *LG* citations.

Firsthand army nursing accounts:

Anon, *Diary of a Nursing Sister on the Western Front 1914–1915* (1916)

K E Luard, *Unknown Warriors: extracts from the letters of K E Luard, RRC, Nursing Sister in France 1914–1918* (1930)

Emily E P MacManus, *Matron of Guy's* (1956).

Interwar Period

Most Reserves and TFNS nurses were no longer required once the influenza epidemic subsided and convalescent and remedial hospitals stopped treating veterans. TFNS members who had rendered satisfactory service until invalided or no longer required were allowed to keep their badge.

A gratuity was paid to Reserves and TFNS for each year of completed satisfactory service, but widespread bitterness was felt at being demobilized with only forty-eight hours' notice. Complaints had been also voiced about the 'serf clause' in army nurses' agreements, whereby they could be summarily dismissed for perceived misconduct, without any right of appeal or redress.

The post-war rise in the birthrate led many to train as midwives and in 1921 Queen Alexandra's Military Families Nursing Service (QAMFNS) came into being. Others took advantage of free emigration passages for ex-services personnel to Canada, South Africa, Australia or New Zealand. This scheme was run for ex-servicewomen through the Society for the

Oversea Settlement of British Women. It was a difficult time to find work and many former military nurses fell upon hard times. Nurses suffering from disabilities resulting from war service might be eligible for a gratuity or pension.

TFNS remaining on the roll reverted to the system of submitting enrolment parchments by 1 January each year. From October 1921, when the Territorial Force became the Territorial Army, the TFNS became known as the Territorial Army Nursing Service (TANS).

In 1926, QAMFNS was absorbed into the QAIMNS, which also gradually from that date took over the work of the QAMNSI in India and Burma.

General Nursing Council (GNC) registration of trained civilian nurses had begun in 1922. By the late 1920s, QAIMNS candidates had to have had three years training in a general hospital training school recognized by the GNC, and from 1931 were required to be state registered. Preference was no longer given to relatives of officers in the armed forces, and candidates were now required to be of pure European descent (i.e., white), rather than British parentage or naturalization. All sisters had to be willing to go abroad at any time. Up to two years' service at home was required before a foreign posting.

Each large military hospital at home and abroad had its own QA mess. QAs were serving in Khartoum in 1925 during the Sudanese mutiny. In 1929, all QAs left Germany with the withdrawal of the BAOR. QAs continued serving in China, Egypt, Sudan, Malta and Gibraltar, as well as India and Burma.

Researching Interwar Army Nurses

Service records for QAs who served in the interwar period are at the time of writing generally still held by the MoD.

The National Archives

Series WO 399 QAIMNS files may include some mention of post-war service, or details of post-war employment or personal circumstances. Many files were opened in the post-war years to answer queries or provide service record details.

WO 100/421 General Service Medal roll includes TANS members awarded the GSM in the interwar period.

The half-yearly *Army List* for this period contains dates of appointment and brief war service details for serving matrons and sisters, but only dates of appointment for staff nurses.

The *Indian Army List* from 1927 includes QAIMNS serving in India, with station, date of present rank and date of completion of Indian tour of duty or age of retirement.

Other Sources

St Bartholomew's Hospital Archives and Museum holds TANS registers from 1921 to 1939.

The BL holds *the Royal Army Medical Corps, The Army Dental Corps and QAIMNS News and Gazette* (1927–1948) which gives brief details of promotions, transfers and postings of serving QAIMNS, including home postings of staff nurses, as well as occasional short obituaries.

General historical accounts:

Ian Hay, *One Hundred Years of Army Nursing* (1953)

Juliet Piggott, *Queen Alexandra's Royal Army Nursing Corps* (1975)

Colonel Eric Gruber von Arni and Major Gary Searle (compilers), *Sub Cruce Candida, a celebration of one hundred years of Army Nursing 1902–2002* (2002).

Chapter 5

VOLUNTARY AID DETACHMENTS

From 1909, following the formation of the Territorial Force Reserve (forerunner of today's Territorial Army), county Territorial Force associations (TFA) used the British Red Cross Society (BRCS), St John of Jerusalem (StJJ) and St Andrew Ambulance associations to raise volunteers to provide first aid and transport for sick and wounded in the event of invasion.

These volunteers were raised in groups of men or women, called Voluntary Aid Detachments, to collect the wounded, take care of them during transport and establish small auxiliary hospitals. A few were formed by the TFA of the county concerned. Men's detachments were planned for collection and transport, women's for rest stations and auxiliary hospitals, but the scheme attracted far more women than men, mostly middle and upper class young women, eager for a patriotic pastime. These women were soon referred to individually as VADs (pronounced Vee-Ay-Dee).

VAD Organization

Voluntary aid detachments were identified by county and number, men's detachments given odd numbers and women's detachments even numbers. Women's detachments had a male or female commandant, male quartermaster, lady superintendent (preferably a trained nurse) and twenty women members, of whom four were to be qualified cooks. Men's detachments had a medical officer and pharmacist instead of a lady superintendent. In practice, many detachments never reached full strength and some women's detachments had medical officers and pharmacists, some of them women. From 1913, women quartermasters were allowed.

A VAD had to be a British subject aged at least 17, pass first-aid and home-nursing examinations and have hospital work experience. Few people took VADs seriously, and hospitals were unwilling to allow them on wards, but some did get a chance to make a few beds, etc.

Detachments were instructed to be ready on mobilization to set up and staff a sixty-bed hospital. In the summer of 1914, the War Office issued lists of everything that had to be provided – including the actual building. May

Cannan joined Oxfordshire 12 Detachment in 1911 when she was 18. As its quartermaster, she had to tackle this terrifying list. By the time an RAMC officer came to inspect their arrangements, she had managed to arrange the loan of an unused wing of Magdalen College, together with promises for all the equipment. By 6 August, the hospital was equipped, scrubbed and ready.

First World War

The BRCS offered the WO 200 ambulances and 1,000 trained nurses, but had been refused. VAD hospitals were not to be used. VAD members would only be used individually if required in military hospitals. Knowing that 3 Southern GH was not yet up and running, May offered their hospital to a very grateful colonel, who had just received a telegram announcing the imminent arrival of a convoy of wounded.

Finally in October, with casualties in France increasing, home detachments were suddenly instructed to mobilize their hospitals. One vicar's daughter answered the telephone and assumed it was someone winding them up – they had endured so much ridicule over the years.

The BRCS organized the vast majority of detachments. The separate aid organizations were brought together for the duration of the war under the Joint VAD Committee of the British Red Cross. Most VADs joined a county detachment but could be transferred elsewhere. Some 'special service' VAD members were posted through BRCS HQ. VADs served as either nursing or general service (GS) members.

In January 1915, the WO began requesting VAD nursing members (over 600 in one week alone) to assist in military hospitals. Nursing members in military hospitals at home were accepted aged 23–38 (later changed to 21–48 or 23–42 for foreign service).

Although working hours in auxiliary hospitals were shorter, VADs in military hospitals were paid and received free board and lodging and travel allowances. County directors forwarded applications from VADs recommended by their commandants for service away from home. Every VAD called up for active service received a letter advising on her duties and attitude, reminding her that the honour of the organization depended on her, with a special prayer on the back. After a probationary period of one month, they signed a six-month contract.

In April 1916, the WO authorized two nursing VADs, two women cleaners and one male orderly per ward of fifty to seventy beds, under a nursing sister. After two months, male orderlies were withdrawn from home military hospitals, and nursing VADs given the same duties as probationer nurses in civil hospitals: sweeping, dusting and cleaning wards, sorting linen and cleaning ward utensils, in addition to any nursing duties they were allowed to perform.

From 1917, VAD nursing members began serving in larger Women's

Army Auxiliary Corps (WAAC) sick bays at home and in France. By August 1917, there were over 3,000 women's detachments. But fresh recruits were in short supply and out of nearly 3,000 nursing VADs posted to military hospitals between April and November, almost 2,000 replaced VADs who had resigned. Many unpaid VADs, discontented about their living and working conditions, left to take up paid employment.

In December 1917, VADs were approved for Women's Royal Naval Service (WRNS) sick bays and a small number worked in home naval hospitals.

VAD nursing, domestic and clerical staff were sent to hospitals in Italy, Malta, Egypt and Salonika. By the end of the war, 90,000 VADs had worked at home and abroad, some coming from South Africa, Canada, New Zealand and Australia.

Trained Nurses

Voluntary Aid Detachments included trained nurses as well as volunteers with first-aid and home-nursing certificates. Red cross nurses had to have certificates showing three years' training in a hospital of not less than fifty beds, a matron's recommendation and a health certificate. Trained nurses (registered on a list) were paid and received free board and lodging.

Trained nurses were employed as matrons, ward sisters and staff nurses in red cross hospitals. By June 1915, about 370 trained BRCS nurses were working abroad, and over 900 in home hospitals. By the end of the war, nearly 9,000 trained and partly trained mostly older retired or married nurses were working in hospitals at home and abroad.

VAD Work in an Auxiliary Hospital

Work in home auxiliary hospitals was voluntary (i.e., unpaid), but VADs signed an agreement to remain for three months, after two weeks' probation.

Apart from trained nursing staff and women who scrubbed floors, auxiliary hospitals were staffed almost entirely by VADs. A VAD doorkeeper checked passes, VADs worked as clerks and secretaries, cooks, laundry maids and orderlies, and each auxiliary hospital had a VAD housekeeper and quartermaster. Quartermasters supervised laundry, issuing the blue and grey suits with red ties worn by military patients.

The ward sister changed dressings, helped by a nursing VAD, before the doctor's ward round. Everything had to be in order, beds lined up, castors all turned the same way. In the afternoons, nursing VADs would be washing bandages or tidying lockers and medicine cupboards. Evenings were occupied with dressings and fomentations, giving medicines and filling hot-water bottles. Lights out was at 9pm, when the night staff arrived.

Auxiliary hospital staff, with QA(R), TFNS, nursing and GS VADs.

Small VAD hospitals were generally more relaxed, with better food than larger civil or military hospitals.

VAD Nursing in Military, Territorial General and War Hospitals

Author Naomi Mitchison served as a nursing VAD at St Thomas's (part of 5 LGH) in 1915. She was clumsy at first. Having had servants all her life, she didn't know how to squeeze a mop or that tea was made with boiling water. However hard they worked, emptying bed pans, polishing lockers, scrubbing floors, the VADs were scolded, or ignored. Only one sister ever explained what was wrong with the patients. Eventually, VADs were allowed to take temperatures and wash patients. Once Naomi was even allowed to sit down – unthinkable, normally – to mark bottles. Beds had to be made with perfect hospital corners tightly tucked in, regardless of patient comfort.

VADs had to hold dishes while the nurse changed dressings, often with the man begging her to stop. Seeing unattractive naked male bodies was a shock. Gas-gangrene wounds smelt awful. Naomi fainted once, but was chastised so much it never happened again. Sleepwalking apparently became quite common among nursing VADs, due to the stress of their work.

Nursing sisters resented these amateurs for devaluing the respect they, as trained nurses, had only recently won. The men compounded this, committing the cardinal sin of addressing VADs as 'Sister' instead of

'Nurse'. They identified with VADs as fellow underdogs, joked and flirted with them. 'Your beauty is only exceeded by your great kindness,' might accompany a request for a hot-water bottle.

But in France, VADs were badly needed and rapidly took on more responsible work.

Nursing VADs in France

In October 1914, two VAD units, including trained nurses, cooks and a driver, led by Katharine Furse, were sent to France to set up rest stations along the lines of communication between the front and the base supply area. On arrival, they responded to urgent pleas for nursing help in 7 SH and a red cross hospital, then set up the first of a number of rest stations on a siding near Boulogne central station, dispensing hundreds of mugs of tea and coffee. In the early weeks they also dressed the wounds of men arriving on ambulance trains.

The VADs were not allowed to smoke or associate with men, earning the nickname 'the starched brigade'. Katharine Furse was determined no moral aspersions would be cast on VADs. Within 5 weeks, they had taken care of 30,000 wounded men passing through Boulogne, and earned VADs a respected role in France.

The first BRCS hospital opened at Wimereux, near Boulogne in November 1914. Olive Dent volunteered as a nursing VAD in France in the summer of 1915. She was issued with brassards (armbands), identity discs

Tug of war between VADs and army nurses at 30 GH sports day – the VADS won.

and an identity certificate. She invested in a camp bed, canvas chair, bath and basin, a ground sheet, sleeping bag, gumboots, an oil stove and collapsible lantern, and arrived in Boulogne with 100 other VADs. They were escorted to a hotel and for the first time Olive shared a room with a total stranger.

Olive was put in a small group sent to Rouen, where an ambulance deposited them at a collection of marquees, tents and hastily erected draughty huts which formed their hospital. They arrived starving hungry, but were only given bread and cups of tea. The reception was as weak as the tea, the sister asking what possible use could they be, without training? In less than a month, the same sister became a staunch friend.

Work was much the same as in home hospitals, with two vital differences. They had to learn to improvise, coping with no hot water, no taps, no sinks, no fires, no gas stoves, not enough cradles, or only 6 wash bowls for 140 patients. Pinching and borrowing became accepted practice. And with the shortage of trained nursing sisters, nursing VADs were suddenly given much more responsible emergency nursing duties. They had to rise to the occasion.

General Service VADs

From September 1915, the WO withdrew NCOs and men working in military hospitals and women general service (GS) VADs took over their jobs as cooks, clerks, orderlies, etc.

GS VADs in military hospitals at home had to be aged 18–50 for paid work as superintendents, dispensers, clerks, cooks, telephone operators, storekeepers, X-ray attendants and laboratory attendants. (Apart from higher, qualified posts like head dispenser, GS VADs in auxiliary hospitals were unpaid.)

From January 1916, women were taken on in military hospitals either as 'general service women' (i.e., GS VADs) or 'labour staff'. The officer commanding a home hospital applied for GS VADs to Voluntary Aid Association county directors, to use local women as much as possible. Otherwise, requests were sent to the Joint VAD Committee. Labour staff (cleaners, kitchen maids and other manual workers) were employed locally by the matron or RAMC officer commanding the hospital.

Employment of GS VADs and labour women was applied to medical units overseas. They now included waitresses, pantry maids, assistants to opticians and dentists, motor transport drivers, mechanics and washers. The age limit for GS VADs in military hospitals abroad was 18–50, as against 19–50 for red cross units abroad.

GS VADs worked in hospitals at home and overseas doing clerical, transport, kitchen, storekeeping and cleaning jobs. They were expected to have basic cooking, laundry and housework or secretarial skills, be handy with tools, and ready for anything. They were described as needing adaptability and discipline, cheerfulness, commonsense and tact. Those with boarding school experience probably found it easier to adapt to army discipline and spartan, shared living.

General Service VADs in France

In April 1916, a small party of VADs replaced male staff at the BRCS post office HQ at the Hotel Christol, Boulogne, sorting and delivering mainly official letters and newspapers to thirty BRCS hospitals and units in the Etaples area. The post office held card indexes of all red cross personnel in France, in case mail needed redirecting. All outgoing letters were also sealed, stamped and tied into bundles after they had been passed by the censor.

Several base ambulance convoys were taken over by women VAD drivers. VAD motor drivers abroad needed at least six months' driving experience, skill at running repairs and a first-aid certificate. They had to pass an initial two-week assessment. Apart from a weekly mess allowance, they were unpaid. Drivers worked shifts, driving up to 150 miles a day, as well as cleaning and servicing their cars, which had to be kept in good running order and were inspected every morning. Aside from transporting patients, they took relatives to funerals or collected people from the railway station.

GS VADs staffed red cross hostels for relatives summoned for men who were dangerously ill. They also ran a nurses' and VADs' convalescent home in France and several rest clubs. VAD cooks staffed invalid kitchens and recreation huts for convalescent camps in France. (Lloyd George's daughter Olwen worked as a VAD cook in France.)

GS VADs in hospitals took orders from officers and NCOs, but their discipline was dealt with by hospital matrons.

Uniform

VAD Nursing Members

Nursing VADs initially wore stiff white collars fastened with studs and starched white cuffs. They wore a dress (bright blue for BRCS, grey for StJJ) with a gathered ankle-length skirt with three tucks at the bottom and long white linen apron 1in shorter than the skirt. The apron had two patch pockets and a bib with a round neck and continuous wide shoulder straps that crossed over at the back and buttoned on to the waistband with linen-covered buttons.

Only VAD nursing members with first-aid and home-nursing certificates wore aprons with a red cross on the bib. Those who had just earned their red cross would wash them to fade the red, so they themselves didn't look so green.

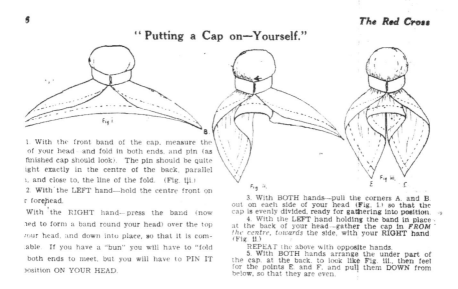

" Putting a Cap on—Yourself."

1. With the front band of the cap, measure the of your head and fold in both ends, and pin (as finished cap should look). The pin should be quite ight exactly in the centre of the back, parallel , and close to, the line of the fold. (Fig. iii.)

2. With the LEFT hand—hold the centre front on r forehead.

With the RIGHT hand—press the band (now ed to form a band round your head) over the top our head, and down into place, so that it is com- able. If you have a "bun" you will have to "fold both ends to meet, but you will have to PIN IT osition ON YOUR HEAD.

3. With BOTH hands—pull the corners A. and B. out on each side of your head (Fig. i.) so that the cap is evenly divided, ready for gathering into position.

4. With the LEFT hand holding the band in place at the back of your head—gather the cap in *FROM the centre, towards* the side, with your RIGHT hand (Fig. ii.)

REPEAT the above with opposite hands.

5. With BOTH hands arrange the under part of the cap, at the back, to look like Fig. iii., then feel for the points E. and F. and pull them DOWN from below, so that they are even.

Instructions for pinning on the nursing VAD cap – hardly an enviable task at 6am! (Courtesy of the British Red Cross Museum and Archives)

Up to 1915 this uniform was worn with a 'Sister Dora' starched cap. From 1915, however, they were allowed soft turned down linen collars, white linen oversleeves (instead of starched cuffs) and white petersham belts, into which they stuck the scissors used for bandaging, dressing and sewing. Skirts were shortened, to 6in from the ground. The cap was replaced by an oblong head veil of white cambric or linen, unstarched, hemstitched all round 2in from the edge. (An embroidered emblem was added in the 1920s.)

VAD Commandants wore red (BRCS) or black-and-white striped (StJJ) dresses, with white apron, cuffs and cap.

GS VADs

BRCS GS officers, commandants, superintendents and quartermasters wore dark-blue greatcoat, jacket, skirt, hat or cap with white or navy blue shirt with detachable white collar, black tie and black patent leather belt. StJJ were similarly dressed, but with dark-grey greatcoat and black jacket, skirt, etc., and grey shirt.

Clerks, typists, storekeepers and telephonists wore a similar uniform with optional white shirt, brown overalls and handkerchief caps (for store-keepers) and dark blue or black hat. Dispensers, laboratory assistants, etc., had similar outdoor uniform, and brown overalls or lab coats. Cooks wore

Two VADS wearing the GS sleeve badge: May Blue in indoor hospital uniform; Nellie Griffith (who served in France as an assistant cook) in outdoor uniform. (Peter White collection)

blue or grey greatcoat, brown overalls, detachable white collars and sleeves or cuffs and a rough apron, with optional jacket and skirt, with shirt, tie and white apron. Pastrycooks had white caps. Waitresses wore overalls and aprons with plain bibs.

GS outdoor uniform had brown shoulder straps. All GS ranks wore on the left sleeve a cloth badge with the BRCS red cross and StJJ white Maltese cross, enclosed in a double circle containing the words 'VAD General Service'.

GS superintendents wore a badge with 'GSS' in white cotton on their shoulder straps (Unit Superintendents had 'US'). Head clerks' and head cooks' badges had HC within a border of white cotton embroidered on a blue or black background above the GS badge. Trained laboratory assistants had a similar badge with 'LA' ('XRA' for trained X-ray assistants). Head laundresses, head waitresses and head housemaids had HL, HW or HH on black on their outdoor coat and on brown on indoor overalls.

Uniform for GS motor drivers included double-breasted belted greatcoat, black mackintosh, jacket and skirt (hem 10in from the ground) or thick breeches, and blue, grey or white shirt, with white collar, patent leather belt and black tie. The greatcoat had loose sleeves fastened at the wrist, a roll collar (worn open or buttoned up over the ears), plain shoulder straps and inserted pockets. They also had a black mackintosh and gabardine stitched peak cap in blue or black. Overalls were worn when cleaning cars. They were allowed one regulation jersey and one grey or blue sweater, black leggings or gaiters, tinted motor goggles, thick boots and gloves and walking shoes.

A leather jerkin for drivers and washing boots for washers could be supplied on loan from the War Department. All motor drivers wore on the left sleeve the GS badge and the BRCS and StJJ emblem in a double circle representing a wheel, surmounted by two upright wings, enclosing the letters VAD in white silk on black.

VADs serving overseas were given a long list of advisable or permissible items, including hot-water bottle, handcream, cold remedies, 'housewife' (sewing kit), tool set, notepaper, etc. They carried an identity certificate, and from March 1915 a special armband (brassard) was issued. This had a

Nursing VAD with shoulder straps showing detachment number and county.

red cross with a red border, an army medical stamp and BRCS stamp with date of issue and number.

In the Mediterranean zone a khaki or white linen jacket and skirt could be worn, with a white sola topi or soft panama hat with regulation ribbon and badge, and white or brown shoes and stockings.

Shoulder titles on outdoor uniform consisted of a cross between the words Red Cross with the county name. The cap badge had BRCS or StJJ badge with a red cross in the centre and county with number of detachment.

Those who had joined a county detachment might wear a badge that identified their county and sometimes also their detachment number.

Trained Nurses

Trained nurses provided their own indoor uniform: dark-blue cotton dress, plain white apron, regulation collar and cuffs and badge, dark-blue belt and black shoes and stockings. Their cap was worn like an army nurses' cap, with double fold turned outwards.

Recognition of Service

A white herringbone War Service Bar was given to VAD nursing and GS members who had served 13 months in a military hospital, or 2,688 hours in an auxiliary hospital over a period of not less than 13 months. An additional bar was given for each further period of 12 months or 2,496 hours. The bar was worn on both sleeves, just below the shoulder.

A scarlet efficiency stripe for VADs working in military and territorial GH, but not war hospitals (i.e., temporary hospitals in infirmaries and asylums), was awarded after 13 months' efficient service, at the discretion of the matron. However, on transfer to another hospital, in practice this stripe was said to have counted for nothing. A VAD with an efficiency stripe could find herself given more junior work than one who had recently joined.

Over 9,000 VADs served abroad, qualifying for campaign medals. VADs were awarded the Military Medal, the ARRC (VADs had to have completed two years to be eligible and only received the second class decoration) and a large number received MiDs or commendations.

In 1921 the British Red Cross War Medal was awarded to over 41,000 home service members not eligible for an official service medal who had given at least 1,000 hours unpaid service (500 for ambulance drivers).

Casualties

More than 400 VAD casualties died during or as a result of war service. A few were killed or drowned as a result of enemy action, but most died from exhaustion and/or influenza in the months following the end of the war. Many others suffered long-term damage to their health.

Researching VADs

British Red Cross Society Museum and Archive

Record cards carry brief service details of personnel who served in the First World War, both VADs and BRCS trained nurses, including those in military and naval hospitals. Information may include dates and place of service, work category and awards. Records are extensive but known to be incomplete. Information on index cards, although not always entirely accurate, may open up opportunities for further research. Alphabetical lists of BRC War-Medal recipients (without badge numbers) are also held.

London Metropolitan Archives

Unfortunately, administrative records of UK military hospitals do not appear to have been preserved. It is worth looking on the online hospitals database (accessible from TNA website) regarding civil hospitals taken over by the WO, but their records may not include this period in their history. Staff records of other civil hospitals partly used as territorial hospitals may be worth investigating, but records of temporary war hospitals (housed in requisitioned public buildings) have almost certainly not survived.

However, LMA holds historical records of some London hospitals that became Territorial Force GH in the First World War, including St Thomas's (5 LGH). H01/ST/C/06/001-003 comprises indexed registers of VADs there, covering 1915 to 1919. Each register includes records of c. 200 VAD nursing members (and some SMPs), giving full name, detachment number, age, address, dates of service including leave and sickness, and brief reports.

The entry on p. 182 of H01/ST/C/06/002 is of interest to anyone familiar with Vera Brittain's description of a brief, unhappy period in autumn 1918 in a 'grim, gloomy' civilian hospital she called 'St Jude's', where the sisters made no attempt to disguise their contempt of VADs. The greater responsibility a VAD had had abroad, 'the more resolutely her ward sister appeared to relegate her to the most menial and elementary tasks' polishing bedrails and sterilizers. St Jude's was in fact St Thomas's, as the brief entry for 'Brittain, Vera Mary, 24, VAD BRCS' shows. Her report bears only the terse remark 'Left on conclusion of provisional month's service'.

H01/ST/NCPH/E/014/001 is an album of photographs, postcards and papers compiled by a Canadian VAD at St Thomas's.

H09/GY/PHYS/C/01/01-02 Guy's Hospital physiotherapy students' records mention former VAD service.

The National Archives

Some classes of documents include brief records of VAD First World War service and mention of previous VAD service may be found in some QMAAC and WRNS service records.

Series WO 95 includes war diaries of medical units abroad, which vary in terms of their content, but may record postings in and out of VADs and are worth consulting for the background detail they offer on the unit and its work. Gladys Constance Crane's BRCS VAD record card shows service in France, but without stating where. Fortunately, her autograph book mentions Rouen in 1917. The war diary of 5 GH (WO 95/4076) records her arrival in March 1917 with three other VADs and subsequent posting to 2 SH on 1 March 1918.

Series WO 399 (QA and TFNS army nursing service records, available on DocumentsOnline) includes a few files on nursing VADs serving in army hospitals, for example, WO 399/15229 concerns VAD Edith Minnie Vowler. WO 399/1083 contains a list of eleven VADs in Salonika who had not renewed their contracts and were to return to the UK, giving surname, initials and hospital at which they had been serving. (Lists of VADs appear in individual army nurses' files in this series, but are effectively impossible to find, unless they have been noted in 'Your Archives'. QA Reserve Charlotte Hookway's file, for example (WO 399/3965), contains a list of staff serving at the Connaught Military Hospital, including seven VADs with surnames and initials.)

Series MH 106 comprises sample hospital admission registers and medical records, of which MH 106/1278 contains records of VAD patients admitted to 19 GH, Alexandria; MH 106/2207 includes medical sheets of VADs. Nursing and GS VADs are also in MH 106/1055, MH 106/1061, MH 106/1065 (2 GH, Havre); MH 106/1280, MH 106/1284, MH 106/1287 (19 GH).

Series PIN 26 contains samples of disablement pension award files, including 300 nurses, with a few VADs. PMG 42/1-12 include brief records of gratuities paid to nursing VADs.

Imperial War Museum

Many firsthand accounts of VADs at home and abroad are held here, including diaries, letters, photographs and documents. They mostly concern nursing VADs.

The WW&S database includes reports on VAD work during the First World War, rolls of honour, lists of decorations and letters and photographs of VADs who died. VADs came from a class that had sacrificed many of its sons. Grieving mothers, facing the added loss of daughters, wrote heartfelt letters to the Women's Work Committee after an appeal for photographs for a memorial album. These photographs and moving letters appear in *WW&S*.

WW&S includes a British Empire Leave Club report, with an alphabetical list of voluntary workers including mention of prior VAD home and foreign service. A few university college reports on women students' war service include brief detail of VAD service.

Online Sources

The *LG* carries notices of VADs mentioned in despatches, and awards to VADs, including Military Medals. Citations for twenty-one VADs and red cross nurses appear in July 1918.

The *BJN* published appointments of trained nurses to home and overseas red cross hospitals during the First World War.

Printed Sources

The *British Red Cross Register of Overseas Volunteers 1914–1918* (reprinted, 2004) comprises several comprehensive (but incomplete) lists including VAD members, with very brief information including destination; GS VAD members' work is indicated by abbreviations

Paul Creswick, G Stanley Pond and P H Ashton, *Kent's Care for the Wounded: a Record of the Work of the VADs* (1915) lists members of all Kent detachments to 1915, with brief history of each detachment

Thekla Bowser, *The Story of British VAD Work in the Great War* (1917)

Vera Brittain, *Chronicle of Youth: Vera Brittain's war diary 1913–1917* (1981)

Vera Brittain, *Testament of Youth* (1933)

Dame Katharine Furse, *Hearts and Pomegranates: the story of forty-five years 1875–1920* (1940)

Lyn Macdonald, *The Roses of No Man's Land* (1980)

Dora M Walker, *With the Lost Generation 1915–1919, from a VAD's Diary* (1970), details work with No. 9 BRCS Hospital and No. 22 CCS.

Chapter 6

MILITARY AND NAVAL MASSEUSES

The rush of civilians offering their services within days of the announcement of war in 1914 included the unlikely sounding Almeric Paget Massage Corps (APMC), advertising in August 1914 for fifty skilled, qualified masseuses to offer to the WO to work in military hospitals.

Origins

Massage had become fashionable in the nineteenth century, when upper class ladies, weighed down by up to 15kg of clothing and constrained by corsets exerting at least 9kg of pressure on their internal organs, turned for some relief to the services of specially trained nurse-masseuses.

Gentlemen, on the other hand, might seek out relief of a rather different kind. In 1894, the *British Journal of Medicine* (*BMJ*) exposed the scandal of London massage parlours where more intimate services were offered. Fearing their own legitimate work would be affected, several nurse-masseuses set up a professional body to protect themselves. The Society of Trained Masseuses (STM), later Incorporated (ISTM), was founded to 'make massage a safe, clean and honourable profession for British women'.

After the Boer War exposed how unfit many young men were, remedial gymnastics was adopted as part of naval and army training. So-called Swedish exercises became popular in schools, although gymnastics for girls was considered very daring. One teacher recalled notes from parents saying 'I do not want my daughter lying on the floor kicking her legs about.'

Almeric Paget Massage Corps

The APMC was named after its founder, Member of Parliament Almeric Hugh Paget. Aware of the effectiveness of massage in rehabilitating the wounded during the recent Balkan wars, he and his American heiress wife Pauline believed this would be the most useful form of assistance to offer the War Office. The APMC honorary secretary, in addition to being a masseuse herself, was Miss Essex Eleanora French, a daughter of Field-Marshal Lord John French. This may explain why the APMC was so readily accepted, when other philanthropic offers of medical aid, especially those involving women, were refused.

Dr Florence Barrie Lambert, the APMC honorary medical officer, had nursed during the Boer War before studying medicine in London and medical gymnastics in Stockholm. By 1914, she was in charge of the 'mechano-therapeutic department' at Charing Cross Hospital.

By the end of September 1914, the APMC had enrolled several hundred masseuses and eleven were already at work in military and territorial GH at Netley, Aldershot, Colchester, Chatham, Woolwich, Edinburgh, Leeds, York and London. By December, over 100 were at work, some voluntary part-time, others paid by the Pagets, who had also opened an out-patient centre in London, at 55 Portland Place.

Headed by Dr Lambert and staffed almost entirely by volunteers, over 100 officers and men were treated daily here as out patients, receiving massage and electrical treatment. One sergeant is said to have quipped 'If the Kaiser saw this, he might say the English Army is being tortured to make it go to the Front.' It wasn't too far from the truth. By the end of 1914, 73,000 injured men had been shipped back to the UK. The WO had embraced massage so readily to speed their return to active service.

One of a set of humorous postcards drawn by a First World War massage patient, which speaks for itself.

Expansion in the First World War

The APMC was still run by the Pagets, Dr Lambert and Miss French, but members came under the orders of the individual doctors under whom they worked. By 1915, over 300 members were working in hospitals all over the UK, full-time and part-time, some voluntary, some paid by the WO and some paid by the APMC. In May 1915, the WO extended their work to convalescent camps and Dr Barrie Lambert was appointed Inspector of Military Massage and Electrical Services, attached to the RAMC, with the honorary rank of major.

All massage workers for military hospitals, camps and depots were to be appointed through the APMC, which would only accept those with ISTM or other approved massage certificates. In the first 9 months of the war, members of the corps gave over 250,000 treatments to nearly 17,000 men.

But the vast numbers of injured meant that demand far exceeded supply of trained masseuses and the APMC started accepting members with lesser qualifications. Under pressure from the ISTM, the WO formed a massage board to oversee APMC enrolment.

In December 1916, the Corps assumed the title Almeric Paget Military Massage Corps (APMMC). The Pagets remained responsible for Portland Place, which now treated 200 officers and men daily, relieving the strain on OP departments of London military hospitals. Otherwise, from May 1917, APMMC members were paid by the WO for duty in military hospitals, convalescent hospitals and command depots. From June 1917 the massage board permitted local masseuses to treat military out-patients. In July 1917, APMMC members were authorized to serve abroad.

Masseuses in military hospitals were paid direct by the WO. Those in convalescent hospitals and command depots were paid by the APMMC, out of a weekly sum received from the WO for their services. Both categories were required to sign six-monthly agreements, which included the controversial 'serf clause', resented by army reserve nurses.

The APMMC grew from 900 members in 1916 to 1,500 in 1918. Over the course of the war, over 3,000 APMMC members (including some masseurs) served with the Corps. About 2,000 were at work when the Armistice was signed. About fifty had served in France, with a few in Italy.

Training

Massage was promoted as a profession in which women could excel. ISTM students were required to be over 21 and of a cheerful, gentle but firm disposition. Training took at least a year. Students studied remedial gymnastics, theory of movement, physiology and anatomy. Electromagnetic therapy had been used for some time to stimulate paralysed muscles and treat sciatic nerve pain. By the end of the war, training in medical electricity took three months.

Many women trained in remedial gymnastics in PT colleges were accepted into the APMC and allowed to take the ISTM medical electricity examination without holding the massage certificate.

RAMC orderlies were eventually also trained as masseurs, together with war-blinded servicemen who proved very adept, although their training initially presented problems since mixed classes were forbidden. It was considered unseemly for lay women to teach men anything involving physical contact, although clearly touching male patients was permissible.

Treatment Work of Masseuses

Over 1.5 million men were wounded in the First World War. Many had shattered limbs which required amputation, or had contracted gangrene or trench foot (from permanently wet feet). Others suffered torso or head injuries, were blinded or developed post traumatic stress, then called 'shell shock'. Thousands of men were injured by shrapnel (sharp metal fragments thrown up by bombs and shells) which often severed nerves, causing muscle and limb paralysis.

Masseuses treated most of these conditions. Massage revived atrophied muscles and restored movement in stiff joints, improving quality of life and 'future usefulness', although combined massage, remedial gymnastics, electricity and hydrotherapy treatments proved more effective than massage alone.

Organization

The clinic at Portland Place became the model for medical and electrical therapy departments in military convalescent hospitals and command depots throughout the UK.

The Army Medical Service divided men into first, second and third class patients. First class (acute) were admitted to the twenty-three territorial GH, to orthopaedic centres or to red cross auxiliary hospitals, some of which were specialist treatment centres. By 1918, twenty orthopaedic centres were being run in converted public buildings in Liverpool, London, Manchester and elsewhere.

Territorial GH used massage for fractures; manipulation or electrotherapy for trench feet; gentle massage for burns and facial injuries; remedial gymnastics for lung damage and massage and gymnastics for the physiological symptoms of shell shock. Sepsis was successfully treated with electrotherapy.

Second class patients were sent to convalescent camps or hospitals. In 1915, the army convalescent camp at Summerdown, Eastbourne, held 3,000 patients, of whom 400 to 500 were given daily massage. Similar camps were established in July 1915, at Dartford and Epsom. Most teams of masseuses in convalescent camps came from PE colleges.

At Summerdown, each masseuse gave twenty to twenty-five treatments daily. This was achieved by treating four patients at once: two on heat treatment, one on electrotherapy and one actually being massaged. Nearly 600 patients were discharged each month, 80 per cent passed as fit to return to the front.

The King's Lancashire Military Convalescent Hospital Blackpool had a gymnasium, a hot exercise room to help break down adhesions, electro-massage and hydrotherapy departments and possibly the earliest use of electric-shock treatment, whereby shell shock patients were treated by an electric current through the brain.

Third class patients needing longer term rehabilitation were sent to command depots. These were set up in the summer of 1915 and gave six months' intensive treatment. At Heaton Park Command Depot, Manchester, neurasthenia, malaria, rheumatism, heart disease and other chronic conditions were treated, with 50 per cent of patients discharged back to active service within three months.

Life as a Military Masseuse

Having learnt massage and Swedish medical gymnastics at a sanatorium abroad, Olive Millard began studying in 1915 for the ISTM examination at the London Ladies' College, which held classes in anatomy, dispensing, massage and medical electricity. Supervised practical treatment of hospital patients was an examination requirement. Olive remembered her first day walking on to wards full of half-dressed men and wondering what she had taken on – 'But now there was no backing out.'

With masseuses in short supply, the BRCS took Olive's earlier experience into account and the WO issued a certificate allowing her to work in auxiliary hospitals while finishing ISTM training, treating nerve damage, frostbite and the varied effects of gunshot and shrapnel wounds.

She qualified in the winter of 1916 and was sent to the new massage department at the BRCS auxiliary hospital for officers at Brighton, which took many amputees. This began two years of very hard work, but the happiest years of her service. The staff comprised 3 men (for heavier work) and 7 women, treating 130 cases daily. Timetables and casebooks had to be kept. Despite the hard work, they had fun. One patient signed her autograph book 'Wounded in the heart by Olive!'

But Olive noticed that as the war dragged on, the wounds seemed to get worse and the men less robust. By 1917, everyone seemed tired and depressed, though no one would admit it. In 1918 the hospital was taken over by the WO, resulting in less pay and much stricter rules and regulations.

Olive returned home to Yorkshire, to join the staff of 2 Northern GH at

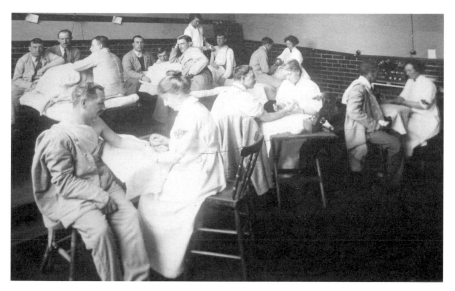

APMMC working to get men back on active service faster – note the universally glum demeanour of their patients . . . (Peter White collection)

Leeds as one of eighty masseuses, treating mostly nerve injuries. Each averaged 110 treatments a week, with 50 working together in a large lecture hall, each sitting at her own plinth where the men came in turn. The monotony nearly drove Olive crazy, but she found nerve and muscle testing in the electrical department more interesting. On a royal visit, she overheard Queen Mary comment, 'What fine, strong women these masseuses look.'

Masseuses did tend to be fitter than most women, but they also worked very long hours at an arduous job – twelve-hour days were not unusual. By September 1918, Olive was feeling the strain. Sent to equip a department to treat war pensioners at Gloucester Royal Infirmary, within a few weeks she had collapsed from overwork.

Masseuses were the Cinderellas of the medical services. They petitioned the WO, complaining they were fully trained, could be sent anywhere in the country, yet could barely survive on their pay, and received no war gratuity, some dismissed at twenty-four hours' notice. A year later, those who were left were finally granted a small increase, but not the gratuity.

Casualties

There is no known roll of honour for masseuses, although the ISTM journal may mention deaths of members during the First World War.

Naval Massage Service

In 1917, the Navy advertised for masseuses with ISTM massage, medical electricity and medical gymnastics certificates to join its massage service, working at Chatham, Haslar and Plymouth.

In April 1917, five nursing sisters for massage and electro-therapeutic work were appointed to the naval hospitals at Haslar, Plymouth and Chatham. Eventually, massage sisters also served abroad at Malta and Bermuda. Head massage sisters and assistant massage sisters served in twos at Haslar, Plymouth and Chatham. Non-residential ordinary masseuses were also appointed to the home hospitals and the ISTM held a waiting list of recommended candidates.

Mrs Elspeth Curphey Kingdon, Head Massage Sister at Chatham, supervised the training of selected male naval sick-berth attendants, who ultimately took over when the Royal Naval Massage service ceased in 1930.

Post-war Military Massage Service

During the war nearly 3,400 masseuses (and masseurs) enrolled in the APMMC and 2,000 were still at work in January 1919, when it became the Military Massage Service (MMS).

Members of the MMS were graded according to qualifications: head masseur/masseuse; senior masseur/masseuse and masseur/masseuse. Each category had three classes: mobile, immobile and part-time. The MMS managed to stop the WO employing untrained masseuses, but they remained very poorly paid.

For several months after peace was declared, the MMS worked alongside a new Pensions Massage Service, attached to the Ministry of Pensions. Plans to amalgamate the two into a national service to co-ordinate treatment of war disabled fizzled out. MMS numbers were reduced to 600 in January 1920, and the Portland Place Clinic closed in December 1920.

Ministry of Pensions centres around the country continued treating injured servicemen, stressing re-education of muscles by massage, electrical stimulation and exercise. In 1919, masseuses were treating war pensioners at the Aberdeen orthopaedic annexe. Tyncastle orthopaedic centre, Edinburgh, treated men who had been discharged too early with nerve damage, debility and unhealed wounds. Newcastle's Royal Victoria Infirmary added an orthopaedic annexe in 1920, treating 500 inpatients and 1,200 outpatients, including ex-servicemen. The BRCS opened orthopaedic clinics for veterans, with eight in the London area by 1920. Much remained to be done for disabled ex-servicemen, but many masseuses were laid off, although some found employment at homes for the disabled.

The ISTMS became the Chartered Society of Massage and Medical

Gymnastics (CSMMG) in 1920. Its members included newly qualified PE college graduates, among the surplus million women who would now have to provide for themselves.

Despite proposals for a reserve massage corps, by 1927 it was decided that in a future emergency only the Voluntary Aid Detachments would provide auxiliary medical services, for which qualified masseuses would be accepted.

The massage profession had advanced considerably in the First World War, demonstrating the effectiveness of physical therapies. In the interwar period it gained an impressive new name: physiotherapy. But Ministry of Pensions work was coming to an end. By 1930, there were only fifty Pensions Massage Service members left. Numbers of war veterans needing treatment had steeply declined and funding shortages led to staff reductions, with the emphasis now on exercise rather than massage.

Uniform

Almeric Paget Military Massage Corps

Early APMC members wore a plain navy blue coat and skirt 'devoid of trimmings' and a black or dark-blue felt hat.

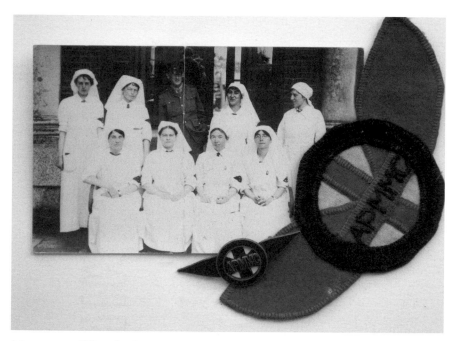

Massage staff Royal Victoria Hospital, Netley, 1918. Cicely Wilcox, back row extreme right, with her APMMC sleeve and cap badges.

Outdoor uniform eventually consisted of dark-blue skirt and jacket with patch pockets, leather buttons and optional belt and dark-blue scarf, worn with black shoes and stockings, white shirt, blue tie and dark felt hat. Skirt hems had to be 6in from the ground. Indoor uniform consisted of a white overall.

Head masseuses in military hospitals wore dark-blue shoulder straps with a scarlet bar; section masseuses a plain dark-blue shoulder strap on outdoor jacket and overall. Ordinary masseuses had no shoulder straps.

When the corps became the APMMC, enamelled hat badges were issued, comprising a blue circle, with the letters APMMC in blue over a winged red cross. A cloth badge was worn on the upper left sleeve of the overall and jacket.

Post-war Masseuses' Uniforms

The MMS badge had white block lettering on a black satin ribbon. Seniority was shown by scarlet stripes on shoulder straps, one for a senior masseuse, two for a head masseuse. The MMS badge was worn on the sleeve of the overall. Their hatband had the letters MMS in white on blue.

The Pensions Massage Service appears to have had a brass hat badge of the letters PMS intertwined, surmounted by a crown.

Researching Military Masseuses

Although APMMC members were paid by the WO, the APMMC was a privately run unit for which very few records have survived. Sadly, there are no known APMMC service records or registers, although members were issued with an illuminated certificate signed by Essex French, showing their dates of service with the APMMC and/or MMS.

London Metropolitan Archives

H09/GY/PHYS/C/01 covers staff and student records of Guy's Hospital School of Physiotherapy from 1907 and includes VAD nurse-masseuses and serving APMC members among various indexed registers of students and past students' record cards.

For example, H09/GY/PHYS/C/01/05/001 comprises index cards with photographs, giving name and address, previous massage and PE experience, examinations passed and massage sister's report. Dora Brooks, aged 26, was a masseuse at Epsom Camp. Dorothy Frances Carter, 29, is described in 1915 as a professional singer, APMC member, Orchard Hospital, Dartford. Margaret Clarke (married surname Hole), 28, 'a good worker and nice girl', APMC Ripon masseuse. Hilda Maud Camilla Dowding (who later served with the APMMC in France) attended from October 1915 to June 1916, working with the APMC at Roehampton: 'Very nice manner. Not strong. Very good to poor patients. Steady, capable, very good worker, worth more training.'

The Wellcome Library

The Chartered Society of Physiotherapy (CSP) collection includes ISTM records covering 1914 to 1918. At the time of writing the full catalogue of this collection is not online. It includes minute books for various committees, membership registers 1895–1975 and printed lists of members 1920–1986. The following relate to APM(M)C masseuses:

SA/CSP/F.1 contains material relating to the APMC from December 1915 to June 1916, including a printed sheet titled 'Massage for the Wounded' describing APMC early history.

SA/CSP/C.2/3/1-8 comprise examination result books for medical gymnastics, massage and Swedish remedial exercises examinations (1906–1942) with number, date, names and addresses and results, arranged by training organization. Results of Swedish remedial exercises examinations between June 1908 and November 1915 (C.2/3/2/1) include a 1913 entry for Eleanor Essex French, giving her certificate number, the fee she paid and her address in Waltham Cross. She trained under Barrie Lambert, sat written and practical 'neuritis', gained 122 marks out of 220 and was awarded a pass.

SA/CSP/D.2/1 ISTM indexed register of members gives certificate number, date of entry, where trained, therapy qualifications and current address.

SA/CSP/D.2/4 ISTM Roll December 1914 to March 1917, an indexed ledger covering numbers 2974 to 4242, with date, certificate number, training, qualifications, date of election to membership, election number and subscription details. Entries include 28 April 1916, 3559, Olive M Millard, 9 Chichester Terrace, Brighton, trained under St Aubyn-Farrar, qualified in Physical Exercises, with Medical Electricity added in June 1918.

SA/CSP/D.1/1/2 CSMMG register of members (1920–1922) includes registered member 484 Olive Mary Millard. Member 140 Kate Walter King (an APMMC member who served in France) is shown at Princess Mary's Convalescent Centre, Rednal, near Birmingham, a 400-bed centre for war disabled.

SA/CSP/P.3/3 includes a folder of reminiscences entitled 'Older Members', including Mary Street who trained at Bart's 1913 to 1914 and was one of the 'first ten' to join the APMC, sent to 2 LGH, Chelsea and later in charge of Reading War Hospital Electrical Department.

SA/CSP/P.4/1/2-4 contains St Mary's Hospital School of Physiotherapy magazine, including reminiscences of service with the APMMC.

The Library holds the journal of the ISTM (1915–1920) at shelfmark S5293.

The National Archives

First World War campaign medal index cards include APMMC masseuses who served abroad, plus a few who came to serve in the UK from Canada, Italy, Australia and South Africa. WO 329/2308, which contains the APMMC service medal roll, shows King, K W, having served in France from October 1918 to March 1919.

Non-APMMC masseuses who served abroad (usually under the auspices of the French Red Cross) will also be found in the service medal index. Those who served with the East African Military Nursing Service are included in Colonial rolls.

If you know where an APMMC masseuse served abroad, it is worth consulting the relevant war diary in series WO 95. WO 95/4076, the war diary of 5 GH, records the departure of Miss Mackenzie, APMMC to Boulogne for demobilization. The medal roll (WO 329/2308) confirms her as M J L Mackenzie, who served in France between August 1918 and March 1919.

Imperial War Museum

WW&S includes newspaper cuttings and information about APMMC history, uniform, WO regulations and specimen agreement forms. A report from the head masseuse at Alder Hey special military surgical hospital gives surnames of masseuses in charge of different sections and describes a typical working day.

Other Sources

If you discover where a masseuse served, it may be worth searching the hospital records database (accessible via TNA website), in case pictorial or staff records for the period have survived. Tyne and Wear Archives service, for example, holds administrative and general records of the Military Orthopaedic Centre, Newcastle upon Tyne for 1917–1929.

The BRCS archive holds record cards for masseuses in auxiliary hospitals, although not for Olive Millard.

Archives of PE colleges may also be worth exploring. Bedford Physical Education Old Students' Association have produced a booklet mentioning ex-student APMMC members.

Online Sources

The *LG* has a few entries of awards, etc. to masseuses.

The CSP website has a bibliography of publications on its history, including a journal article on the history of massage in the Royal Navy (J Stockton, 'The history of massage and physiotherapy in the Royal Navy', *Physiotherapy*, January 1994), see www.csp.org.uk.

The Times online archive includes letters from disgruntled military masseuses, describing service conditions.

The *BJN* published items on the APM(M)C, with some mention of individual members, including a list of eleven APMMC members who rendered valuable services during the war, giving their names and where they worked, for example, 2 Scottish GH Edinburgh, the military convalescent hospital Ashton-in-Makerfield, etc.

A list of command depots may be found at www.1914-1918.net.

Printed Sources

Dr Jean Barclay, *In Good Hands: the history of the Chartered Society of Physiotherapy 1894–1994* (1994)

Jane H. Wicksteed, *The Growth of a Profession* (1948)

Olive Millard, *Under my Thumb* (1952).

Researching Naval Massage Sisters

The National Archives

Navy List – massage sisters with their place of posting are listed immediately beneath the QARNNS (Queen Alexandra's Royal Naval Nursing Service).

ADM 104/171 massage sisters register (covering 1917–1930, with brief service details and remarks on conduct, temperament, physical fitness), is on microfilm. Miss Irene Chabot, ISTM qualified, appointed in August 1917 to Plymouth Hospital, resigned in January 1930. As head massage sister her temperament is variously described as 'even', 'cheery, equable and kind', 'cheerful and determined' and 'impulsive and enthusiastic'. She is considered 'a very capable masseuse, with an extensive knowledge of the scientific and theoretical side of her profession . . . a lady of marked and forceful personality'.

ADM 1/8483/55 concerns the establishment of the naval massage service in 1917, including appointment of Eila D Ewart, first head massage sister, previously with the APMC at the Command Depot, Alnwick.

Institute of Naval Medicine

The QARNNS archive includes journal articles on the history of the naval massage service and a list of massage sisters (1917–1930) including twenty-three temporary ISTM-trained masseuses employed in the post-war period. (This list appears to be incomplete, omitting qualified masseuse Miss Janet Hirst, who served for three years at Haslar in the early 1920s.)

Chapter 7

FIRST AID NURSING YEOMANRY

The 'Fanys', as they became universally known, began as a small team of young volunteer horsewomen trained, rather improbably, to render first aid to wounded men on battlefields.

Origins

The FANY were formed by Edward Charles Baker, an imposing ex-cavalry sergeant major who had served in the Soudan campaign, where in his own words he had 'the misfortune to be wounded'. Made painfully aware of the lack of stretcher bearers, he dreamed up a plan whereby after the battle women on horseback would give first aid and rescue the wounded.

This idea remained dormant until 1907. The Scout movement had just been formed, and many girls were disappointed they could not join. With the help of his daughter Katie, Baker started a mounted first-aid corps for young women and by 1909 had already approached the War Office, hoping to affiliate them to the new Territorial Force. The reply firmly stated that military experience had shown that such an organization would be totally unsuited to work on battlefields.

This deterred neither him nor his troupe. Members had to be aged 17–35, over 5ft 3in tall and enrol for at least a year. They were given military style ranks and trained in first aid, home nursing and horsemanship, borrowing Gamages department store's van and horses for practice driving. They put on competitive displays at the Territorial Forces Exhibition and paraded across London on horseback in smart scarlet military style dress uniforms, raising funds to buy an ambulance wagon.

However, dissension in the ranks led to twelve members resigning to form the Women's Sick and Wounded Convoy Corps, led by Mrs St Clair Stobart. Other powerful personalities took over the remaining group, headed by Lilian Franklin and Grace Ashley-Smith. Baker and Katie faded out of the picture and by 1912 a Grenadier Guard officer had become their honorary colonel. Addressed in military fashion, by surname and rank, their ranks included second lieutenant, sergeant-major, sergeant, corporal and trooper. Numbers grew. They learned signalling from a signalling

A pre-First World War FANY camp, showing post-1910 uniform. (Peter White collection)

officer, bandaging and stretcher drill from RAMC sergeants and rode in Hyde Park and on Hampstead Heath.

Their links with the army encouraged them to hold weekend camps in Surrey. On one occasion they joined ASC territorials for an overnight route march, and to their delight dealt with a concussion case, who had fallen while mounting his horse. The Brigade of Guards lent them equipment, the RAMC allowed them to help out in the camp hospital at Pirbright, army instructors taught them drill and stretcher work and in 1913, they were allowed to take a small part in field exercises.

Pat Beauchamp went along to their camp at Pirbright, attracted by a newspaper photograph of 'a girl astride on horseback, leaping a fence in a khaki uniform and topee'. That was the 'sort of show' she fancied joining.

The FANY in the First World War

When war broke out, the FANY were among the first to offer their services to the WO and the BRCS, and like other independent units were refused.

While Franklin looked for a role for them at home, Ashley-Smith was invited to open a hospital in Antwerp. The German advance put paid to that. Ashley-Smith got caught up in the retreat but managed to escape back to the UK via Holland.

She soon crossed the Channel again with a party of trained nurses, nursing orderlies and a motor ambulance – of which there were very few at that date. In October 1914 they opened a hospital in old school buildings in Calais, treating Belgian refugees and soldiers. They also ran a special motorized bath (nicknamed 'James', which toured round giving 250 baths a day), a canteen and more motor ambulances helping the French, Belgians and occasionally also the British. In 1915 two members were caught in a gas attack at Ypres, and drove British casualties to safety.

Pat Beauchamp remembered the innocent excitement when it was her turn to drive the ambulance up to the Belgian front line. After a passing party of soldiers was blown to pieces and more shells fell close by, they all hesitated. Someone suggested turning back. 'Rather not, this is what we've come for,' another said, and they were soon making straight for the noise of the guns.

Off-duty from working at the hospital, the FANY helped run YMCA canteens for troop trains passing through Calais and formed a small concert party to entertain the troops. They cheerfully accepted every hardship and every request – a headache for those raising funds and running the office at home. But they refused to compromise their independence by placing themselves under the BRCS.

They had, however, always wanted active service with the British Army. Ultimately, ASC officers helped broker an arrangement whereby the FANY were commissioned by the British Red Cross Joint War Committee to run a base convoy for 35 GH. On 1 January 1916 the FANY started the first women-run motor ambulance convoy attached to the British Army, 364 Motor Transport (MT) Convoy, on a hill overlooking Calais. The cars were owned and maintained by the BRCS, the ASC supplied petrol and oil and the unit was given help, advice and support from the Deputy Assistant

FANY drivers. (Peter White collection)

Director of Transport. Official driving tests for the FANY were held at the Base MT Depot.

Within a few weeks numbers had grown to twenty-two Fanys, two male mechanics, twelve ambulances, three lorries and a motorcycle. Their work consisted of unloading patients from trains, transferring them from hospitals to hospital ships and unloading the very bad cases from the St Omer canal. At other times, they might be detailed to chauffeur a matron or other VIPs.

After sleeping under canvas for a few months, they were finally moved into hastily erected huts, which proved more draughty than the tents. Driving wounded men on narrow cobbled roads with deep mud either side demanded great concentration. You could tell by the expression on a driver's face, as well as the speed of her car, whether she was loaded up or returning empty to base. Over the following cold winter, a few volunteers had to stay up all night, starting the cars every hour so the radiators would not freeze. A normal day consisted of parade – sometimes with overcoat hiding pyjamas – before 'brekker' at 8am. Fatigues might include tidying the camp, weeding flowerbeds, or clearing ashes out of the hot-water boiler before cleaning huts, engines and vehicles.

The FANY now concentrated their energies on ambulance transport. A second FANY convoy for the British began at St Omer in 1918, this time in a permanent camp with Nissen huts and a comfortable mess. After the Armistice, these units worked with the War Graves Commission, although the Calais convoy continued until May 1919.

Their bravery and good humour made the FANY hugely popular with the troops, who claimed that their name stood for 'First Anywhere'. Their quasi-military appearance and ranks were somehow more acceptable than they might have been at home. The Fanys were young and reckless, out for fun and adventure, but they were also determined, hardworking and committed to proving themselves equal to any situation.

Recognition of Service

Mostly young, enthusiastic, upper class amateurs who could afford to work unpaid, the Fanys' spirited fearlessness won them many awards and MiD. Out of 450 members on active service, the FANY gained at least twenty-eight MiD for individual bravery and were awarded nineteen Military Medals, as well as Belgian and French decorations, including twenty-seven Croix de Guerre.

Casualties

Seeing them drive unscathed through heavy air raids, French villagers concluded that God protected the Fanys. Their one casualty, Eveline Fidgeon Shaw, died of dysentery in France in August 1918.

However, Sergeant Henrietta M Fraser was badly wounded rescuing French soldiers and Driver Catharine Marguerite Beauchamp Waddell (Pat Beauchamp) lost a leg below the knee in a collision with a train in 1917 while with the Calais convoy. She had to pay for her own artificial limb (servicemen got them free) and when the FANY office employed her part-time to augment her small disability pension, most of it was then docked, leaving her no better off.

Between the Wars

The FANY were among the first women sent into Germany after the Armistice, to repatriate French POWs.

At home, FANY drivers delivered over 200 ambulances to BRCS directors in 76 counties, under a Joint War Committee scheme to use ambulances from France in rural districts, taking emergency cases to hospital.

The FANY chose not to disband after the war, seeking a useful national peacetime role. The Brigade of Guards helped keep them going, lending equipment and teaching drill, signalling and map reading at their annual training camps at Pirbright.

They began voluntary driving for hospitals and advertised themselves as trained in first aid, stretcher drill, map reading, mechanical repair work and home nursing. In May 1926, at twelve hours' notice, the WO summoned them to help during the General Strike. Many older members had retired and recruitment had fallen off since the war. It took nearly the whole strength, with members coming from all over the country and even returning from abroad, to provide nineteen with their own cars to drive for the WO, while ten took over ambulances at Kensington Barracks and several drove for the police. A total of sixteen Fanys were sent to Aldershot, mainly replacing RASC drivers on essential transport work during the strike.

The following year they were given official recognition and an entry in the *Army List* (as a voluntary reserve transport unit at the disposal of the WO for service in any national emergency) joining army nurses and former women's auxiliary services at Armistice Day parades to the Cenotaph.

The FANY remained a voluntary unit, totally dependent on members' subscriptions, but their RASC training now became official, with classes for theoretical and practical mechanics, the right to take parts of the RASC driving tests and examinations in mechanics and administration. This helped raise the standard of their work and consolidate their association with the army. Other army units contributed first aid, anti-gas training, map reading, cookery and drill, but the FANY remained otherwise entirely self-sufficient, with its own officers, NCOs and drivers, mechanics, cooks and clerks.

They provided transport for hospitals all over the country and FANY sections sprang up in London, Aldershot, Derby, Glasgow, Northumberland, Yorkshire and even Kenya. Two women doctors joined in the 1920s. About 100 members attended a yearly 3-week training camp under canvas at Pirbright, giving displays of their work, using RASC members as casualties.

In 1933 Princess Alice became President of the newly titled 'First Aid Nursing Yeomanry (Ambulance Car Corps)' to reflect their role as a largely motor transport corps. They had tried to change their name altogether, but were stuck in the public mind as 'the Fanys'.

Uniform

In the early days, members' dress uniform consisted of black-peaked scarlet cap and military style scarlet tunic with stand-up collar and elaborate frogging, a navy blue bell-shaped skirt with three rows of white braid near the hem and black patent leather riding boots. Troopers wore khaki or light-blue service dress. Mess dress consisted of a scarlet monkey jacket with pale-blue facings, over a white muslin dress with red sash. Scarlet and pale blue became the FANY colours.

In 1910, a more practical service uniform was adopted: khaki divided skirt, white blouse and tie, khaki military style tunic and khaki pith helmet.

During the First World War, FANY members wore all-khaki uniform with badges depending on their unit or section. The British section wore BRCS badges; Belgian and French sections wore their respective military transport badges. Photographs show FANY drivers swamped by shaggy goatskin fur coats, issued by the French army. At some stage in the war, their distinctive, soft, round khaki cap without a peak was adopted, with their equally distinctive badge, a Maltese cross within a circle, symbolizing sacrifice and unity.

Researching the FANY

Since they remained an independent unit, no service records relating to FANY members are held in the public domain. The Royal Logistics Corps Museum, which houses RASC records, appears to hold no record of them, other than an article in the *RASC Journal*.

The National Archives

Most FANY members served in France during the First World War and nearly 380 are included in the medal card index. WO 329/2334 contains the FANY British War and Victory service medal roll and WO 329/2933 those who earned the 1914–1915 Star. HS 7/7 has a brief chronology of the FANY and MH 106/1495 a brief register of hospital admission and discharges of FANY Convoy members to 4 SH, Longuenesse, in 1919, some entries described as 'VAD FANY' and others as 'FANY Convoy'.

Imperial War Museum

The *WW&S* database contains a report of the first FANY annual dinner in 1919, with over 330 names. *WW&S* also lists FANY foreign decorations, members of the first unit in France and a report on the work of the FANY up to 1917.

The IWM holds copies of the *FANY Gazette* and Beryl Hutchinson's accounts of the Calais and St Omer convoys.

Online Sources

The website of FANY (Princess Royal's Volunteer Corps) carries some information on FANY history. Research queries may be addressed to their archivist at hq@fany.org.uk, for which a small charge will be made.

The *LG* contains Military Medal citations to FANY and notifications of foreign awards. (The *BMJ* online and *BJN* online are useful sources for mention of awards to individual FANY members, particularly if a *LG* entry cannot be found.) The *BJN* online includes articles on the pre-First World War FANY.

Printed Sources

Pat Beauchamp, *Fanny Goes to War* (1919, reprinted 1940 with photographs as *Fanny Went to War*) has many references to fellow FANY members (including the original eighteen Calais convoy members)

Irene Ward, *F.A.N.Y. Invicta* (1955) includes much detail, many names, indexed, and lists of recipients of awards

Hugh Popham, *F.A.N.Y.: the story of the Women's Transport Service 1907–1984* (1984) draws on interesting archive material, indexed with many names.

Chapter 8

MEDICAL WOMEN WITH THE ARMED SERVICES IN THE FIRST WORLD WAR

Employment of women doctors with the armed services during the First World War began at a very early stage. By the end of the war, several hundred had served both part-time and full-time, treating servicemen and women at home and abroad.

Origins

When Florence Nightingale took her band of nurses to Scutari, the struggle for women to qualify as doctors was only just beginning. One woman became an army medical officer (who clashed with Nightingale) and rose to be Surgeon General. But she had had to pass herself off as a man. It was only when she died in 1865, that Dr James Barry's lifelong secret was discovered.

Over the following half-century, beginning with Elizabeth Garrett, women fought to enter the medical profession. Once qualified, they were restricted to treating women and children, either running their own practices or working in public health and education.

Many were active women's suffrage supporters. When war was declared in 1914, suffrage societies funded independent medical units staffed by women. One such unit, the Women's Hospital Corps (WHC), set up their own all-women hospital in Paris, treating French wounded. Led by Dr Louisa Garrett Anderson (Elizabeth's daughter) and Dr Flora Murray, it became a showcase for women surgeons' abilities, attracting many visitors. Within a few weeks, in October 1914, with the RAMC floundering under the influx of thousands of British casualties, several WHC doctors were seconded to dress the lightly wounded in a British military hospital.

Women's Hospital Corps Work with the Army

The RAMC made full use of the next WHC unit, opened at Wimereux in November 1914. This ran successfully for several months until the WHC

WHC doctors in Paris. Marjorie Blandy is standing centre left; Rosalie Jobson standing centre right; Flora Murray seated far right; Louisa Garrett Anderson seated centre right. (The Women's Library/Mary Evans Picture Library)

were approached in early 1915 to open a 500-bed military hospital in London. The WO offered them a former workhouse infirmary in Endell Street, Covent Garden, which had been requisitioned for use as a military hospital. The DGAMS Sir Alfred Keogh (instrumental in overturning the army's reluctance to employ women doctors) quietly arranged for senior WHC doctors to take a course in army hospital administration at the QA Military Hospital, Millbank. In March 1915, a horrified RAMC colonel handed over the keys and Endell Street Military Hospital was successfully run and staffed by women from May 1915 until 1919.

Ruling their own environment and with their own smart uniform, the WHC spent most of the war immured from the problems of other women doctors working with the army.

Work with the RAMC Abroad

In January 1915, one woman doctor joined an RAMC unit in Calais as an anaesthetist and was followed by six more, but they did not work in large numbers with the RAMC until 1916.

As the main reception centre for the evacuation of thousands of sick and wounded from the Dardanelles, Malta was dotted with military and red cross hospitals. An outbreak of malaria in Macedonia had brought increasing convoys of patients in July 1916, requiring tented extensions to the hospitals and more medical personnel.

Between August and December 1916, parties of women doctors who had responded to a WO appeal were posted to Malta under contract to the WO. By the end of the year over eighty had been sent, proving 'a most welcome reinforcement and an innovation attended in every way with the happiest results'. Their duties were mostly medical, with some surgical and laboratory work.

In April 1917, following the sinking of several hospital ships, the policy of evacuating patients to Malta changed. Five general hospitals were mobilized from among the medical staff on the island. As 61 to 65 GH, they left for Salonika in May 1917.

Work on Malta correspondingly lessened and a number of medical women were sent to Egypt. In early 1918, eight were posted to 45 SH, a collection of huge marquees set up by the seashore. They handled the routine work, dealing with surgical, medical, eye and ear conditions. The hospital quickly expanded to 2,000 beds with infectious cases ranging from measles to diphtheria and typhus. After several weeks, 45 SH was ordered to Salonika and the medical women dispersed to hospitals around Cairo. By this time, medical women were also serving in military hospitals in Alexandria. Others had returned to work in UK military hospitals.

Medical Officials with the QM/WAAC

The formation of the women's auxiliary services (the WAAC, WRNS and WRAF) led to employment of more women doctors.

From February 1917, when WAAC camps and hostels were being set up, newly enrolled women were examined and treated if they fell ill by RAMC officers or WAAC officials with nursing VAD training, while discussions were held about appointing women doctors to oversee the health of the women now in the army's care. The new WAAC Controller-in-Chief, Mrs Chalmers-Watson, herself a qualified doctor, recognized the importance of maintaining the women's health and fitness, if they were to confound critics who argued that women lacked stamina for the work they were taking on.

Eventually, women doctors were authorized to be appointed to an auxiliary section in the RAMC, for medical treatment of the WAAC. WAAC units had been in France since late March 1917. The medical women arrived in October 1917. By November 1917, twenty-seven full-time medical women had been appointed for the duration of the war.

Dr Jane Turnbull was appointed Controller of Medical Services and Dr Laura Stewart Sandeman, who had helped organize enrolment medical boards, Controller of Medical Services Overseas, based at the HQ of the Director Medical Services, Lines of Communication. There were two area medical controllers (AMC North, stationed at Boulogne, AMC South, at Rouen) in charge of nine women 'medical officials' and based at Boulogne, Rouen, Calais, Etaples, Le Havre, Dieppe and Abbeville. Each was responsible for between 400 and 1,200 women.

At home, recruiting medical controllers were attached to a number of recruiting areas. Part-time immobile medical officers were locally employed in provincial cities and at nine centres in London, to serve on WAAC medical selection boards.

AMCs advised on the health and welfare of the women in their areas and inspected hostels, camps, kitchens, workshops, stores and anywhere Waacs worked, as well as sick bays and hospitals with WAAC patients. They were expected to submit recommendations and might be called as consultants to see any WAAC patient in their area, or serve on WAAC medical boards. On Jane Turnbull's initiative, two hostels were opened, one for unmarried mothers, the other for VD sufferers.

Medical officials' duties included routine medical inspections and office and camp inspections. Those attached to large camps held daily sick parades. Each camp of more than forty women included a small hut or dormitory sick bay, with a small kitchen and duty room. Hostels had a small bedroom set aside. Queen Mary's Camp, Calais had a large sick wing, with two wards, a surgery and bedroom for the nursing VADs attached to the camp. Smaller units included a hospital forewoman or nursing orderly on the strength.

Medical officials saw women who had reported sick each morning and made daily rounds of sick-bay patients. Women needing more than forty-eight hours' care were sent to special 'sick sisters' sections of military hospitals, set aside primarily for nurses. Each medical official took charge of WAAC hospital patients in her area, under the supervision of the RAMC officer in charge.

Many women were malnourished and ignorant of personal hygiene and dental care. Medical officials gave hygiene lectures and vaccinations and were expected to report poor working or living conditions, bad food or concern about hygiene to the RAMC area medical officer (AMO).

Status of Medical Women Working with the RAMC in the First World War

From 1915, medical women had begun working in UK hospitals alongside RAMC officers. They were soon accepted and given medical and surgical practice that would not have come their way in civilian practice. Some went on to make their mark in specialist fields.

But many also suffered daily humiliations in the course of their work, due to their lack of army status. They had been promised equal pay, but were not given the travel and board allowances temporary RAMC officers received. One woman had a chit from the Assistant Director Medical

Services stating that her rank was that of a temporary officer of the RAMC, paid less than a Civilian Military Practitioner (CMP). The same man later informed her that she was not entitled to a travel warrant, because she was a CMP.

Men in the women's care were left to conclude that they were inferior doctors, as they had neither rank nor uniform. Without uniform, they had great difficulty travelling, especially abroad. While army nursing sisters and VADs travelled first class, women doctors were forced to join ORs in third-class carriages, or masquerade as nurses or officers' wives. Without badges of rank or commissioned status, they could not enforce any instruction given in the course of their work. One woman described how a corporal unloading an urgent case ignored her instructions, forcing her to appeal to a sergeant to enforce them.

Some, like Louisa McIlroy, were given specialist posts. Yet, however long they had worked with the army, even senior consultants remained junior to the most recently appointed RAMC subaltern. The final straw came when medical women were refused servicemen's tax relief, on the grounds that their work in military hospitals was 'not of a military character'.

One woman returning from Malta smuggled out a number of colleagues' letters detailing their grievances. The Medical Women's Federation (MWF) used these to outline the problems, arguing for the women doctors to be granted temporary commissioned rank. They were told this would require an Act of Parliament not feasible in wartime, and simply offered the same uniform as QMAAC officials, with RAMC cap and collar badges.

QMAAC medical women were already wearing this uniform. They had been promised honorary rank in a special auxiliary section of the RAMC, and demanded to be gazetted, since QMAAC officials were gazetted. An entry finally appeared in the *London Gazette* in November 1918. Its position and wording affronted them even more, suggesting they were enrolled with the QMAAC rather than employed in an auxiliary section of the RAMC. The WO refused to acknowledge the error, but subsequent entries added the words 'Auxiliary Section, RAMC attd.' – the only tangible evidence of the existence of their auxiliary section of the RAMC.

Uniforms of Army Medical Women

WHC uniform consisted of a khaki skirt, shirt, tie and belted tunic jacket with high lapels, button-flap hip pockets and a buttoned belt. Medical officers had distinguishing red shoulder straps with the WHC initials embroidered in white. Those at Endell Street wore RAMC collar badges.

Medical women with the QMAAC wore the QMAAC officials' uniform of drab felt hat (or Burberry cap, or brown straw hat) khaki shirt and tie, skirt and tunic jacket. The hem was to be 8in from the ground for home service and 9in for foreign service. Stockings were to be khaki, not transparent, with brown shoes or boots, with leggings or gaiters. Khaki drill could be worn in summer and light-coloured shirts on home service. The tunic had a cloth belt fastened in front with two large buttons 6in apart, two bellows hip pockets, dull cherry red RAMC shoulder flashes and bronzed RAMC buttons. They wore RAMC collar and hat badges, but WAAC rank badges, which they weren't happy about.

WAAC officials wore badge motifs of roses and fleurs-de-lis to denote higher rank, rather than stripes or crowns. The medical recruiting controller and AMCs wore one fleur-de-lis on their shoulder strap, equivalent to a major's crown.

One AMC in France, who regularly inspected camps and units, complained that her rank badge only compromised her position, with jokey comments about 'the Boy Scout's badge'.

Other RAMC-attached Medical Women

Dr Florence Barrie Lambert, reputedly the first woman doctor working in military hospitals to wear a uniform, apparently also carried a personal letter from Sir Alfred Keogh, permitting her to wear the RAMC badge.

Otherwise, medical women (even those working in army hospitals abroad) were initially not issued a uniform. This laid them open to accusations of being 'slackers' not on war work – most women were in uniform (or wearing 'on war work' badges) by the midpoint of the war. Some medical women serving abroad apparently devised their own unofficial khaki uniforms.

Following the MWF intervention on their behalf, medical women serving on contracts with troops abroad or at home were allowed to wear the QMAAC officials' uniform with RAMC buttons and badges but without the Sam Browne belt. In Egypt, medical women wore a uniform of tussore (a coarse, brownish Indian silk) or khaki drill in the wards; some COs apparently insisted on the Sam Browne belt.

Recognition of Service

Several medical women were mentioned in despatches. May Thorne, said to have been a tower of strength for all women serving on Malta, received a military OBE.

Casualties

Some medical women's contracts with the Army were terminated due to ill health. Only one appears to have died on active service with the armed forces. Isobel Addy Tate is buried in the stone-walled cemetery at Pieta, Malta, between two army nursing sisters' more modest headstones.

Isobel Addy Tate's grave in Pieta cemetery, Malta. (By kind permission of Brenda Schacht)

Women Doctors with the WRNS in the First World War

When the Women's Royal Naval Service was first formed, Wrens were attended by naval or civilian medical officers, or examined by WAAC medical boards. In February 1918 a woman MO (Miss Annie Forster) was appointed as a temporary WRNS medical assistant director and medical women were contracted at an hourly rate to serve on medical boards to examine WRNS recruits.

In April 1918, Dr Dorothy Christian Hare (one of the first RAMC-attached women sent to Malta in August 1916) was appointed WRNS assistant director (medical) to replace Dr Forster as medical adviser to the WRNS director and a woman doctor was appointed in Edinburgh to conduct WRNS medical boards. In addition to her administrative duties, Dr Hare travelled round inspecting WRNS quarters and working conditions. Eventually, three more women doctors were employed, one to examine new recruits and two to attend the Edinburgh and London depot hostels.

QMAAC medical boards continued examining WRNS recruits and invalids, but by August 1919 it became necessary to co-opt medical women on to boards dealing with WRNS invalids.

Uniform of WRNS Medical Officers

WRNS medical officers appear to have worn the WRNS officers' uniform of dark-navy double-breasted jacket, skirt, white shirt and black tie with tricorne hat and WRNS officers' blue lace sleeve bands with diamond, according to rank: medical assistant director had four bands; deputy medical assistant director had three. From November 1918, women doctors on the WRNS HQ staff wore scarlet cloth (signifying the medical service) between the stripes.

Women Doctors with the RAF in the First World War

After the Women's Royal Air Force (WRAF) was formed in April 1918, QMAAC medical boards examined WRAF recruits, but other medical

Dr Lily Baker (left) with Alice Chauncey, Maresquel. Dr Baker is clearly seen wearing similar uniform to the WRAF officer beside her, but with crux anasata *RAF medical branch collar badge. (Courtesy of RAF Museum London)*

duties were eventually taken on by about a dozen women doctors working with the Medical Branch of the RAF.

Their work was similar to that of medical women with the QMAAC (attending WRAF patients, conducting inspections and giving 'hygiene' lectures at depots and hostels) but they could also be called on to treat RAF personnel.

Letitia Fairfield was appointed WRAF Inspector of Medical Services in June 1918.

She acknowledged the medical women's debt to Sir Matthew Fell, first director of RAF medical services and Sir Godfrey Paine, who as Master-General of Personnel was responsible for the Air Ministry Order by which the medical women were given honorary rank, to be used in official communications. An example of this may be found at TNA in AIR 2/2840 in a memo signed 'Hon. Lieut. Col. RAF Woman Medical Director'. (Honorary rank differed from commissioned rank, which would have conferred power of command over men.)

From 30 August 1918, the RAF officially took over from the QMAAC medical care of WRAF (except enrolment medical boards) and undertook to supply WMOs to hospitals and RAF units where their services might be found necessary.

Rank appointments were:

	Rank equivalent (RAF officers initially had army titles)
Woman Medical Director (stationed at the Air Ministry)	Lieutenant
Area Medical Superintendent (stationed at Area HQ)	Major
Senior WMO (special responsibility, i.e., presiding on officers' boards)	Captain
Junior MOs (stationed at RAF hospitals, WRAF hostels and other RAF formations)	Lieutenant

Lily Anita Baker, an eminent gynaecologist who had served on WAAC medical boards, became Area Medical Superintendent for the WRAF Midland Area, and went out with the WRAF to serve in France and Germany.

Uniform of RAF Women Medical Officers

RAF medical women wore similar uniform to that of WRAF officers, with the *crux anasata* badge worn by RAF MOs on their lapel and sleeve stripes of the honorary rank to which they were appointed.

Interwar Period

By the early 1920s, the women's services had disbanded, many military hospitals closed and male colleagues returned to reclaim civilian practices. Medical women had gained general practice, the respect of the medical branches of the armed services, as well as service medals and other awards. A few contributed to medical research, but women doctors largely retreated back to pre-war areas of practice.

Researching Medical Women who Served with the Armed Forces in the First World War

Medical Women Attached to the Army

It's important to bear in mind that medical women were attached to the RAMC or employed with the army in five different ways:

- As WHC members, practising initially in France, then 1915–1919 running Endell Street Military Hospital in London, funded by the WO, treating British soldiers and some servicewomen;
- As individuals on yearly contracts to serve in military hospitals abroad from 1916 onwards;
- In the 'RAMC auxiliary section' comprising medical women attending QMAAC at home and in France;
- As individuals serving in military hospitals at home, on monthly contracts;
- As immobile part-timers, employed as CMPs on an hourly basis, serving locally to their own practices to conduct medical examinations or medical boards relating to servicewomen.

The 1911 census illuminates the background of medical women who joined the armed forces. Some ran their own practices, some worked in public health, while others were still at medical school. Some had army family backgrounds.

First World War campaign medal index cards (TNA DocumentsOnline) are normally a helpful tool when researching service women. However, many medical women who served abroad with the RAMC either appear on medal rolls relating to earlier service with independent units or are missing, having perhaps not applied or not realized they were eligible for a service medal. May Thorne does not seem to have applied for or received the service medal to which she appears to have been entitled. Her entry in the AMS 'Lady Doctors' register, showing her embarkation for Malta with the first party of medical women on 2 August 1916, seems to be the only official record of her service.

Women's Hospital Corps

The National Archives

No service records of WHC medical women are held at TNA, other than medal index cards and medal rolls.

WO 95/4104, the war diary of 13 SH merely refers to 'lady doctors'. However, the campaign medal roll that lists WHC 1914 Stars (WO 329/2504) states 'lent to the 13th Stationary Hospital, Boulogne' beside the entries for Marjorie Blandy and Rosalie Jobson. (In other instances where medal index cards exist for medical women, there may be more information on the medal card than on the medal roll.)

Imperial War Museum

Dr Flora Murray resisted the Women's Work Collection's request for information about the WHC, not wanting them compartmentalized as women's work. Sadly, therefore, although the *WW&S* database has nominal rolls for other suffrage unit members with women doctors, it appears to have no lists of WHC staff who served in France or at Endell Street.

Flora Murray's account of the WHC, *Women as Army Surgeons*, is full of interesting anecdotal detail, however, mentioning some of the medical women by name.

The Women's Library

TWL holds letters, a scrapbook relating to Endell Street Military Hospital in 1916 and a photograph of the original seven women doctors.

Medical Women Serving Abroad in Malta, Salonika and Egypt

Army Medical Services Museum

Brief service details for *c.* 130 medical women who signed full-time contracts before April 1917 are held in a register at the AMS. (Later registers appear to have existed but not survived.) This register is titled 'Lady Doctors' – the women themselves preferred the title 'medical women'. Beginning with women doctors posted to Malta in August 1916, it typically gives full name, qualifications, date of birth, dates of postings and country, or home command, and sometimes the hospital(s) in which the woman served, or other brief comments. Rosalie Jobson is included, with her posting to the Eastern Command in December 1916.

The register includes mention of medical women on the strengths of GH mobilized in Malta for establishment in Salonika. Further information may be found in war diaries of these hospitals.

The National Archives

Series WO 95 holds war diaries of military hospitals abroad where medical women were employed. WO 95/4936 contains war diaries of several GH

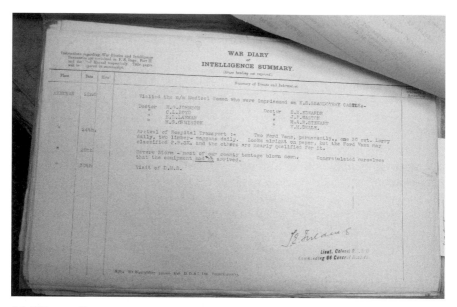

64 GH war diary, naming medical women 'imprisoned' aboard HS Llandovery Castle. *(TNA WO 95/4936)*

mobilized from Malta to Salonika, including mention of the medical women who accompanied them.

On 2 July 1917, eight medical women are listed embarking on HMT *Abbassieh* for duty with 62 GH. Lifebelts had to be worn all day and kept beside them at night. They were escorted by two small warships, both of which struck mines, forcing them to return to Malta. They sailed again escorted by Japanese destroyers and must have reached Salonika with some relief. While the hospital site was prepared, the medical women were ordered to wait on hospital ship *Llandovery Castle*. They joined the site in late July, being instructed in Army Medical Service regulations while the last hospital marquees were erected.

WO 95/4746, the war diary of 45 SH at El Arish (near the Palestine border), mentions only 'lady doctors' reporting for duty in January and February 1918. They are named when leaving the unit in April, having perhaps by then proved themselves worthy of individual mention.

WO 329/2324, the medal roll that includes (under Nurses 9) a section titled 'Lady Doctors Hospital'. This is largely a misnomer. The first page does list nursing sisters at the WHC hospital, Paris, known as the Lady Doctors Hospital. The list, however, continues with medical women who served abroad with the RAMC in various capacities, giving dates and countries in which they served, including with the QMAAC in France. (Those who served solely on Malta only received the British War Medal.) The list is incomplete.

The Wellcome Library

The Medical Women's Federation Collection offers a window on the experiences of women doctors working with the RAMC and holds obituaries of medical women.

Whereas the MWF used quotes from medical women anonymously in their pamphlet on their grievances (see *WW&S*), SA/MWF/C.159 contains typed copies and some of the original letters, with their names and where they were serving.

The doctor who smuggled her colleagues' letters home to avoid the censor is revealed here as K Waring. (The AMS register records her full name: Katherine Ada Waring, embarked for Malta 12 August 1916, serving with 61 GH Salonika from July to December 1917.)

SA/MWF/C.165 contains more letters from medical women serving at

Entry for Katherine Ada Waring in 'Lady Doctors' register – her date of birth appears on the reverse. (Courtesy of AMS Museum)

Malta and Salonika, together with a list of fourteen in Cairo and seventeen in Alexandria in 1918.

Other Sources
The *WW&S* database contains reports on the work of hospitals in Malta and an account of medical women in Malta and Egypt.

In November 1917 five medical women serving in Salonika were mentioned in despatches in the *LG*, under the heading 'Medical Women (attached Royal Army Medical Corps)'.

Civilian Medical Practitioners

The National Archives
WO 162/35 includes lists dated October 1917 naming twenty-five immobile women doctors employed intermittently on a part-time hourly basis in the four home commands to serve on WAAC medical boards.

RAMC Auxiliary Section (Medical Women with the QMAAC)

The National Archives
First World War campaign medal index cards for some of the sixteen QMAAC medical women who served in France appear to be missing. Others are included on the 'Lady Doctors Hospital' medal roll pages, or were serving earlier in another capacity when they earned their service medals.

AIR 2/90 contains a file that describes in detail the organization of QMAAC medical services.

Imperial War Museum
The *WW&S* database contains a précis of the medical services for QMAAC in France (ref. Army 3.27/10) and details of the MWF grievances, quoting some RAMC auxiliary women.

Sixteen medical women attached to the QMAAC in France (Army 3.27/14) are listed, with detail on certain individuals, including Zilla Scruby, who became Controller of Medical Services for the WAAC clerical section working for the American Expeditionary Force at Bourges. (She does not appear in the AMS 'Lady Doctors' register, as her initial appointment would have been in a later register which has not survived.)

Online Sources
Appointments announced in the *LG* that appear from November 1918 effectively provide a nominal roll of women doctors employed for the medical care of the WAAC (and later the WRAF), with full names, rank titles, professional qualifications and dates of appointment.

Rosalie Holmes' entry shows her appointed June 1918 as a 'medical official' offering medical care to QMAAC. Her entry (under her maiden surname, Jobson) in the 'Lady Doctors' register, records her as working in the Eastern Command between December 1916 and August 1917.

She has two campaign medal index cards (under maiden and married surnames) only mentioning WHC service, with date of embarkation as 15 October 1914. But Louisa Garrett Anderson's letter (at TWL) of 27 September 1914, clearly says 'We have been joined by two more doctors from London, Marjorie Blandy and Rosalie Jobson, who are just qualified and who will be very useful in the capacity of dressers.' Blandy and Jobson were lent to 13 SH, Boulogne. The 13 SH war diary (WO 95/4104) entry for 29 October 1914 records that two supply trains brought about 1,400 slightly wounded casualties and continues, 'Got six Red Cross nurses and four lady doctors to assist with dressings.' Intriguingly, Flora Murray only mentions two women. The four are not named in the war diary.

The *LG* and *BMJ* both include army appointments of medical women, the latter with some obituaries, which may offer more information (not always entirely accurate) on First World War service.

Researching WRNS Medical Women

The National Archives

Appointments of women doctors as WRNS officers appear in the micro-filmed register of First World War WRNS officers' appointments (ADM 321/1-2). Entries are very brief, including name and qualifications, date of appointment, establishment, rank and dates of service.

Other Sources

The *WW&S* database (IWM) contains items outlining medical arrangements for the WRNS including mention of medical women appointed and/or employed on a pro rata basis.

The MWF Collection (WLL) includes a *Medical Women's Federation Journal* article on the medical service in the WRNS in the First World War.

The *LG* includes appointments of WRNS medical assistant directors.

Researching Women Doctors with the RAF Medical Service

The National Archives

AIR 2/92 includes a file on medical women with the RAF which names six.

Other Sources

The MWF collection (WLL) holds papers of Letitia Fairfield, copies of MWF Journal articles and transcripts of talks on medical women with the armed forces.

The *BMJ* contains some obituaries of medical women who served with the RAF in the First World War. The *LG* mentions some RAF medical women, including Miss Ruth Balmer, MB (described as Honorary Captain, RAF Medical Service) awarded a military OBE for distinguished service in North Russia.

Chapter 9

RAF NURSING SERVICE AND PMRAFNS

Motto: *'nec aspera terrent'* – 'nothing shall deter us'

The RAFNS was created as a temporary service in 1918, shortly after the establishment of the RAF. Made permanent in 1921, it was renamed Princess Mary's Royal Air Force Nursing Service (PMRAFNS) in 1923.

For most of the First World War, the army and navy had their own separate flying sections, the Royal Flying Corps (RFC) and the Royal Naval Air Service (RNAS). Sick or injured RFC airmen were nursed by army nurses; those in the RNAS by naval nursing sisters.

In June 1918, shortly after the RFC and RNAS combined to form the Royal Air Force, the new temporary RAF Nursing Service was announced. Its members would join new RAF medical centres or replace army and navy sisters currently nursing airmen in units being taken over by the RAF medical branch. Miss Lucy E Jolley (who had served in France with the QAIMNSR) was appointed acting principal matron.

RAF Nursing Service

Applications for the RAFNS were invited from August 1918. Candidates had to have British parents, be aged 25–45 and either single or widowed, with at least three years' training in a civil hospital of over 100 beds. Those accepted joined initially as staff nurses. The service comprised matron-in-chief, matrons, superintending sisters, sisters and staff nurses, all appointed only for the duration of the war.

Among them were recently resigned army and naval nursing sisters, to replace those serving at what were now RAF medical units, in the London area, Cranwell and Blandford, as well as WRAF depots in Glasgow, Sheffield and Birmingham, convalescent centres in Matlock and Hastings, and training camp station sick quarters (SSQs) around Salisbury Plain.

Some sisters were posted to comfortable billets in rural surroundings, like the convalescent hospital at Matlock Hydro, Derbyshire, with tennis courts, a ballroom – although nursing staff were not allowed to dance with patients – and a nearby teashop. Other postings were less well appointed. Nurses might arrive on a winter's day to find themselves billeted 'like shop girls' at the YWCA hostel.

The vast Blandford Camp in Dorset, taken over by the RAF, had a hutted hospital. The nursing sisters commuted 4 miles and back every day by lorry, with the camp milk churn slopping over their uniforms. Despite gumboots and macs, they got soaked walking between wards in wet weather. Night duty involved carrying a swaying hurricane lamp and stepping between sparsely laid duckboards, over muddy rat-infested tracks.

In November 1918 Lucy Jolley was succeeded by Joanna Margaret Cruickshank, a veteran of the QAMNSI. The RAFNS was less than six months old when the Armistice was signed. Faced with peacetime cutbacks, the RAF fought to keep its own medical branch, with its unique medical specialisms.

By 1919, the three RAF hospitals (Halton, Cranwell and the RAF Officers' Hospital, Finchley) were staffed entirely by RAF nursing sisters, with one serving at the SSQs at Netheravon and Henlow. VADs were appointed as nursing orderlies, cooks, etc.

By 1920, RAFNS sisters and staff nurses were serving in hospitals, SSQs, training camps and convalescent centres. There were four WRAF hostels and eight air/airship stations, each with a nursing sister. Ten were serving at the officers' hospital at Hampstead and fourteen at Blandford camp hospital. The remainder worked either at Matlock or Hastings.

Plans to administer the RAFNS as a branch of the QAIMNS crashed and

RAFNS nurse seated with RAF medical staff, flanked by WRAF. (Peter White collection)

burned. The Air Ministry wanted the two services to remain separate, with QAIMNS members seconded to the RAFNS for three years, during which time they might be required to serve in ones and twos on isolated RAF stations. The QAIMNS Matron-in-Chief recoiled at the idea of her nurses working unsupervised. Joanna Cruickshank, having served in India where postings could be much more isolated, had no such qualms. She wanted a modern, progressive service that endorsed the independence women had gained during the war.

In January 1921, the RAFNS became a permanent branch of the RAF, comprising matron-in-chief, three matrons, sixteen sisters and twelve staff nurses. In 1923, Princess Mary became patron of the now renamed PMRAFNS. Their new title even more of a mouthful, PMRAFNS members took to calling themselves 'PMs'. By the mid-1920s numbers had increased to four matrons, four senior sisters, twenty-five sisters and over eighty staff nurses. During this period, PMs went out to Baghdad, Hinaidi (also in Iraq), Palestine and Egypt.

The RAF justified its existence in the interwar period by patrolling the British mandate countries of the Middle East (former enemy colonies, administered by the Allies) as well as India and Africa, quelling uprisings sometimes simply by buzzing the protagonists. The first ten RAFNS sisters left in September 1922 to take over from army sisters at 23 British Combined Services Hospital, Baghdad. In 1923 another hospital opened in Basrah, hospitals in Palestine and Aden were taken over by the RAF and more PMs sailed abroad. (They were not officially permitted to fly.)

The youngest nursing service was expanding, advertising posts with the promise of foreign postings at a time when many former army nurses needed employment. Temporary openings for staff nurse candidates aged 24–40 were announced in 1923, on yearly contracts, with the possibility of transfer to the permanent service.

PM postings abroad offered the luxury of servants, a leisured colonial lifestyle of riding and tennis and paying social calls – or working in stifling humidity, running with sweat, plagued by flies, with limited water supplies. Faraway stations where European women were few and far between encouraged marriage – necessitating retirement.

Otherwise, the RAF medical service was exciting and progressive. RAF Halton's old wooden huts were finally abandoned and a light, airy modern hospital with rubber flooring and the latest specialist equipment opened in 1927, including beds for airmen's wives and children, and six for nursing sisters. The early 1930s saw the opening of a third RAF hospital at Uxbridge where PMs enjoyed single bedrooms, with hot and cold running water.

Uniform

RAFNS matrons wore blue winter serge and alpaca summer dresses, with soft collars and cuffs, blue muslin cap, blue cape and bonnet, summer and winter cloaks. Matrons with nursing duties also had washing dresses and aprons.

Superintending sisters and sisters wore blue serge or blue cotton dresses, with soft collar and cuffs, white aprons, blue cloth cape, washing dresses for working on the wards, straw hat in summer and a wide-brimmed, four-cornered black felt hat (known as a 'Dick', after Dick Turpin) in winter.

Staff nurses had similar uniform, with white caps and black shoes and stockings. Trench-coat mackintoshes and gumboots were permitted in winter.

Blue tippets (shoulder capes) were worn, with the RAFNS badge at each front corner. This comprised a crowned laurel wreath enclosing the letters RAF between outstretched wings, upon a scroll bearing the legend 'R.A.F.N.S.'.

Early uniforms were pale blue but this impractical colour soon gave way to the more familiar air force grey-blue, introduced in the autumn of 1919.

In the 1920s, blue dresses were replaced by white cotton worn with white linen collars, cuffs and aprons, with air force blue tippet shoulder cape. The yard-square white lawn veil cap was embroidered in one corner in blue with wings surmounted by a crown. White stockings and shoes replaced black. A long blue satin mess dress with satin shoulder cape could be worn for formal evening occasions. Sisters also had white duck (rough cotton or linen) overalls, with pearl buttons and long sleeves, detachable at the elbow.

Following the change to PMRAFNS, RAFNS badges worn on the tippet were replaced by the RAF medical caduceus of Mercury (a winged staff intertwined by two snakes).

PM outdoor uniform comprised grey-blue jacket and skirt, white shirt and black tie, black shoes and stockings. This outfit was worn with a double-peaked storm cap (similar to the WRNS cap) or the black quatrecorn 'Dick Turpin' hat. The latter was nearly abandoned in the late 1920s, when shingled hair became fashionable, but successfully altered slightly.

Rank stripes were worn on cape shoulders, or at the wrist of jacket sleeves. Staff nurses wore dark-blue braid; sisters the same with a single pale-blue stripe; senior sisters and matrons had maroon braid with pale-blue stripes, wider for matrons.

Before 1927, two styles of white ward dress existed, home service and overseas. From 1927, medium-weight white drill ward dress was worn both at home and overseas.

Researching RAF Nursing Sisters

The National Archives

Individual service records remain with RAF Records, and may only include members of the permanent service.

Some naval nursing service records mention service at RNAS stations, prior to formation of the RAF. (ADM 104/163 shows QARNNS Reserve Eva Gladys Beard at Roehampton Air Station.)

AIR 49/382 contains, in addition to a short history of RAF nursing 1918–1941, a nominal roll of 166 RAFNS members who joined the service between 1918 and 1923 (including temporary staff nurses listed at the end). This roll gives surname and (usually) initials and shows date of joining and leaving (prior to 1923), with brief reason for leaving. It also includes dates of former war service with prefixes 'VAD', 'A' or 'Army', 'N' or 'Navy', and 'T' (TFNS), opening up the opportunity of research into RAF nursing sisters' earlier careers and confirming an identity.

Miss Blair (no initials) is shown on the roll as still serving in 1923, having been appointed in December 1918, following service with the Navy between February 1917 and October 1918. The *Air Force List* confirms her as Sister Emily Mathison Blair, serving at Manston, Kent. Emily M Blair's brief QARNNSR service record will be found in ADM 104/164.

First World War QA(R) and TFNS service records (series WO 399) do not normally include mention of service with RAFNS. However, WO 399/8937, the QAIMNSR service record for Ethel Whittingham, includes a note 'appointed permanently to RAFNS' dated 29 January 1919, suggesting that the nominal roll in AIR49/382 is incomplete, since her name does not appear. Katherine Christie Watt, who served in France with the QAIMNSR (see WO 399/8784), does appear on the roll, appointed to the RAFNS in January 1919.

Permanent members of the RAFNS appear in the *Air Force List* from 1921, in order of seniority, with full name, date of appointment to rank and place of posting.

Series AIR 2 contains administrative files including AIR 2/93, which concerns the establishment and future of the RAFNS, its rules and regulations, with mention of some early RAFNS members.

Some First World War medal index cards mention service with the RAFNS, although qualification for medals relates to earlier army service.

RAF Museum London

Holdings contain over 200 (PM)RAFNS uniform items and insignia, with a permanent PMRAFNS display.

Imperial War Museum

Holds reminiscences of PMRAFNS service from 1923.

Online Sources

The *BJN*, *Flight* magazine and the *LG* online contain some appointments, awards and resignations for RAF and PMRAFNS members. The *BJN* and

Flight magazine include a few obituaries and further information on the service itself, as well as announcements of embarkation for foreign postings for RAFNS in the early 1920s. In 1922, for example, the ship and date of departure are announced, with surnames and initials, of matrons, sisters and staff nurses for duty in Iraq.

Printed Sources

Mary Mackie, *Sky Wards: a history of the Princess Mary's Royal Air Force Nursing Service* (2001), a vividly detailed history of the service. Its appendices list RAF hospitals and medical units at home and overseas

Andrew Cormack and Peter Cormack, *British Air Forces 1914–1918 (2) Uniforms of the RAF* (2001), for more detail on uniform.

The nominal roll in AIR 49/382 includes M Welch joined on 4 November 1918. The career of Marion Welch, an early RAFNS member, may be traced in the *Air Force List* from her appointment as a Sister at Halton in 1921. *Flight* magazine dated 7 March 1929 includes mention of the award to her of an RRC for 'exceptional devotion and competency' nursing in air-force hospitals at home and in Iraq. The *BJN* carries her obituary in 1938, describing how she turned down the opportunity to become PMRAFNS matron-in-chief to marry Harold Lampard, secretary of the Baghdad YMCA.

Chapter 10

QUEEN ALEXANDRA'S MILITARY FAMILIES NURSING SERVICE

Motto: '*Vincit Amor Patriae*' – 'love of country conquers'

From the mid-nineteenth century, a few beds in regimental hospitals were allotted to soldiers' wives and children and midwifery training was given for women with 'a fair education'. From 1885, hospitals for soldiers' wives and children had a qualified midwife matron.

In 1921, in response to the post-war baby boom, QAMFNS was formed to provide midwifery and nursing care in Military Families hospitals, for army wives and children. The service consisted of matrons, sisters-in-charge and staff nurses. Applicants had to have British parents or be naturalized British subjects, aged 24–35, with a certificate of not less than three years' training and service in medical and surgical nursing in a civil hospital, plus the certificate of the Central Midwives' Board (CMB).

The QAMFNS badge ('A' surmounted by a crown within an oval consisting of the words 'Queen Alexandra's Military Families Nursing Service') was worn when in uniform, with a silver collar badge on the point of the collar of the coats and greatcoats of members of all ranks.

From January 1927, QAMFNS was absorbed into the QAIMNS, which became responsible for nursing wives and children of the British Army wherever they were stationed.

Researching QAMFNS

At the time of writing, QAMFNS members' service records remain with the MoD.

The National Archives

Series WO 399 includes a few army nurses who also served with QAMFNS. WO 399/8530, for example, relates to the transfer in 1927 of QAMFNS member Mary Cox Urben to the QAIMNS.

The *Army List* gives appointment dates and rank of QAMFNS, including staff nurses. Many had previously served as army nurses and entries for matrons and sisters include details of war service. Jessie MacGillivray, for example, served in the QAIMNSR with the Egyptian Expeditionary Force between 1916 and 1918, in Greek Macedonia, Serbia, Bulgaria, European Turkey and the Islands of the Aegean Sea. (Her QAIMNSR service record WO 399/5393 may mention appointment to the QAMFNS.)

Series DV 7 holds the CMB Roll and Register of Practising Midwives, on which serving QAMFNS should be found.

Online Sources

The *LG* carries appointments, etc., for QAMFNS and the issue of 14 January 1927 lists of matrons, sisters and staff nurses transferred in order of seniority to QAIMNS, including Miss J MacGillivray, ARRC.

The *BJN* also includes appointments and promotions to QAMFNS.

Chapter 11

NAVAL NURSING SERVICE

M odern naval nursing began with the Royal Naval Nursing Service
in 1884, renamed Queen Alexandra's Royal Naval Nursing
Service in 1902.

Origins

Formal nursing for sick and disabled naval men began at the end of the
seventeenth century, when the Royal Naval Hospital opened at
Greenwich. Many ships and landbased hulks (unseaworthy ships) were
also put to use as hospital ships. Female nurses were employed at
Greenwich and on several naval hospital ships, the surgeon of one hospital
ship suggesting women were 'more easily got and more fit for nurses or
washing than men'. By the 1760s, the Royal Naval hospitals at Haslar (at
Gosport, near Portsmouth) and Plymouth (beside Stonehouse Creek) had
opened.

Female nurses at Greenwich were mostly disabled sailors' wives or
sailors' widows. They were expected to be fit and strong, sober, humane
and of good character. For such low-paid, menial work, although
inevitably a few bad apples helped deserters to escape or pilfered patients'
belongings, they were probably mostly decent and honest but likely,
through the stresses of the job, to succumb to the consolations of alcohol.
Nursing on naval vessels and in naval hospitals was otherwise carried out
by convalescent patients and old sailors.

In 1847, Admiral Sir Edward Parry tried to raise the standard of nursing
at Haslar, by appealing for respectable women to train as naval nurses. He
did not attract a single applicant; such was the status of women nurses at
that date.

By the outbreak of the Crimean War, in 1854, policy had moved towards
all-male nursing in naval hospitals and as sick-berth attendants aboard
naval vessels. Within weeks of Florence Nightingale's departure to Scutari,
however, the Admiralty was looking for female nurses to improve the
nursing care of 120 wounded marines and sailors in the naval hospital near
Therapia, on the Bosphorus, to replace shiftless naval ratings and marines
and inefficient Maltese nurses.

Mrs Elizabeth Mackenzie, a daughter of the eminent Scottish theologian

Dr Thomas Chalmers but not a trained nurse, was selected to lead the small party eventually chosen. Accompanied by her husband the Reverend John Mackenzie, she set out in January 1855 with Miss Erskine, 'a lady of experience', and five 'well-trained real nurses' over 30 years of age and with at least six weeks' hospital nursing experience. Of these, two were ladies, while the other three were professional nurses of a lower social class.

The expedition was an experiment – to be repeated in other naval hospitals if it proved successful. They set off wearing black straw bonnets, grey cloaks and a badge with 'Therapia Hospital' sewn in large blue letters, which Mackenzie admitted made her look like 'a person of a slightly eccentric turn, who rejoices in dressing rather oddly'.

The medical staff at the hospital (a large ramshackle wooden building) put them to work as soon as they arrived. One of the responsibilities passed to Mackenzie was washing patients' bedlinen and clothes, the backlog having been done by Mary Stanley's party. Knowing her nurses felt themselves above such heavy menial work, Mackenzie found a Maltese woman to do the laundering and, contrary to the hospital's previous experience, persuaded marines and bluejackets to do the ironing. 'They did not know their value until we found it out,' she wrote. 'The men were so helpful to us at ironing and folding and would have done anything for us which I explained to the gentlemen to be because we never spoke to them as if they were dogs!'

The hospital boasted a higher survival rate than at Scutari and Koulali, being small, better situated and never excessively overcrowded. Nevertheless, the work was demanding, many men with massive cannonball injuries, or frostbitten fingers or feet that had to be amputated.

Eliza Mackenzie, described as 'imaginative, sensitive and sensible', was clearly endowed with what would now be called empathy and diplomacy, able to smooth ruffled feathers and conceal squabbles between her nurses from the medical staff. But the 'admirable service' she and her team rendered at the Crimea did not immediately lead to respectable women nursing in naval hospitals. The delay was as much to do with the need to establish nursing as a respectable occupation as with reluctance on the part of the naval authorities.

'Lady' nurses, keen to administer broth, read at bedsides or comfort the dying, were unwilling to perform the more distasteful practical tasks involved in nursing sick or injured, especially of the opposite sex. Support was, however, growing for Florence Nightingale's belief that nursing the sick involved knowledge, skill and training, along with sympathy and willingness to undertake menial tasks.

In 1860, the Nightingale nurse training school opened, in association with St Thomas's Hospital, London. Other large hospitals began to offer nursing training, with live-in accommodation in nurses' homes, to safeguard nurses' respectability. Over the next twenty-five years, nursing became established as skilled work, with growing acceptability as an occupation for a gentlewoman. In 1884, Nightingale claimed that she had 'raised nursing from the sink'.

In 1880, only about a dozen female nurses were employed in naval hospitals. But in 1881 the director general wrote that he could see no reason why 'as highly respectable female Nurses are employed in our Civil Hospitals, our sailors should any longer be denied the invaluable benefit of good nursing in our Naval Hospitals'. Nursing was now 'useful work for ladies of character and culture, assisted by a staff of respectable under Nurses' – these last he envisaged as 'upper housemaids from good families'. Recommended improvements in naval hospitals included introducing a small number of trained nursing sisters 'of the position of gentlewomen' under a head sister, in each hospital.

Royal Naval Nursing Service, 1884–1902

In 1884, the Admiralty appointed three head nursing sisters at Haslar, Plymouth and Chatham, each with a small staff of nursing sisters. The head sisters had equal rank, although their hospitals ranked in importance: Haslar, Plymouth, Chatham. They had all served in Egypt with the Army Nursing Service in 1882, and two had served in army hospitals.

The new naval nursing service outlined nursing sisters' duties and responsibilities and, vitally, enabled them to fulfil them, by giving them a position of respect and authority in the naval hierarchy, second to naval surgeons. The nurses had to learn naval terminology – the ward became the 'deck', shifts became 'watches', the toilets 'heads', the nurses' ward office the 'cabin'.

Nursing sisters were pronounced a great improvement. They showed 'professional knowledge and skill . . . of incalculable benefit'. Their presence had 'a restraining and humanizing influence over the patients' bringing 'order and decency' to the wards. Patients benefited from their gentleness and skill at applying dressings and bandages, although their sex and social status precluded them from nursing 'afflictions of the middle third of the body'.

Regulations stipulated that candidates aged 30–48 could be appointed as head sisters, aged 25–40 as sisters. They would be borne on the established list of the Civil Service and eligible for pensions, after retirement at 60. Furnished apartments with a mess room, reading room, kitchen and offices were provided, heating and lighting all found, with a bedroom for each sister and sitting room and bedroom for the head sister. All nursing sisters were required to join the mess, of which the head sister was president. Wines 'or other stimulants' were not allowed in bedrooms unless as a medical prescription. Visitors were only allowed 'at the discretion of the Principal Medical Officer and the Head Sister under proper precautions'.

All sisters were liable to be transferred to other naval hospitals at home, and in the event of war, abroad, as well as, exceptionally, to hospital ships.

They were assisted in the wards by male stewards and sick-berth attendants. Sick-berth staff carried out most of the practical nursing. The nursing sisters were responsible for ensuring patients were kept clean and that all prescribed medicines, diets, etc., were administered. They also assisted at surgical operations and were required to report any misconduct or dereliction of duty by the sick-berth staff.

The regulations firmly established the nursing sisters' status in the hospital 'as officers of the Hospital, taking a position immediately after the surgeons . . . at all times to receive the respect due to their position'. Nursing staff had uniformed maidservants, were addressed as 'Madam' on the wards and travelled first class.

All sisters were entitled to medical attention while sick, on full salary. The MO of each hospital decided their working hours, but where possible they were to be allowed two hours daily for recreation and were given thirty-two days' leave a year, one afternoon off every fortnight and one Sunday every month.

Numbers gradually increased as the system extended to other naval hospitals, at home and abroad, at Malta, Hong Kong and Bermuda, with over fifty naval nursing sisters by the early 1900s.

Recognition of Service

The first naval nursing sisters to receive campaign medals were three aboard the hospital ship *Malacca* treating the sick and wounded from the Benin Expedition of February 1897, awarded the East and West Africa Medal with Benin 1897 clasp.

Queen Alexandra's Royal Naval Nursing Service

Naval nursing was included in the re-organization of military nursing in 1902, when the service formally became Queen Alexandra's Royal Naval Nursing Service (QARNNS), under the control of the medical director general of the Navy.

The service still consisted of only two grades, head sister and nursing sister, the former normally drawn from the ranks of the latter. (The title 'matron' in naval hospitals was used for the person in charge of the laundry.) Candidates were required to have at least three years' training at a large civil hospital, have nursed male patients, have British parents or be naturalized British subjects. Conditions of service were much the same as before, except that they were appointed aged 25–30 and served twelve months' probation prior to appointment.

Their pension varied between 30 and 70 per cent of final salary, depending on length of service. A head sister retired normally at 55, a sister at 50, but could be compulsorily retired at any time. (Those who had joined prior to 1901 could continue to 60 as before.)

Nursing was still largely done by male sick-berth staff instructed by the nursing sisters, who supervised a larger number of wards than in a civil hospital, as they were only involved in nursing, not washing patients, changing beds, etc.

A day sister took charge of four to six wards of fourteen beds each, assisted by a sick-berth steward. There were two night sisters who each took charge of half the hospital, one surgical, the other medical, responsible for administering medicines, feeding, etc. They served on night duty for a month, on rotation.

In 1911 a new intermediate grade, 'superintending sister', was introduced. A total of seven superintending sisters were appointed, as senior sisters at Gibraltar, Malta, Hong Kong and Portland naval hospitals and second sisters at Chatham, Haslar and Portsmouth. Sick-berth staff were given more nursing duties and their training increased from six to twelve months.

QARNNS Reserve

The QARNNS Reserve was set up in 1911, to expand the naval nursing service in the event of war. Arrangements were to be made with the main civil hospitals to supply a quota of nurses in time of war, selected by the matrons from among the best nurses they could spare when the time came. Each hospital would be paid a small donation to compensate for the inconvenience. QARNNS Reserve would work under the same conditions of service as regular naval nurses.

Matrons of hospitals with reputable nurse training schemes were asked for volunteers among their nursing staff to have their names placed on a roll submitted every six months to the Admiralty medical department. Each matron made a commitment to the number of nurses she could provide at six hours', two weeks' or longer notice.

First World War

Prior to the First World War, naval hospital ships were anchored in port in peacetime, but in wartime had followed the Fleet, taking wounded sailors on board and returning with them to port, where they either treated patients in their own sick berths or transferred them to land-based hospitals.

During the First World War, the greater numbers of casualties and increased speed of hospital ships emphasized their role in transporting the wounded. Naval hospital ships stopped following the Fleet, operating instead as CCS, carrying out emergency treatment in addition to ferrying patients back to base hospitals at home (much like army hospital ships), or, for example, from Gallipoli to Malta, often carrying many times more wounded and sick than the number of beds. (The *Drina* had capacity for 221 beds, but on one occasion carried 900 patients.)

In 1914, the QARNNS comprised about seventy members. It was estimated about 250 would be needed, but for the first 6 months only about 100 Reserve nurses were added to the strength.

Four were 'lady probationers', formerly VAD nursing members, attached to the service in 1915. Their numbers rose to eleven in 1917, but were reduced to two by the end of the war.

QARNNS continued to serve at the RN hospitals at Haslar, Plymouth, Chatham and Portland, the Royal Marine Infirmary at Deal, the RN Cadets' sick quarters at Osborne and Dartmouth, and the sick quarters at Shotley. They also nursed at new naval establishments, including sick quarters at Queensferry at the mouth of the River Forth, where an important wartime naval base had been established.

In 1916, nursing sisters (often sent in twos, a regular and a Reserve) gradually began to take over the posts of home-based male sick-berth attendants, to relieve them for service at sea.

QARNNS did not nurse at sea, except on hospital ships. These were generally refitted merchant steamers or passenger ships, where the sisters had their own cabins, work room and mess room. They took temperatures, administered medicines and treatments, and looked after the general condition of the patients. Each ship typically carried two regular and two Reserve QARNNS nursing sisters. In January 1918 four sisters survived the torpedoing of the hospital ship *Rewa*, sunk off the coast of Devon.

Naval nurses also served on the hospital ship *Plassy* which spent the early months of the war plying backwards and forwards across the Channel, carrying wounded. In 1915 it sailed to the Dardenelles,

First World War QARNNS Reserve on the China. *(Peter White collection)*

anchored off Mudros and joined other ships taking wounded from Gallipoli. Hilda Chibnall (who received the ARRC) remembered 'endless struggles' to get them clean and combat the exhaustion and mental shock many were suffering when they arrived on board, their clothes 'stiff with blood and sand, alive with vermin, and almost black with flies'. Providing clean bedlinen was a constant problem.

In 1917, due to the increased submarine threat, QARNNS on hospital ships in the Mediterranean were replaced by male sick-berth attendants.

QARNNS served at two of the three naval hospitals abroad, at Malta and Gibraltar. Nursing sisters at Hong Kong had been recalled for war work at home from 1915 to 1919.

Casualties

Ten QARNNS nursing sisters are recorded as having died in the First World War, most from sickness, but one serving on HMAS *China* was killed by a mine explosion at Scapa Flow in August 1918, and three died in the accidental explosion of ammunition that sank HMS *Natal* in December 1915. They had been serving on the SS *Drina*, and invited to a filmshow aboard the *Natal*, leaving the fourth on duty.

A memorial tablet erected at Haslar Hospital in 1922 commemorates medical staff who died in the First World War, including eight naval nursing sisters.

Interwar Service

Several hundred nursing sisters passed through the Reserve in the First World War, a few going on to join the permanent service.

In the immediate post-war period, nursing sisters continued serving on the hospital ships *Berbice* and *St Margaret of Scotland*, helping with the re-patriation of POWs.

By the end of 1920, all Reserve sisters had left the service. Numbers were further reduced by the resumption of sick-berth staff in posts where they had been temporarily replaced, the closing of temporary sick-berth accom-modation and the closing in the 1920s of certain naval establishments.

In 1923, the QARNNS comprised three head sisters, seven super-intending sisters and sixty-five nursing sisters. Numbers rose slightly in 1926, with four head sisters, at Haslar, Plymouth, Chatham and Malta. In 1927, the senior head sister at Chatham was appointed head sister-in-chief, a new administrative post, taking over the medical director general's nursing staff inspection, selection and supervision responsibilities. She continued serving at Chatham.

Nursing sisters served during the interwar period at Haslar, Plymouth, Chatham, Dartmouth, Shotley, Malta and Hong Kong, and for limited periods at other naval establishments. Olga Franklin (later to become matron-in-chief), a probationer at Chatham in 1927, described how hot water to wash in was brought by a maid each morning, but coal fires were only allowed in the sisters' bedrooms once a week. A posting to Malta brought the luxury of electric fires in cold weather and a cup of tea with the hot water every morning.

At Chatham, a fancy dress dance was held each New Year's Eve in the medical mess library, with punch at midnight to celebrate the New Year promotions.

In 1935 the title head sister-in-chief was changed to matron-in-chief, in line with the other armed service nursing services.

Uniform

Early naval nurses wore grey serge gowns with white aprons, winter and summer cloaks and a navy blue short cape.

In the 1890s, head sisters and sisters wore a navy blue serge dress with Geneva badge (red cross on white background encircled in gold) on the sleeve above the right elbow, long blue cape, white muslin cap, linen collar and cuffs, white apron and navy blue straw bonnet with navy blue ribbon, plus summer and winter navy blue tweed cloak with sleeves. In hot weather (as at Malta) white cotton blouses with cuffs and badges were worn with a blue or white skirt.

After re-organization, the Geneva cross was incorporated into the QARNNS badge, which comprised a red cross on a white ground in a gold border, with Queen Alexandra's monogram above – two As in red, interlacing an anchor and cable, surmounted by a crown. The badge was worn on the right breast.

Dresses were now navy blue linen with scarlet cashmere cuffs, with a long button-through navy cloak and bonnet, white apron and white gloves. Muslin caps were replaced by white handkerchief veils with an embroidered crown in one corner. A blue tippet (short cape) piped with red was also introduced. Belts were optional, of white petersham, which the nurses had to provide themselves. The white metal clasp had an anchor surrounded by leaves and surmounted by a crown.

QARNNS Reserve nurses were supplied with the uniform of a naval nursing sister, but nurses who preferred to continue wearing the uniform of their own hospital were permitted to do so.

Researching Naval Nurses

The National Archives

Greenwich Hospital, 1700s and 1800s
TNA holds registers with brief details of nurses employed at the Royal Greenwich Hospital, between 1704 and 1865. These comprise entry books

(ADM 73/83-86). Entries include name, dates of service and whether Discharged Dead (died while serving), 'Run', Resigned or Expelled, with some remarks such as 'transferred to school infirmary', superannuated or discharged 'for being married'. Aside from names and dates of death, there is little positively to identify these women, although ADM 73/85, covering 1783–1863 includes wives and widows of seamen, with names and details of husbands' service and occasional brief remarks on a few black sheep, expelled 'for indecent conduct with a pensioner', or fined for missing pillow cases or neglect of duty. ADM 73/86 records dates of appointment, death, discharge or resignation, suggesting a somewhat higher status than earlier colleagues. Except for ADM 73/85, organized alphabetically and ADM 73/86, arranged by nature and place of work, names are otherwise entered chronologically, with index registers in ADM 73/87-88.

ADM series 354 and 45 include records mentioning a few individual women nurses employed on hospital ships and in naval hospitals from 1740 onwards.

Royal Naval Nursing Service 1884 Onwards, Including QARNNS and Reserve

Naval nursing service records from 1884 onwards are available on microfilm.

ADM 104/43 is an indexed register of naval nursing service/QARNNS sisters from 1884 to 1909, showing name, rank, date of birth, establishment, date of entry and discharge and where discharged to, with remarks, including appointment references and dates. Grace Hamilton Mackay, appointed in October 1884 after training at Bart's, served at Malta and became head sister successively at Plymouth, Haslar and Chatham. The remarks note that at Haslar, she 'refused to carry out orders as to continuous nursing'. The Navy Board expressed 'grave displeasure' at this insubordination, which included 'giving information to public press and questioning inspections'. She was transferred to Chatham in 1902. Here, after she complained about the new quarters and nursing sisters remaining in wards at meal hours, it is noted that any further instance of such conduct would require the necessity of dispensing with her services without pension. Her service record is marked as transferred to the new register, 1 April 1909.

ADM 104/43 also includes service records for the three nursing sisters who accompanied the 1897 Benin Expedition.

ADM 104/95 comprises annual reports of nursing sisters (1890–1908), each year listed in order of seniority, giving name, age, where stationed, dates of service and brief remarks on character and work.

ADM 104/96 Nursing Sisters' and Ward Masters' establishment book. This is indexed by establishment (hospital, etc.) and lists staff in roughly chronological order between 1912 and 1927, giving name, rank, date of appointment and discharge, with reason.

ADM 104/161 is a large indexed register of permanent naval nurses' service records (1894–1929 with summaries of pre-1909 service), with date of appointment, rank, hospital or hospital ship appointed to, date of joining, date of discharge, cause of appointment, next of kin details, brief remarks on conduct, ability, tact, 'zeal', sympathy with patients, temperament, efficiency in medical and surgical nursing, and 'special notations'. Some entries are extensive, in tiny script.

Ethel Anne de Blaquière, born in 1877 and trained in Dublin, joined at Plymouth in 1905, served all through the First World War and was posted to Haslar in 1922, retiring in 1927, at 50. Early in her career, she is described as zealous with considerable ability, although not amenable to discipline and somewhat flighty and fond of amusement. Towards the end of her career, she is regarded as slow, lazy and unintelligent, a bad example to junior sisters, with 'entire lack of zeal and interest in her profession'. Nevertheless, she was one of a handful of QARNNS who attended the funeral at Westminster Abbey of Queen Alexandra in 1925.

ADM 104/161 also includes the service record of Agnes Wotherspoon Baird, born in 1885, who began as a Reserve nurse from Bart's (St Bartholomew's) Hospital. (There are therefore also entries for her in ADM 104/163.) She served during the war on the hospital ships *Plassy* and *Karapara* (which transported wounded from Gallipoli) and is described as cheerful with above average sympathy but only average zeal and tact. As the years pass after the end of the war, she becomes quiet and sensitive rather than bright and cheerful and is invalided out in 1926.

ADM 104/161 also reveals the fate of Grace Hamilton Mackay. Her entry seems to have been transferred to the new register in order to record all the special notations about her. One entry in the 'general remark' column reads – 'Has worked well looks after officers.' Otherwise, a further complaint about new messing arrangements is recorded. This precipitated a court of enquiry and on 19 April 1909 she was invalided out of the service, with a pension of £128 5s 9d pa.

ADM 104/162-165 comprise filmed registers of QARNNS Reserve nursing sisters' service details, covering 1914–1919. They also include lists of candidates for hospital ships and waiting lists of those who had applied for entry into the service. Several entries on different pages will often be found for the same person. Entries for individual Reserve nurses are quite brief, rather haphazardly entered, with comments, matron's report, dates of service and postings. They can be quite difficult to decipher, but repay the effort!

Hilda Chibnall, who served on a hospital ship treating the wounded from Gallipoli, has two entries in ADM 104/162, which show her discharge from hospital ship *Rewa* to Plymouth Hospital in September 1915, and record one of the fleet surgeons writing that 'Miss Chibnall is a lady and has much more influence over the S.B. staff. She is the sister who was such an excellent example to the other three sisters and the S.B. staff by serenely going on dressing cases when the first batches of bullets began

Page from QARNNS Reserve service register, showing part service records of Hilda Chibnall and Constance Hayden. (TNA ADM 104/162)

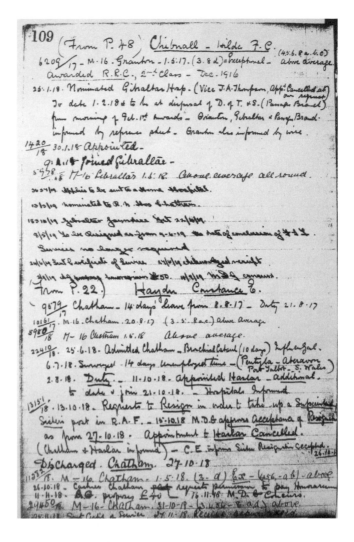

striking the decks and ship's sides.' (Another entry for her appears in ADM 104/165.)

ADM 104/161-165 include service records of the naval nurses who died during or as a result of service in the First World War. Eva Gladys Beard (ADM 104/161) died in Haslar Hospital on 14 March 1920 from influenza and bronchial pneumonia. ADM 104/163 records the exact time of Mabel Edith Grigson's death on Malta, in October 1918, from amoebic dysentery and heart failure.

ADM 137/3608 holds the report into the tragic accidental explosions aboard HMS *Natal*, naming the one QARNNS and two Reserve sisters who died. (Their service records will be found in ADM 104/161 and 163.)

ADM 1/8483/55 contains a copy of the *Regulations for QARNNS Reserve*.

ADM 171/133 comprises the microfilmed roll of naval war service medals for the First World War, including QARNNS.

From 1885, RNNS head sisters appear in the *Navy List*. From 1889, nursing sisters are also listed. First World War entries for QARNNS include first name and where serving; Reserve nursing sisters and 'lady probationers' have initials and where serving.

It is possible to ascertain from the *Navy List* that in 1918 QARNNS Sisters Mary L Hocking and Dorothy G Bryant were serving aboard hospital ship *China*, together with Reserve Nursing Sisters A E Richardson and L C Chamberlain, whose service record in ADM 104/162 identifies her as Louisa Charlotte Chamberlain, nominated for hospital ship *China* in December 1917 while serving at the RN Infirmary at Deal, who joined the *China* in February 1918. Her name subsequently appears on the Roll of Honour, having died in August 1918.

Royal Naval Museum

Their collections include early photographs of naval nurses and First World War QARNNS, with some ephemera.

Institute of Naval Medicine

The Institute of Naval Medicine Historic Library holds the collections of the former RN hospitals at Haslar and Stonehouse.

Online Sources

The *BJN* carries naval nursing general announcements as well as individual appointments, RRC decorations, etc. for RNNS and QARNNS nurses.

Printed Sources

Kathleen Harland, *A History of Queen Alexandra's Royal Naval Nursing Service* (1990)

Captain C M Taylor (ed.), *Nursing in the Senior Service 1902–2002, Personal Histories of Queen Alexandra's Royal Naval Nursing Service* (2001) includes firsthand accounts of naval nursing service.

Chapter 12

INDIAN ARMY NURSING SERVICE AND QAMNSI

The Indian Army Nursing Service (IANS) was set up in 1888 to provide nursing care for sick British soldiers serving in India.

Origins

In nineteenth-century India, units of British Army regiments were stationed in garrisons throughout India. British and European officers and

The first Indian Army Nursing sisters, April 1888. Catharine Loch is seated centre with four nurses. (Royal British Nursing Association collection, by kind permission of King's College London)

men also served in the Indian Army. Nursing in Indian military hospitals was carried out by male medical orderlies of the Military Subordinate Medical Service. Many sick or wounded British soldiers died from lack of skilled nursing, but a scheme put forward by Florence Nightingale in 1867 for trained female nurses in military hospitals in India was rejected as unnecessary.

However, twenty years later, Lady Nora Roberts, wife of the new Commander-in-Chief, India, had more success. Raising money from the regiments, Lady Roberts set up station hospitals and special wards for sick officers (who were otherwise forced to stay in seedy clubs and hotels or rely on the hospitality of friends).

The Government of India and the India Office (its opposite number in London) funded a small number of trained nurses as an experiment. Two lady superintendents (Miss Loch and Miss Oxley) and eight handpicked nursing sisters went out in 1888 to nurse in Rawalpindi and Bangalore.

They had expected merely to supervise the nursing of serious cases, but found themselves teaching the male orderlies basic nursing care. Some doctors had no idea what nurses could or should do and their duties over-lapped with those of the Eurasian assistant surgeons, whose relationship with the nursing sisters became – and remained – somewhat strained.

The success of the experiment was largely due to Catharine Loch. Diplomatic in her dealings with the medical services, Loch was also a warm and caring leader of her small flock. Her letters home vividly described the violent climate – freezing cold, stifling heat and dust storms that blotted out the sun, covering everything in a thick layer of sand. Later that year, armed with some rudimentary firing practice and belted-on revolvers, Miss Loch and four nurses accompanied the Black Mountain Expedition in north-west India.

By 1891, fifty-two IANS members were serving at a few of the largest military stations in India and Burma, in two and threes and even singly, huge distances apart. A military nurse in India had to be very self reliant, physically strong to withstand the climate and seasonal demands of the work, able to sustain good relationships in a small community and above all not attract gossip. For this reason, selection was restricted to well-bred gentlewomen, for fear of bringing nursing into disrepute.

Nursing duties varied depending on the MO in charge of the station. From 1894, the training of soldier orderlies, who carried out most nursing duties, became more formal. The nursing sisters worked in shifts, so there was always one on duty, in charge of several wards.

Organization

By 1897, every large military hospital in India had IANS nurses. The service comprised four lady superintendents, nine deputy super-intendents (later called senior nursing sisters) and thirty-nine nursing sisters, but many more were needed in the smaller stations, where many patients still died due to inadequate nursing.

A lady superintendent served at each of the military commands, having authority over all the subordinate stations within her command. She made a yearly inspection tour, reporting to the principal MO on the work and conduct of the nursing sisters. The deputy superintendent was responsible for management and discipline of the wards but also shared in the work and offered advice. Absolute loyal obedience to her was insisted upon, not always easy in a situation where two or three were living and working together.

Applicants had to be aged 25–35 and were appointed for five years, renewable for a further five years. Only if passed as physically fit by a medical board could they serve a third term, and in very exceptional circumstances, a fourth. After fifteen years they became eligible for a pension.

Life in the IANS

Successful applicants were ordered to embark about a month after appointment. Quarters were usually comfortable and spacious, sometimes with a private sitting room. The government only supplied basic furniture. Nursing sisters had to provide their own bedlinen, crockery and cutlery. It was possible to live fairly comfortably, and keep a horse and trap. The senior sister usually did the housekeeping.

Sisters could be moved from one station to another. Hospitals in India varied considerably, some without running water, others without electricity. The climate usually dictated the nature of the work, with 'dull' quiet periods before an outbreak of fever, dysentery or pneumonia. There were very few surgical cases. Transfer in summer to a cooler hill station could involve living and nursing in huts or tents, but most sisters had to stay in the plains all year round. They might be on duty for fourteen hours, with wards full of enteric fever (cholera) cases, working in temperatures well above 100 °F. During the monsoon, even the salt on the table turned 'into a little puddle before one's eyes', and clothes not made of wool always felt wet. Glorious views and balmy moonlit nights made up for some of the inconveniences.

Lady Roberts had set up convalescent homes for nursing sisters who fell ill. Homesickness surfaced most on short leave periods, so it was helpful to have family or friends in India during the five years before long leave in England was permitted.

Queen Alexandra's Military Nursing Service for India

In 1901, the committee considering the re-organization of the Army Medical Department and Nursing Service recommended the amalgamation of the ANS and the IANS as a new combined service. Six months later the QAIMNS was established. However, the India Office, fearing dilution of the high moral standard of the IANS, opted to carry on running its own nursing service, which in 1903 became Queen Alexandra's Military Nursing Service for India (QAMNSI). QAMNSI nurses were recruited and selected by a nursing board in England.

A new grade of senior nursing sister was introduced. The establishment now consisted of lady superintendents (one for each command), senior nursing sisters (one at each station) and nursing sisters. Normally, three sisters working in a station hospital would work alone in three shifts, alternating on a weekly basis. Two months' leave on full pay was granted annually. After five years' service, sisters could take a year out on two-thirds pay, with free passage home and back. In Burma four nursing sisters served a two-year tour of duty, being eligible for a hill-station posting on their return to India.

Recognition of Service

Small IANS parties accompanied frontier expeditions, in 1888, 1892 and 1895, for which they received campaign medals, and in 1899 the RRC. QAMNSI who served during the First World War (in France and Mesopotamia) received campaign medals, with several RRCs and 10 MiDs.

QAMNSI in the First World War

In 1914, out of ninety-one QAMNSI members, seventeen were mobilized in India for service with three medical units of the BEF in France, named after the stations from which they had come, for example, the Rawalpindi British General Hospital at Wimereux. They also served with two CCS.

In November 1915, nearly all were recalled to the Rawalpindi, prior to posting to two general hospitals in Mesopotamia (now Iraq). The belief that white women would not stand the climate may have influenced the decision to send QAMNSI members. In March 1916, the remaining sisters were recalled urgently to India, where need for trained nurses was so great that 600 were sent from the Australian nursing service.

Interwar Period

In July 1919, nearly sixty QAIMNSR and TFNS members were serving in India. Many QAs and former QAs began to be sent out from the UK to serve in India on temporary yearly contracts. By November 1919, about 250 temporary nurses had been appointed, to allow the release of the Australian nursing sisters and give permanent staff much-needed leave of absence.

During the early 1920s former army nurses were invited to apply for temporary QAMNSI posts as staff nurse midwives, to serve in Military Families' hospitals or work alone with one Indian woman helper. The influx of these temporary nurses dissolved any remaining fears of sinking moral standards. Short service contracts proved more practical, allowing more easily for resignation on marriage (a fairly frequent occurrence) and forestalling the health problems which developed with long exposure to the Indian climate.

From 1926, QAIMNS took over nursing in India, filling all vacant posts in military hospitals for British troops in India, for tours of duty not exceeding five years. The QAMNSI continued concurrently, until the last members retired in the late 1930s.

Uniform

The IANS wore a scarlet cape and white dress with scarlet cuffs, white apron, stiff collar and rank buttons. Early nursing sisters wore fez-like white caps. From about 1900, they wore white and grey 'sailor hats', possibly straw boaters. Photographs of QAMNSI show similar uniform, but with sleeve rank stripes, veil caps and soft collars.

Researching the Indian Army Nursing Service/QAMNSI

Not all British nurses in India belonged to the IANS or QAMNSI, nor should the Indian Army Nursing Service be confused with the locally recruited Nursing Service for Indian Troops/Indian Military Nursing Service (the latter established in 1926), although the IANS is often referred to as the Indian Nursing Service in official documents.

British Library

The India Office Records collection, part of the British Library Asia, Pacific and Africa Collections (APAC), contains a large amount of material relevant to the search for individual IANS, QAMNSI and QAIMNS nurses who served in India.

The IANS became a highly prestigious nursing service to which many applied, but few were selected. Each nurse had to provide a reference confirming that her family was 'of respectability and good standing in society, and that she possesses the tact, temper, and ability qualifying her for the appointment'.

IOR/L/MIL/9/430-432 comprises bound ledgers listing the large number of Indian Nursing Service candidates between December 1887 and May 1920. As well as recording rejected candidates, these ledgers formed a waiting list for a future vacancy of accepted candidates.

Entries are indexed and include name, address and personal details, with father's occupation, giving an idea of those who were acceptable –

daughters of brewers, architects, builders, farmers, engineers. The entries also note nursing training and experience and some brief remarks – 'have seen the lady who seems a good sort', a comment made about Gilmore, Mary Gertrude, appointed in 1902.

Application papers relating to the service of successful candidates may be found at IOR/L/MIL/7/11617-11803 for those appointed between 1887 and 1919, catalogued in rough chronological order under initials and surname. M G Gilmore has two catalogue entries, one of them in the above series, L/MIL/7/11671. This includes papers bound into a dark-blue ledger, relating to the service of Miss Mary Gertrude Gilmore. They include her formal letter of application in 1899, when she was nursing at St George's Hospital, London and a letter from Cape Town in 1900, where she was serving in the South African War. A form headed 'Indian Nursing Service' states that her name will be retained on the list of candidates so long as she remains within the age limit for admission or until her appointment, stressing that the number of vacancies is small compared with the number of qualified candidates. A declaration form shows her as single, 32 next birthday, born in India, her father worked in the Indian Educational Department, she had been educated at home by a governess and was not a member of any sisterhood or society. Her state of health is left blank, but we learn that she trained at St George's for three years. Her papers include letters of recommendation, and printed conditions of appointment.

Reference to the service of individual members of the IANS/QAMNSI may be found in many different files in Collection 262, IOR/L/MIL/7/11316-11616 1886–1940, including resignations, new appointments, etc. Some nurses' surnames are given in the catalogue descriptions. If you have an approximate date of appointment (this may appear in the *LG* or *BJN*), a search of possible documents covering appointments for that date should prove fruitful.

IOR/L/MIL/7/11373 1902–1923 appears to contain papers relating to Gilmore's appointment in 1902. A file relating to 'Sick leave to count towards service in special case of Miss M G Gilmore' is at IOR/L/MIL/7/11423 dated 1913. The surname Gilmore is also mentioned in the catalogue description of IOR/L/MIL/7/11364 1899–1952, although this may relate to Lady Superintendent A M Gilmore, whose retirement is contained in a list of QAMNSI promotions, resignations and retirements published in the *BJN* in 1923.

Annual confidential reports on QAMNSI members from 1902 to 1920 are in IOR/L/MIL/7/11383, 11392, 11446, 11516, etc., including nursing sisters transferred to the MEF in 1915 (11447). The reports show where the nurse was serving and include comments and reports, which didn't always concur with one another. One woman is described as 'hysterical' in two reports and 'excellent' by the MO.

Guidance notes on the preparation of the report give some insight into the qualities required: energetic, tactful, self-reliant, compliant with the wishes of those over her, 'desire to live pleasantly with those with whom she is located' and with 'knowledge of the customs of good society to enable her to act as a gentlewoman at all times'.

IOR/L/MIL/7/4007, 1909, concerns claims from nursing sisters at Peshawar for the India General Service Medal (1908) with North West Frontier clasp.

Collection 234 contains references to IANS RRC recipients in the late 1800s and early 1900s, and 1891–1918.

IOR/L/MIL/7/11361, dated 1899–1916, and IOR/L/MIL/7/11397 contain uniform details.

IOR/L/MIL/7/11572 concerns the grant of pensions to dependants of deceased members of the nursing service, 1925.

Collection 262 contains numerous files concerning temporary appointments between 1919 and 1924, e.g., IOR/L/MIL/7/11502 and IOR/L/MIL/7/11488-89 (temporary nurses appointed between 1919 and 1925). IOR/L/MIL/7/11534, 11536, 11538 and 11539 hold confidential reports on QAMNSI members 1921–1935. IOR/L/Mil/7/11488-11508 comprise files relating to temporary appointments between 1918 and 1934, including many surnames. Some of the catalogue descriptions list surnames; others cover a part of the alphabet, for example, surnames Runton to Stroud are in 11503.

The National Archives

WO 145/1-3 the RRC registers include IANS/QAMNSI recipients.

WO 222/2134 contains a report on QAMNSI work in the First World War, including names of nursing sisters and hospitals.

Series WO 95 contains war diaries for hospitals and CCS where QAMNSI worked – see WO 95/4095, WO 95/4096 and WO 95/344.

QAMNSI nurses who applied for First World War campaign medals will be found in the DocumentsOnline index and on the service medal rolls WO 329/2352 and WO 329/2348.

Online Sources

www.london-gazette.co.uk. The *LG* carried notices of some but not all IANS/QAMNSI appointments, promotions and resignations, as well as MiD and RRC awards.

rcnarchive.rcn.org.uk. Some IANS/QAMNSI appointment notices appear in the *BJN* and its predecessor. The *BJN* of 20 September 1902, for example, announces that Sisters Robinson, Campbell, Harris, Hayes and Lingard of the IANS have applied for and obtained re-engagement for another term of five years. These journals also include articles on the IANS. The *BJN* publicized the Government of India's request for fully trained nurses on short contracts in the early 1920s and published notices of ladies appointed as (temporary) staff nurses, giving names and dates of departure.

Early nurses travelled on troop ships, but it is worth searching outbound or incoming passenger lists (at Findmypast.co.uk and Ancestry.co.uk respectively), especially for a post-First World War appointment, to find out when a nurse sailed to India. This will give a rough date of appointment and whether she sailed with other nurses, which is useful if her surname doesn't come up in a search of the BL/APAC catalogue. It is worth searching for files containing the surnames of other nurses who were appointed at the same time, and checking files of temporary appointments which cover the year she would have been serving in India.

www.bmj.com/archive. The *BMJ* includes some articles, notices of appointments and RRC awards concerning the IANS/QAMNSI.

Printed Sources

The BL holds copies of the *Royal Army Medical Corps, the Army Dental Corps, and Q.A.I.M.N.S. News and Gazette*, from July 1927. These contain very little relating to QAIMNS, but do carry *LG* announcements, with postings including to Allahabad, etc.

The *Indian Army List* (TNA hold some copies; the BL/Asian and African Studies reading room has a more complete set) lists serving sisters with their rank and (other than in wartime) where they were stationed.

The IANS appear between 1891 and 1903. From July 1903, QAMNSI dates of appointment, present grade, station serving at, dates of leave or sickness are included. Mary Gilmore's postings can be followed, from Wellington in 1903 to Bangalore, then Secunderabad until 1908, when she took her year's home leave on two-thirds pay, having served five years. In 1909 she was posted to Quetta, then Secunderabad, then Allahabad in 1914. By now she had become a senior nursing sister. In 1915 she was back in Bangalore, and by 1918 on to her third period of service. She was awarded the RRC, returned in April 1919 to Secunderabad and took another year's leave in 1920. Each grade was listed in order of seniority. In 1925, just before her retirement, Mary Gilmore's name finally arrived at the top of the list.

Post-1926, the *Indian Army List* includes both the QAMNSI still serving and the QAIMNS currently serving in India, under separate headings, showing where each nurse was serving. The QAMNSI list shows date of completion of present period of service, and whether first, second, etc. The QAIMNS list includes staff nurses and shows date of completion of Indian tour, or age of retirement. In 1927, QAMNSI Chief Lady Superintendent Wilhelmine Walker (who also superintended the separate Indian Military Nursing Service) is shown at Simla, with four lady superintendents, fifteen senior nursing sisters and ten nursing sisters, while the QAIMNS in India were headed by Miss C G Stronach, as Principal Matron at Poona, with one

Part of the QAMNSI entry, Indian Army List, *January 1902, showing Catharine Loch still at Rawal Pindi. (TNA Crown copyright)*

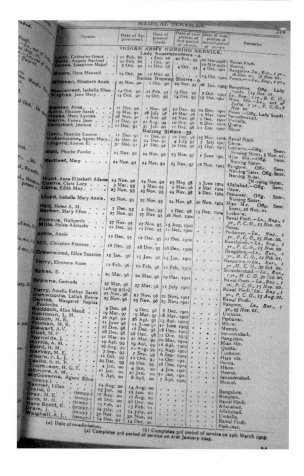

Matron at Secunderabad, thirty-six sisters and nine staff nurses. By 1937, only 6 QAMNSI members remained, whereas 200 QAIMNS were serving in India.

QAMNSI also appear in *Thacker's Indian Medical Directory.*

Norman Gooding, *Honours and Awards to Women to 1914* (2007) contains much detail of awards to INS nursing sisters, with helpful references.

A F Bradshaw (ed.), *Catharine Grace Loch, Royal Red Cross, Senior Lady Superintendent Queen Alexandra's Military Nursing Service for India. A Memoir* (1905), available online as an ebook, gives much fascinating detail on the early history of the IANS.

Lily Grace Petter served with the QAIMNSR during the First World War. Her QA(R) service file at TNA (WO 399/5301, under her married surname McNair, although she did not marry until 1921) reveals that she considered emigrating under the ex-service free passage scheme, but instead went on to serve in the QAMNSI. Outgoing passenger lists at Findmypast.co.uk show her sailing from Liverpool to Bombay in September 1919.

Her name was not in the list of applicants in the register of permanent appointments, IOR/L/MIL/9/432, although it covered the period up to May 1920. The passenger list showed that she travelled with a large party of nurses, only a few of whom figured in the applicants' register. Her surname did not appear in a search of the IOR collection, but the departure of her fellow nurse passengers was announced in the *BJN*, although again without mentioning her name.

Several documents in Collection 262 listed the surnames of her fellow passengers at the right date. One of these, IOR/L/MIL/7/11502 'Appointments of Temporary Nurses' covering the letter P in the alphabet, contained a contents list that did include her name, and papers relating to her appointment. These comprised her official acceptance as passed by the nursing board for temporary QAMNSI in July 1919, application form giving details of education, health, the hospital where she trained, a brief resume of her war service and letters, including one asking if she could sail with her friend Miss C Gabbett – the passenger list of the *City of Marseilles* shows that she did.

Constance J M Gabbett had the ideal background – her father had been a colonel in the Indian Army. She was appointed for regular service. IOR/L/MIL/7/11488 contains the nursing selection board report listing those appointed – including Constance Gabbett. It also gives comments on others and lists of those invited to apply for temporary appointments as sisters or staff nurses. There were twenty-six applications received for seven permanent vacancies. Of these, twelve were rejected without interview. The successful applicants including Constance Gabbett received £20 outfit allowance, instructions on uniform requirements and notice that passage to India would be arranged at an early date.

The file lists those sailing on the *City of Marseilles* (the passenger list shows their occupation simply as 'nurse'), those permitted to re-engage for a further five years and resignations (often for marriage). Constance Gabbett resigned for this reason in December 1920.

WOMEN'S AUXILIARY SERVICES

Chapter 13

WOMEN'S AUXILIARY SERVICES IN THE FIRST WORLD WAR

Introduction

Women's catering, clerical and technical work with the armed forces began during the First World War with the formation of the Women's (later Queen Mary's) Army Auxiliary Corps (WAAC), the Women's Royal Naval Service (WRNS) and the Women's Royal Air Force (WRAF).

Women were enrolled, rather than enlisted, signing up for twelve months or the duration of the war, whichever was the longer period. After enrolment, they would be sent to a hostel, depot or camp for a medical examination, initial training in saluting, drill, service routine and customs and to receive their kit. For many, it was the first time they had undressed in front of a stranger or lived away from home, since most girls only left home when they married.

Women who enrolled as mobiles could be posted anywhere. Living communally in a hut could be difficult for those who hadn't experienced boarding school, but it broadened outlooks and wearing uniform was a great leveller. Foreign postings (for which they were given identity certificates and discs with their service number) were an exciting revelation for those who would never normally have travelled abroad.

It was difficult to foster team spirit among immobiles, who worked from home, and were collected on a lorry every day before roll call and drill. The women sometimes went on route marches, singing as they marched. Many shortened their skirts and hair, became fitter and healthier and grew in confidence. Service life had many rules and regulations, but there were also cunning ways of getting round them, aided and abetted by servicemen, who offered lifts, illicit boat trips or flights on aeroplanes and airships.

During the course of their work, the women came under the respective Army, RN or RAF senior officers where they worked. The WAAC officials, WRNS and WRAF officers were in charge of their discipline and welfare. Some were more humane and approachable than others.

Some hostels had normal mattresses, but other servicewomen slept on army 'biscuits', three separate square pads, piled neatly with their folded bedding at the foot of their beds every day before hut inspection. Larger hostels had a small sick bay, some with a live-in nursing VAD. Small women's wards were set aside in hospitals, including Endell Street Military Hospital, and a special QMAAC hospital opened at Isleworth. The Spanish flu epidemic at the end of the war took its toll on servicewomen concentrated in hostels and camps.

After the Armistice, work for the women's services increased, following the clamour for men to be demobilized as soon as possible. By summer 1919, however, public opinion had turned against women still in uniform at taxpayers' expense, and the women's services gradually disbanded. Some left without a backward glance, others found it difficult after service life to step back alone into the outside world.

Employment other than private domestic work was hard to find. Several hundred women took advantage of the government free passage scheme for ex-service personnel to resettle in Australia, South Africa or Canada, run through the Society for the Oversea Settlement of British Women.

The WAAC owed its formation in early 1917 largely to the work of two groups of women: Army Pay Department (APD) temporary clerks and Women's Legion (WL) cooks and drivers.

Army Pay Department

During the First World War, temporary civilian women clerks were taken on by the APD to work in army pay offices (APOs) all over the country.

The story goes that in the early weeks of the war, Woolwich APO was inundated with separation allowance claims for wives of the newly mobilized territorials as well as the surge of patriotic volunteers. Seeing how desperate and exhausted the captain of the claims section looked, the ordnance depot CO offered his wife to address envelopes.

This lady and a few of her friends set themselves up at tables in the barracks garden. Others joined in, all working non-stop. Unfamiliar with army procedure or abbreviations, they inevitably made mistakes, like misreading 'Bdr' as brigadier, instead of bombardier. Nevertheless, the arrangement worked well until October, when the WO got wind of it. The unauthorized volunteers were banished and forty temporary female clerks appointed to administer separation allowances, with Post Office Savings Bank female clerks as supervisors.

This workforce continued day and night trying to clear the mountain of paperwork. In January 1915, the WO capitulated and officially began employing women in APOs. Mixed sex offices, with women working alongside men, had previously been taboo. Numbers rapidly grew (especially after 1916, when male APC clerks were transferred to infantry

Badge worn by women of the Army Pay Department, with 'WOMEN'S ARMY SERVICE' embroidered in white around the letters APD. (Peter White collection)

regiments) to over 28,000 female APD clerks with 279 lady superintendents by the end of the war.

From 1917 onwards, temporary female APD clerks aged over 17 signed agreements to serve for the period of the war and four months afterwards. Most worked in UK APOs, and were not permitted to volunteer to work abroad. They had no uniform, just a small black cloth badge. A selected few were sent to France in April 1917, among the first members of the WAAC.

Researching APD Clerks

The National Archives

Reference to earlier APD service is occasionally found in surviving QMAAC or WRNS service records.

Imperial War Museum

WW&S has a shortlist for the first clerks and typists to be sent to France, UK APO inspection reports and a list of seventy APD lady superintendents, with address, appointment and previous employment details.

Alice Mary Sartain, an APD bookkeeper, was shortlisted to go to France in April 1917. Her QMAAC service record has not survived, but the

QMAAC service medal roll (WO 329/2310) shows her as WAAC enrolment no. 1, embarked on 16 April 1917.

Adjutant General's Corps Museum

A record book contains names of lady superintendents; the museum also has photographs of First World War female clerks.

The Women's Legion

Motto: *'Ora et Labora'* – 'prayer and work'

Not to be confused with the women's branch of the British Legion, an entirely different organization, the Women's Legion was set up in 1915 by Lady Londonderry, in response to the call for women workers to release men for active service. Thousands of women soon enrolled as catering and domestic workers, drivers, gardeners and semi-skilled industrial workers.

Suggestions of employing women experienced in plain cooking to feed the expanding ranks of the army led in August 1915 to 100 WL cooks being sent for a six-month trial period to take over the cookhouses of army convalescent camps at Dartford, Epsom and Eastbourne. They compared very favourably with hastily trained male recruits, producing appetizing meals with less waste. The experiment extended to other convalescent camps and command depots, then officers' and sergeants' messes, the RFC and cadet battalions.

The WO hired WL cooks, waitresses and cookery instructors (to train soldier cooks). Some came from domestic service; others were qualified domestic science teachers.

Organization

The WL initially comprised ambulance, canteen and cookery sections, growing to include agricultural, general and motor transport sections, each with its own HQ and commandant. Ordinary WL members were known as Legionaries. Cookery and motor transport became known as the military sections. The WO paid the workers in these sections; WL administrative workers were volunteers.

Military Cookery Section

Employment of WL cooks at army camps was formalized in February 1916. By August 1917, over 6,000 WL cooks, waitresses and kitchen helpers were working in 200 British camps, on a ratio of 14 women catering for 1,000 men. WL cooks and waitresses formed the core of the new WAAC sent to

France in spring 1917, and most cookery section members were gradually absorbed into the WAAC.

Motor Transport Section

The WL supplied the army with twenty women drivers on a trial basis in spring 1916. Within six months this number had doubled. Khaki-clad women were soon driving army cars, motorcycles and lorries all over the UK as the WL Motor Transport (MT) section replaced men as ambulance and motor drivers for the ASC and RFC. The WL supplied uniforms, on which they were allowed to sew the ASC or RFC shoulder title.

Drivers were accepted from ten approved driving schools. Training courses were later held at a WL training centre at Teddington, near Twickenham. By the end of 1917, about 1,500 WL MT drivers had enrolled. During 1918, an average of fifty enrolled every week.

Some were wealthy aristocrats; others were garage owners' daughters. Some became motorcycle despatch riders. Others drove lorries in convoys, sometimes for twenty hours without a break. Those who chauffeured staff officers suffered much tedious hanging around and waiting. Chauffeuring could be unpleasant if you drove someone you didn't get on with and WL drivers' vehicles were sometimes sabotaged by the ASC men they were replacing. Molly Coleclough was sent to Morpeth with her sister Bardie. Molly delivered stores in an ancient van while Bardie, the better driver,

WL drivers wearing ASC cap badges. (Peter White collection)

chauffeured the ASC colonel. They went to the pictures for the first time, learnt to dance and play poker.

MT section members were employed as superintendents, head drivers, or squad leaders, mechanic drivers, probationer drivers, commercial drivers and garage washers. All cars, ambulances and box vans up to 15 cwt (excluding for home defence and mobilization) were driven by women.

The WL MT section was planned to be absorbed into the WAAC, but they rebelled, backed by the ASC companies to which they were attached. The several thousand home service drivers were allowed to stay in the WL, although between April and July 1918, 500–600 of them transferred into the newly formed WRAF.

The WL also supplied drivers to the Canadian Forestry Corps, and the New Zealand and Australian forces.

After the Armistice, WL drivers had the chance of going to France, to relieve RASC drivers. Molly went in the early summer of 1919. The work mainly consisted of transferring patients between hospitals, and driving German POWs to and from work. Most drivers took off-duty tourist trips to the front line, still a sea of mud, dugouts, craters and half-buried tanks, with people clearing debris, ammunition dumps and barbed wire.

Other WL Sections

The Mechanics section, formed in 1917, trained and employed WL members in semi-skilled aeroplane construction work. Its members were absorbed into the WAAC, some transferring to the WRAF on its formation. Large numbers of clerks, telephonists and unskilled storeswomen were also employed, attached to the ASC.

The Sailors and Soldiers Work section, known as War Service Legion, trained disabled servicemen to make gold lace for uniforms. The other WL sections had no army association.

Casualties

Ten WL members are recorded as having died, mostly drivers. A Motor Drivers Compassionate Fund was set up to help those injured in accidents.

Post-war

Former members of the MT section helped distribute food supplies during the railway strike in 1919. In 1927, the WL MT section was officially recognized as a voluntary reserve transport unit, for use in times of national emergency, with an entry in the *Army List*.

Uniform

WL members wore khaki outdoor uniform and a distinctive brooch badge, designed by Lady Londonderry.

Cap badges for higher ranks were solid metal, enamelled red for motor transport, turquoise for canteen and later household service, green for agricultural, purple for horticultural, yellow for clerical, orange for mechanical and pink for HQ staff.

Some WL buttons have the letters WSWL. The full name of the WL appears to have been 'War Service Legion and Women's Legion', modified to 'War Service and Women's Legion'.

WAAC forewoman wearing WL badges on her collar. (Peter White collection)

Researching the Women's Legion

The National Archives

WL documents are sometimes found in surviving QMAAC service records of former WL members (see DocumentsOnline).

WO 162/65 holds lists of home service QMAAC put forward for recognition of good service. These include frequent mention of former WL service, giving length of service and sometimes where served.

WO 162/62 relates to the decision for home drivers to remain WL members and those abroad join the WAAC, listing several hundred motor drivers and washers serving either at home or abroad, stating in some cases where they were serving.

A small number of First World War campaign medal index cards mention WL service. A few files relate to death or injury of WL drivers.

Mary Hackney's WL enrolment form. (TNA WO 398/97)

Imperial War Museum

Rank and section badges are displayed in the online collection. *WW&S* contains a history of and reports on WL work, including drivers supplied to Canadian Forestry Corps camps and attached to RASC companies.

National Army Museum

Reports on the Women's Legion are among papers of Lady Londonderry held here.

Other Sources

The Canadian National Archives (see *Library and Archives Canada*'s collection RG9-III-Vol. 2660 and B1 Vol 2659) holds lists and documents relating to WL drivers attached to the Canadian Forestry Corps.

The Liddle collection has MS recollections, documents, photographs and badges relating to WL service.

Printed Sources

Molly Coleclough, *Women's Legion 1916–1920* (1940).

Chapter 14

WOMEN'S ARMY AUXILIARY CORPS

Corps motto: 'Steady!'

As the war progressed and women substituted for men in many occupations, the army became increasingly dependent on locally engaged civilian women, whom they had no powers to direct or retain. This situation came to a head in 1916, following the deployment of WL cooks and waitresses in army camps.

After several conferences to discuss female labour, a scheme emerged by which civilian women were brought into the army, initially in France, where the first WAAC draft stepped ashore on 31 March 1917. Eventually, 10,000 mainly domestic workers, clerks and telephonists substituted for men in France and about 40,000 served in the UK, some 7,000 transferring to the WRAF when it was formed.

Organization

The WAAC was headed by a chief controller in London, Mrs Chalmers Watson. She later took the title of controller-in-chief, with Helen Gwynne-Vaughan as chief controller in France.

Rank titles for this first corps of women serving with the British Army smacked of the factory rather than the military. Women in supervisory positions were called 'officials' rather than officers, titled as: deputy chief controller, controller, assistant controller, area controller, recruiting controller, unit administrator, deputy administrator and assistant administrator. Quartermistresses were also appointed. NCO-equivalent rank were titled forewomen; the ordinary rank and file called 'workers'.

WL cookery section members and some APD clerical staff formed the nucleus of the new corps. Women signed on for the duration of the war, but were enrolled rather than enlisted, and not subject to army discipline. They enrolled initially as mobiles, who could be posted anywhere in the UK or in France, billeted in hostels, huts or tents in camps. From December 1917 an immobile branch was formed. Immobiles worked in the vicinity of their homes and generally lived at home. They were liable to a week's rather than a month's notice and not always required to wear uniform.

The WL military cookery section was gradually absorbed over the course of 1917. At the end of 1917 it was decided the home service MT section would remain WL members, but WL drivers serving in France had to join the WAAC.

The 'Waacs', as they were familiarly known (even after April 1918 when they became Queen Mary's Army Auxiliary Corps), worked at bases and on the Lines of Communication in France; and at home in command, garrison and regimental depots, offices and camps. Those serving abroad were classed as 'camp followers' and could be courtmartialled, but not for desertion or going AWOL and could not be punished by the CO. Women serving at home came under civil law, following the agreement they signed. They could be discharged without notice for misconduct or breach of their contract, and under the Defence of the Realm Act (DORA) liable to six months' imprisonment for being AWOL or not performing their duties. For other misdemeanours they could be fined, have privileges withdrawn, or given fatigues, usually scrubbing floors or peeling potatoes – catering or domestic workers were given lists to write.

By October 1917, nearly all cooking, domestic, clerical, postal, telegraph, telephone and signalling work in France was being done by women. Experienced GPO telephonists replaced men at base exchanges as telegraphists and telephonists and took over smaller exchanges in depots and camps.

Waacs worked for the BEF in the Calais, Rouen, Boulogne, Dieppe and Etaples areas, in instruction schools, in some Expeditionary Force Canteens, and after the Armistice at GHQ. In 1918, about 500 WAAC clerks and domestic workers worked in Tours and Bourges for the American Expeditionary Force. Waacs were gradually also employed as store-women, bakers, machinists and to do other technical work with the RFC and ASC. WAAC drivers were attached to a depot, on call to officers needing a driver.

The Waacs had the excitement of being the first women in uniform – apart from army nurses and red cross workers – to serve in France. Living in communal huts was an eye-opener for many, exposed to frank barrack-room chat. They shared a sense of camaraderie with the men; although their lives were rarely at risk, they understood conditions in France, unlike the men's families at home.

At home over the course of 1917, 7,000 WL cooks, waitresses and domestic workers enrolled in the WAAC, but the MT drivers and car washers, who coveted their special relationship with the ASC and RFC, remained in the WL.

A training camp for 1,000 women moved to Bostall Heath, near Woolwich, where the camp had its own hospital, dramatic society and band. Officials were trained at a cadet wing. Waacs worked in the London

District, Aldershot, Scotland, Ireland, Northern, Southern, Eastern and Western Commands. Home strength reached 40,000, but enrolment fell far short of numbers required.

Young women working away from home alongside men were a daring innovation. Rumours of immorality among Waacs in France were fanned by the press, adversely affecting recruiting. An official investigation found a few cases of pregnancy, but less than in the population as a whole. Some people felt the stories had been spread by gullible civilians taking servicemen's jokes and boasting too literally.

During the spring 1918 German offensive, WAAC women cooks, clerks and signallers carried on working within range of the guns and under

Rose Rattle in uniform, with WAAC armband and shoulder strap, six months after the name change to QMAAC. (By kind permission of Michael Ayden)

constant threat of air raids. At St Omer, the Directorate of Signals intervened against an order to withdraw 142 women telephonists and telegraphists, arguing that they were all indispensable and must remain at their posts.

In April 1918, Queen Mary assumed the title of Commander-in-Chief of the Corps, now renamed Queen Mary's Army Auxiliary Corps.

Women previously employed in munitions were needed as turners, machinists and fitters in engineering shops. Rose Rattle had been a lathe worker in a munitions factory. In October 1918, she applied to join QMAAC as a machinist with the ASC. By the time her application was processed, the war was over and she was posted to France as a filing clerk. The last few QMAAC members, working in France for the War Graves Commission, were demobilized in September 1921.

Life in the WAAC

Elizabeth 'Johnnie' Johnston learnt to drive, but her parents felt it was too dangerous an occupation, so she applied to the WAAC for a post as telephonist and was accepted for foreign service. The main receiving depot for new recruits was the Connaught Club (Edgware Road, London) but those posted to France reported to the Hotel Metropole, in Folkestone. After her long journey, tired and homesick, Johnnie was on the verge of tears; her roommates made her laugh instead, although she still cried into her pillow that night.

She was vaccinated and inoculated, drilled and issued her uniform, all of which she had to mark with her name. The shoes felt so heavy, she could hardly lift her feet.

Quarters in France were a draughty Nissen hut, winter spent huddled round its stove, summer baking under its corrugated iron roof. But firm friendships were forged and there was always something to do – dances, whist drives, camp concerts. The YWCA ran recreation huts (known as 'blue triangle huts') and shops. Workers were only allowed to socialize with NCOs and privates. Roll call was at 7pm, unless you had a late pass. Johnnie and some friends went to a concert which overran past the time on their pass – the men who were driving them home were still on stage!

Uniform

Officials wore a khaki single-breasted tunic jacket with side but not breast pockets (to avoid emphasizing the bust), cloth belt and bronze buttons, at first with the royal arms, later the corps badge. This was worn with a blouse and tie and a daringly short skirt, 12in (30cm) off the ground. Khaki caps with khaki crêpe de Chine veils at the back were later replaced at home by round brown felt hats, and in France by peaked caps.

Officials' rank badges, similar to those of the WL, were bronze roses and fleurs-de-lis (instead of crowns and stars):

Controller-in-chief	–	a double rose and single rose
Chief controllers	–	one fleur-de-lis and two roses (later a double rose)
Deputy controllers	–	fleur-de-lis (later, fleur-de-lis and rose)
Unit administrators	–	three roses
Deputy administrators	–	two roses
Assistant administrators	–	one rose

Unfortunately, the Army seldom realized what WAAC rank badges meant. Controllers had shoulder straps with blue cloth inset; recruiting controllers had green; administrators had orange. Those who had served in the WL were permitted to wear their WL badge on their collar. Forewomen wore a cloth laurel wreath encircling a rose on the upper sleeve (see illustration on p. 135); assistant forewomen a laurel wreath.

Drivers wore a khaki tunic like the upper part of the workers' coatfrock, with khaki skirt, brown shoes, gaiters and gloves.

All workers in France wore uniform, consisting of a khaki gaberdine coatfrock with a buttoned cloth belt and washable collar, brown shoes, khaki stockings and gaiters, a single-breasted army greatcoat, with two pockets, brown felt hat and brown shoes. Workers had brown collars, but

Waacs in front of their hut in France. Note the non-regulation uniform necklines, etc. (Peter White collection)

forewomen wore pale collars, which workers often imitated. Eventually in 1919 workers were allowed pale collars, although stocks of brown collars had to be used up first.

Necklines were customized, illicitly unbuttoning the top button to make a more attractive V-neck. A certain amount of 'wilful destruction of uniform' also went on, shortening coatfrocks and greatcoats by cutting several inches off the bottom rather than simply turning them up. Hats tended to fade and lose their shape. The greatcoat became sodden and very heavy in wet weather, so they were allowed to buy themselves waterproof mackintoshes. These were ordered to be worn without belts. They bulged suggestively at the front, and the order was rescinded.

At home, only those whose duties required 'regular attendance at camps or other military formations' were authorized to wear uniform. Immobiles tended to wear khaki overalls when working, a cap where necessary and an armband. Home service Waacs were supposed to wear a blue armband, with the letters 'WAAC' (later 'QMAAC') in white, to distinguish them from other women in khaki. (The Navy and Army Canteen Board uniform was very similar.) They were always losing these armbands.

Members' occupations were shown by coloured insets on their shoulder straps: brown for clerks; red for domestic workers; claret for drivers; purple for women in other employments, including storekeepers, gardeners (tending graves in France), painters (who repainted ambulances), aircraft assembly workers. QMAAC patrols (appointed from August 1918) wore coatfrocks with a black armband with red lettering and a white lanyard with a police whistle.

Recognition of Service

Assistant Administrator Geneste Penrose, an artist in charge of French women dyeing camouflage material in the Northern Special Works Park at Aire, was one of a small number of QMAAC awarded the Military Medal. For several months when the town was being shelled and bombed, the coolness she displayed encouraged the workers to carry on.

Casualties

During the 1918 spring offensive, Camp II at Abbeville received a direct hit, destroying most of the WAAC hut accommodation. Many had sheltered in the HQ cellar, but several were injured. A week later, on 30 May 1918, eight Waacs were killed outright in Camp I at Abbeville, and another died later. An additional six were wounded. Three Military Medals were awarded to women who helped in the rescue.

About 200 QMAAC are recorded as having died during or as a result of war service.

Researching Queen Mary's/Women's Army Auxiliary Corps

On 7 September 1940, the first night of the Blitz, nearly 1,000 German aircraft bombed London. Many high explosives and incendiaries fell in the area surrounding the docks. Firemen were soon fighting blazing warehouses, including in a tiny street called Arnside Street, just south of Walworth Road. This street held a large government storage repository.

Huge numbers of First World War army personnel records and administrative papers were consumed by fire or damaged by water. Only about one-third of men's army service records, the so-called 'burnt documents', were salvaged. Other records kept in the Arnside store included those of women who served in the QM/WAAC. These were even more catastrophically destroyed – of 57,000 women who passed through the service, only the records of 7,000 survived, with documents missing or too water-damaged to read.

If you don't find a record for the woman you are researching, it may not quite be the end of the road. A few brief sources on individual service may be found elsewhere.

The National Archives

The filmed QMAAC service records (series WO 398) are available to search and download at DocumentsOnline.

Surviving QMAAC records include officials as well as workers, but the extent of the destruction comes home when you search for a number of women. My search for the first women enrolled – the cooks, waitresses and clerks who formed the first units in France in the spring of 1917, whose names appear in service number order on the medal roll – produced none. The destruction seemed more complete among these lower service numbers. Other searches produced perhaps two or three, out of a dozen names. It's sad to search in vain for the records of interesting QMAAC members, like Johnnie Johnston and Geneste Penrose, or the journalist and novelist Winifred Holtby, who became a QMAAC forewoman.

If your search is fruitless, the next step is to search WRAF records, also on DocumentsOnline. Nearly 7,000 QMAAC members transferred to the WRAF when it was formed. (Surviving WRAF records do not include officers and are much briefer than QMAAC records, often comprising a simple certificate of service.)

Ivy Partington's WRAF service record includes her WAAC enrolment form as well as her 'statement of the services' form, which has her WAAC service number crossed out and WRAF service number substituted, giving her date of posting as category A (clerk) to Folkestone, her transfer to the hostel at Mortimer Street and official date of transfer to the WRAF, endorsed by a special stamp.

First page of Rose Rattle's QMAAC application form. (TNA WO 398/183)

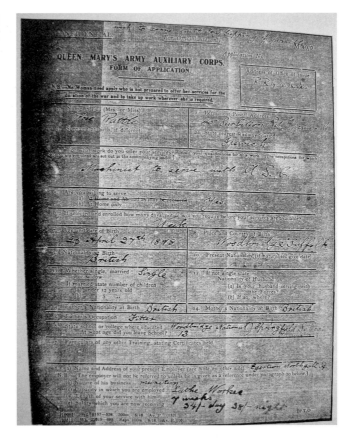

Frances May Pontos enrolled in the WAAC in July 1917 as a shorthand typist. Her WRAF 'statement of the services' form shows her appointment to the GHQ of the director general of transport in August 1917, transfer to the London hostel, then Hastings in December and to the WRAF on 1 April 1918.

If the woman you are researching served abroad before the Armistice, it is also worth searching the First World War campaign medal index (at DocumentsOnline) and consulting the corresponding medal roll, which may give a little more information.

Winifred Holtby was studying at Somerville College, Oxford when girls not intending to be doctors or teachers were invited to volunteer for service with the QMAAC. She was so excited, all the way down to the boat at Folkestone saying to herself 'I'm going to France! I'm going to France!'

Holtby's medal index card shows her as 'F/Woman' service no. 46506, entitled to Victory and British War medals, but 'Theatre of war first served in' and 'Date of entry therein' are not filled in. However, the corresponding medal roll (WO 329/2312, to which the reference QMAAC/101 B9 page 944 on the card refers) gives her dates of service in France, arriving only a few days before the Armistice, but staying until 8 August 1919.

A few home service Waacs came from abroad, qualifying for a British War Medal (not the Victory Medal). Deputy Administrator Sarah Pollard not only has a medal index card but a whole medal roll page to herself, which states that she came from New Zealand via Canada, shows the date she applied to the WO to do war work, the dates she joined the WL and transferred to the QMAAC, the date she resigned, 30 November 1918 and that by May 1921 she was Mrs Robson.

Similarly, some officials who did not actually serve in France appear on the medal roll as having acted in a 'conducting' role, accompanying QMAAC drafts across the Channel. Nearly forty women appear on the QMAAC medal roll for this reason. Most only made one conducting trip, perhaps taking the chance to see QMAAC on active service in France. The first Chief Controller, Mrs Alexandra Mary Chalmers Watson, appears in this way, apparently conducting on 5 June 1917. She had actually gone to check on how Helen Gwynne-Vaughan was running the WAAC in France.

The campaign medal index includes cards for recipients of a Silver War Badge. These refer to the relevant page on the QMAAC SWB roll (WO 329/3246), which gives service number, rank, full name, badge number, dates of enlistment and discharge, cause of sickness (usually simply 'medically unfit') and whether served at home or overseas.

WO 162/65 holds lists of home service QMAAC officials and members put forward for special recognition (mention in the *LG* or an OBE, MBE, etc.) for length of service and devotion to duty. This represented an attempt to reward the service of those who did not qualify for service medals. Each Command was invited to put forward lists of names. These lists, apart from name, rank, service number and category, generally show where they were serving – 'School of Musketry, Strenshall', or '22 Camp, Ripon', etc. Some include more detailed remarks, with length of service and previous service in the WL. Some names are mentioned several times, with differing information.

Unit Administrator Olive Bartels, awarded the OBE in December 1920, features on four different lists, the amount of information varying each time. If a home service Waac's name appears in the *LG*, it is worth searching WO 162/65 for possible further information. At the time of writing, there are plans to digitize series WO 162. This will be very helpful, as the lists include names not in the *LG*. Elizabeth Elsden, for example, is listed as a forewoman cook at Warwick, aged 63, who had served in the WL before enrolling in QMAAC.

WO 162/62 holds lists of several hundred WAAC drivers and car washers, compiled in early 1918, following the decision that home service WAAC drivers would remain in or transfer to the WL, while only WAAC-enrolled drivers could serve in France.

WO 162/16 contains nominal rolls of personnel surplus overseas in autumn 1919, including thirty-nine QMAAC fitters, mechanics, turners, electricians, checkers (mostly workers but some forewomen), giving service number, rank, surname and initials, trade and category. WO 162/29 includes nominal rolls and details of individual WAAC telephonists. WO 162/54 contains names, addresses and service numbers of former QMAAC members who applied to emigrate, mainly in late 1919 to Australia, under the ex-services free passage scheme.

Series MH 106 contains sample medical registers and military hospital patient medical sheets (loose, in rough alphabetical order). Aside from medical details, they may give age, rank, unit, length of service and other details. Among QMAAC officials' sheets in MH 106/2211 (which include some workers and forewomen), we discover that Unit Administrator Mrs L M Albutt, admitted from Bostall Health, 'has just closed down a unit at Dover and feels very tired indeed'.

MH 106/2208-11 contain QMAAC medical sheets. MH 106/1055, MH 106/1061 and 1065, all admissions registers, include a few pages of WAAC patients.

WO 95/84 and WO 95/85, the QMAAC BEF controller-in-chief and area controllers' war diaries, may be downloaded at DocumentsOnline. WO 95/84 contains appendices attached to the war diary of the Abbeville Area Controller, with drafts of about 270 personnel, listing service number, surname, initials, category, sometimes the name of the official in charge and other brief details including postings. B H Annand, head cook, A M Bean, cook, and K Bentley, head waitress, top a list of twenty-seven domestic staff posted for duty at the Fourth Army Infantry School of Instruction. (The campaign medal index reveals them as Barbara H Annand, Alice M Bean and Kate Bentley.)

In addition to detail on early WAAC units in France, the diary includes names of QMAAC officials. On 31 March 1917, Deputy Unit Administrator Miss F M Finlay arrived at Boulogne with fourteen women, en route for the Expeditionary Force Canteen Officers' Club, Abbeville. Two women, E P Shalders and K Woodward, were appointed as NCO equivalent (the rank of forewoman not yet created). This was fortuitous, as Miss Finlay developed measles and was admitted to 16 GH. The first pages of the QMAAC workers medal roll (WO 329/2310) identify this early group of women, including Ellen Pat Shalders and Kate Woodward, by the date of their arrival in France.

The *Army List* provides a source of information on rank and date of appointment of officials. They are listed in order of seniority and included in the index at the back of each volume, which gives column number against each name and initials – women are easily identifiable by the prefix Mrs or Miss.

Similarly, the *LG* between September 1917 and May 1920 lists appointments, with date and rank titles, of WAAC/QMAAC officials.

Imperial War Museum

WW&S holds QMAAC nominal rolls of honour. These include officials and members, with service number, rank and full name, some also giving category and date and place of birth, date and place and cause of death. They include the eight women killed by the Abbeville bombing raid and Elizabeth 'Johnnie' Johnston, who tragically fell to her death from the tower of St Ouen, a church in Rouen.

The database also has brief information on camps and units in France and officials working in these, with (not always favourable!) comments. A report of the controller-in-chief's inspection in October 1918 of all QMAAC units serving with the BEF in France covers over sixty units, camps, telephone exchanges, etc., including offices and quarters, rest camps, etc.

Winifred Holtby was posted as hostel forewoman to a signals unit that had moved to a chateau in woods at Huchenneville, following the bombing of Abbeville. In the preface to Holtby's *Letters to a Friend*, the QMAAC official in charge, Jean McWilliam, another ex-Somerville student, describes the QMAAC unit as hidden in the orchard of the chateau, comprising twenty-eight telegraphists, eight telephonists, two stenographers, two typists, one forewoman waitress, three cooks and five or six general domestics. McWilliam had the luxury of a small bedroom in the gardener's cottage of the chateau. The setting was beautiful, but a lonely posting for a woman official, so Holtby was sent to be hostel forewoman. She slept in the open loft of the cottage. The women lived initially in tents, in a sea of mud, crossed by duckboards. One false step, and the mud sucked their shoes off. Ultimately, German POWs built huts for them. The male telegraphists, telephonists and engineers had a camp on the other side of the orchard.

Jean McWilliam's QMAAC service record hasn't survived – but a glimpse is offered in WW&S in the report of the controller-in-chief's inspection (Army 3.13/114). Under the heading 'A.D.R.T. Huchenville' where Miss McWilliam was Deputy Administrator, the visit on 15 October mentions that the members of the unit were just about to move into their new huts, having been sleeping in two lofts in some discomfort. (Had the tents been hidden for the visit?) While commenting that Miss McWilliam, who had only just arrived, seemed interested in her women and determined to settle down and do her best, the report ends 'She has not been at all satisfactory up till the present.'

WW&S also includes minutes of conferences, inspection reports, copies of administrative correspondence, Helen Gwynne-Vaughan's personal diary, newspaper and magazine cuttings, and details of the setting up of the WAAC. There is some information on individual officials and a few copies of the *WAAC Magazine* (January and March 1919), giving officials' appointments and transfers.

The IWM also holds a run of the *QMAAC Old Comrades Association*

Gazette, a neglected source of much information on individual QMAAC members and units. It leans towards officials and those who emigrated abroad (under the assisted passage scheme for ex-servicemen and women), but not exclusively. It includes messages from ex-QMAAC wanting to re-contact those they served with or reminisce about old times, and contains many names and interesting details about their service, news of their post-war activities and birth, marriage and death announcements.

Rose Leeson, writing from New York, mentions half a dozen names of QMAAC who worked with the American Expeditionary Force at Bourges who are also in New York and writes, 'Please put in the Gazette that "Some Hut girls from Bourges are nearly all over this side and the rest had better hurry up!"'

Great warmth exudes from these messages, and nostalgia – for example, for the ordnance office where 12,000 women worked surrounded by 5 million men! Some Waacs took holiday trips back to their old hunting grounds, which were often already vastly changed. In Rouen, all huts had disappeared by 1922.

Maud A M White describes how she and three other Waacs went to Berlin with the British Military Mission before peace was actually signed. Miss H G Myers, in the office of the medical controller at York, took up a post with the BAOR base at Antwerp as a shorthand typist. In November 1922, Mabel Johnson writes that she is still working for the army at Catterick Camp, as a civil subordinate.

The IWM also holds official photographs and manuscript and taped recollections of QMAAC service, together with documents and other items of memorabilia.

National Army Museum

The WRAC collection includes papers of Helen Gwynne-Vaughan, memoirs and memorabilia of former WAAC members and copies of the *QMAAC Old Comrades Association Gazette*.

Printed Sources

Dame Helen Gwynne-Vaughan, *Service with the Army* (1941)
Roy Terry, *Women in Khaki, the Story of the British Women Soldier* (1988)
Shelford Bidwell, *The Women's Royal Army Corps* (1977)
E M Barton and M Cody, *Eve in Khaki: the story of the women's army at home and abroad* (1918)
Maud Onions, *A Woman at War: being experiences of an army signaller in France* (1929)
F Tennyson Jesse, *The Sword of Deborah, firsthand impressions of the British Women's Army in France* (1918).

Chapter 15

WOMEN'S ROYAL NAVAL SERVICE

Motto: 'Never at Sea'

T he WRNS was announced in November 1917 and became the first women's service to have its own officers. Numerically the smallest women's service, it prided itself on its smart uniform and the high standard of its members.

Origins

When war was declared in 1914, the Royal Navy had no room for women, other than the few nursing sisters in naval hospitals. Vera Laughton, daughter of a naval historian, recalled trekking to the Admiralty to offer her services 'as a humble scribe', only to be told 'We don't want any petticoats here.'

As the war progressed, however, the navy needed to be paid, kitted, victualled and maintained. Naval dockyards grew larger and other shore establishments sprang up around the coast. This expansion generated much paperwork. Most yards took on temporary male civilian clerks, but by spring 1915, when more were clearly needed but candidates thin on the ground, the Civil Establishments branch suggested employing women.

Responses ranged from wholehearted support (Chatham naval stores) to flat denial of the desirability or practicality of such a scheme (Dartmouth RN College), deeming dockyards unsavoury places for respectable women and the cost of extra lavatory and office facilities (it was still widely considered unseemly for the sexes to work in the same room) prohibitive. However, some naval offices, particularly in the East Coast Command, were already employing women as clerks and typists, thanks to the Auxiliary Patrol.

The Auxiliary Patrol comprised fishing trawlers and drifters brought into the navy for mine-laying and mine-sweeping. They still sometimes went out fishing. Part of the proceeds (called the Fish Profits Fund) could be spent 'for the benefit of the service'. This financed office, mess accommodation and lavatory facilities for women clerks.

Local fisher girls and fishwives (practised at repairing fishing nets) were taken on as casual labour at naval docks, making and repairing wire nets (lengths of wire netting with floats and mines attached) strung in the waters around ports, to snare enemy submarines.

Some yards also employed women sorting seamen's clothing and folding banknotes to pay wages and by 1917, although strong resistance remained in some places, women clerks were firmly ensconced in naval offices. Many were officers' wives and daughters.

In spring 1917, the Controller of the Navy proposed sharing the WAAC with the army. By the autumn, when a response from the War Office was still not forthcoming, the decision was taken to set up the navy's own women's service.

It was an open secret that Dame Katharine Furse was about to resign as commandant-in-chief of the women's VADs. She was very popular and it was on the cards that many of her staff would follow her – the perfect ready-made nucleus for a new women's service. Sure enough, the new service, with Dame Katharine as director, was announced at the end of November.

Early Days

By early January 1918, when recruiting for 10,000 women began, the new service was already being referred to as the 'Wrens'. Women were initially only recruited for home service, at large naval bases or isolated small stations, as chauffeurs, wireless telegraphists, writers (naval-speak for clerks), cooks, stewards (officers' mess waitresses), workers to repair and

WRNS and RN officers conferring at Crystal Palace WRNS training depot. (Peter White collection)

clean aircraft on naval air stations, wireless operators and women for cipher work (decoding and coding messages).

Vera Laughton had rushed to enrol and became the first appointed officer, sent to HMS *Victory VI*, a Royal Naval Volunteer Reserve training depot at Crystal Palace, where she was to train the first Wrens.

The first enrolled were mainly those already working as civilians, including motor drivers at the Admiralty. Many applicants were young shop girls and clerks, the minimum age of 18, as most women were already on war work.

The original appeal had emphasized immobiles living near a naval base, but recruits from inland rather than port areas had come forward. Attempts were made to enrol the largely reluctant female civilian employees, who did not fancy drill, did not relish becoming mere ratings rather than 'lady clerks', or signing on 'for the duration', not knowing how long that would be. What if their fathers were posted elsewhere? What if they were gossiped about, like the Waacs?

Civilians in their mid-teens who could not enrol until they reached 17½ were employed in many places. Civilian women tracers had been employed since February 1916. (Some continued as civilians until after the war and through the 1920s.) Magnetic mine testers at Immingham were seconded from munition factories and never joined the WRNS.

Organization

The WRNS consisted of officers, subordinate officers and women, known as ratings. (The naval term 'rating' refers to a seaman being 'rated' according to skills and work performed.) WRNS ratings could be promoted to leader, section leader or chief section leader (equivalent to RN leading seaman, petty officer and chief petty officer).

The hierarchy comprised director, deputy director, assistant director, deputy assistant director, principal, deputy principal and assistant principal. Initially, all officers were required to be mobile. Eventually, immobile officers were accepted, but directors, principals and quarters supervisors had to be mobile. Officers were either administrative or non-administrative. They wore the same rank badges, but non-administrative officers did not rank higher than principal.

Administrative officers were responsible for the welfare and discipline of the women in their division. Non-administrative officers were normally employed on decoding and complicated accounting work or confidential secretarial duties.

The WRNS was organized into administrative areas called divisions, including London, Scotland, Ireland, South West, Humber, Harwich, Chatham and Bristol Channel. Each division was administered by a divisional director or a deputy divisional director, and included two or more sub-divisions, depending on its size. Each sub-division came under the control of a principal, and comprised two or more companies under a deputy or assistant principal. Smaller units might have a chief section leader in charge.

Training

The two-week induction consisted of squad drill and lectures on the traditions and customs of the navy. The aim was to instil discipline, general efficiency, smartness and *esprit de corps*, as well as a working knowledge of the standing orders and service regulations. Officers were to be saluted and addressed as 'Ma'am' – Katharine Furse later likened it to the bleating of sheep.

Officers' training at Ashurst, a large house in Sydenham, lasted four weeks, with thirty to fifty in each intake. Training included drill and PE, lectures on naval tradition, customs, etiquette and organization, as well as WRNS organization, with role-playing exercises. Naval officers gave the lectures until WRNS instructors took over. After an examination and personal assessment, trainees were initially appointed as principals, assistant principals or quarters' supervisors.

Eventually, fifteen principals ran the WRNS College for Officers, the Crystal Palace training depot and various WRNS units at Great Yarmouth, Tynemouth, Inverness, Cranwell, etc. Non-administrative officers were trained in decoding at the Signal School, Portsmouth.

Chief Section Leaders (CSL) and Section Leaders (SL) were initially trained with their WAAC counterparts, the forewomen. They studied forms, discipline, hygiene, management of women, drill and games. Tact and courtesy were also stressed.

As the service established itself, technical training courses were set up for stores ratings, writers, cooks, despatch riders and drivers.

Categories of Work

As WRNS work expanded, occupations were divided into categories, lettered A to H. These letters occasionally appear on WRNS ratings' service records.

A. Clerical and Accountant Branch, including senior writers as decoding or ledger clerks, writers (shorthand typists), general clerks, stores clerks and victualling stores assistants.

B. Household Branch, including stewards (waitresses), cooks trained in large-scale catering, cleaners and laundresses.

C. Motor drivers and garage workers (car washers). Driver applicants were tested, and either passed, needed further coaching or failed. WRNS drivers drove all types of cars and vans, except heavy lorries. London drivers had to learn what taxi drivers call 'the Knowledge' to navigate around London. Motor drivers chauffeured officers or acted as couriers, for which motorcyclists were also used.

D. General Unskilled Branch, comprising orderlies, messengers, porters, unskilled storewomen and packers.

E. Postal workers, including telegraphists and switchboard telephonists as well as mail office sorters, noting transfers and working in dead letter offices.

F. Miscellaneous Branch, including bakers, gardeners, tailors and pigeon women, who helped look after carrier pigeons used by the RNAS (later RAF). Tailors repaired or altered uniforms to fit.

G. Technical Branch. These skilled workers included engineers, fitters and turners (making small replacement parts for destroyers, turning brass spindles, cutting screw threads, etc.), tracers, electricians, aircraft hands (mostly on fabric work – sailmaking and doping), photographers, technical storekeepers, depth-charge workers, mine-net workers, gas-mask workers and boiler cleaners.

Tracers traced exact copies from blueprints. Draughtswomen (more skilled) made scaled-up enlargements of instructional diagrams, working at the Signal School, Portsmouth, the Whale Gunnery School and in the Paravane Department of Portsmouth Dockyard.

Gas-mask workers assembled new gas masks and cleaned, tested, repaired and repacked gas masks.

Depth-charge workers tested, cleaned and re-set the time fuses of depth charges.

Electrical testers at the Signal School tested valves and circuits. Semi-skilled wiring hands assisted a skilled artificer. Gyro testers adjusted the gyro-steering apparatus for torpedoes.

Net-mine workers were employed wherever mine nets were used against submarines. Not all were absorbed into the WRNS. They sat on the quaysides, or in open sheds, crooning in harmony as they worked. They helped shift the heavy wire nets from the patrol boats, repaired them, set the floats and spliced the cables. They also cleaned and prepared mines.

Sailmakers at Lowestoft helped on the cumbersome work of making new sails for the trawler patrol or repairing gunshot holes. At Plymouth, they supplied the destroyer patrol with canvas gun covers, sail bags, etc., using palm (a stiff leather glove) and needle, as well as sewing machines.

Armourers cleaned, painted and tested mines and torpedoes.

Boiler cleaners worked on board trawlers, inside steam engine boilers, chipping limescale off with hammers. Boat cleaners were attached to coastal motor-boat bases.

H. The Signal Branch included wireless telegraphists at the Admiralty, Aberdeen and Stockton-on-Tees, receiving and logging signals received.

WRNS Abroad

The WRNS had been planned as a shore-based home service. In March 1918, plans for Wrens in several French ports were scuppered by an Admiralty order stipulating that they could not be drafted to stations abroad in numbers of less than five. Waacs were seconded instead.

In early July 1918, however, the WRNS Mediterranean division began at Gibraltar, a tiny but strategically vital British naval base, to which eventually four officers on cipher duties and two CSL shorthand typists were posted. Gibraltar's steep, stony roads made short work of WRNS-issue shoes.

Mediterranean divisional HQ was established on Malta, expanding to forty-seven officers and ratings, mostly in the offices of the British commander-in-chief. Women civilians worked in HMS *Egmont* (a depot ship) and the admiral superintendent's offices. Oppressively humid in spring and autumn, Malta was nevertheless a lively posting. After the June 1919 Malta riots, however, WRNS ratings were only allowed out in pairs, and escorted to and from work by armed blue-jackets.

The tiny WRNS presence in Genoa was the minimum allowable – one officer and four ratings. They shared messing and recreation with GS VADs and were eventually transferred to Malta, where the division closed in October 1919.

Plans to expand the WRNS to other countries were abandoned after the Armistice, when further substitution ceased. Having set out for Tunisia, two decoders had to be recalled from Marseilles, but Wrens had already arrived in Egypt and the SNOs at Port Said and Alexandria, overloaded with paperwork, fought to keep them.

In January 1919, Wrens were sent to Zeebrugge and Ostend. They included telephonists, senior writers and shorthand typists, with a cook and general domestic for their hostel, and later motor drivers and postal clerks. Hopes for the WRNS to serve on the Rhine (alongside QMAAC and the WRAF) sadly came to nothing.

Transfer to the WRAF

On the establishment of the WRAF in April 1918, transfer of 2,000 WRNS on RNAS stations was supposed to take immediate effect. In practice, however, it was delayed and Wrens continued serving at former RNAS air stations. The Air Ministry supplied their accommodation, rations, stores and pay. The WRNS provided their uniforms, kept their records and were responsible for their discipline.

The WRNS continued recruiting for air stations until October 1918, when arrangements were finally made for transferring WRNS at air stations gradually by divisions. Those wishing to remain Wrens were posted elsewhere. By late November, all WRNS had been transferred.

Post-war

Recruiting ended after the Armistice. Most divisions never reached their full complement, partly for lack of accommodation. The need for separate WRNS quarters was exploited by SNOs who didn't want women on their stations. They could simply delay providing it.

The Crystal Palace training depot became an army demobilization centre. Most immobiles there were discharged on the spot, with a week's pay. It was the terms of their agreement, but some felt very bitter.

In the early months of 1919 demand for WRNS remained high, however, as they increasingly shouldered the administrative work of naval demobilization. The Chatham assistant paymaster rang Edith Crowdy, Deputy Director WRNS, in February 1919, asking if she had any spare as they were 'in an awful hole for want of clerks'. He told Crowdy the Wrens had been extremely useful, certainly causing no friction with the men – most were engaged to naval ratings.

Nevertheless, the Admiralty, while praising their contribution, announced the demobilization of the WRNS. As the WRNS contingent in the Peace Parade on 19 July 1919 passed them, a group of admirals broke into spontaneous applause. But units closed, women were gradually discharged, until at the end of October 1919 the WRNS finally ceased to exist.

Some Wrens continued working for the navy as civilians. A WRNS Friendly Association was formed in 1920, becoming the Association of Wrens, which continues to this day.

Life in the Wrens

Many men seemed reluctant to accept women at first, and some had not relished being released for front-line service. An early WRNS motor driver remembered vehicles being sabotaged – terminals disconnected, tyres let down, water poured in petrol tanks. But WRNS cooks and stewards brought better standards of service as well as more appetising meals, and WRNS clerks proved more conscientious.

Lectures on naval history and customs helped WRNS recruits to feel part of the romance of service at sea. They learnt to talk about watches instead of shifts, the deck instead of the floor, the galley instead of the kitchen, the mess room instead of the dining room. Instead of making a mistake, they struck a rock. This, together with a generally more friendly reception from the men (for whom they represented novelty, excitement and a taste of home), fostered pride in belonging to the senior service.

Some worked in beautiful coastal areas, with wonderful views. Much of the work, however, was tedious, repetitive and demanding. Some divisions made more effort than others to organize off-duty activities, water polo matches, swimming contests and dances. There were also of course illicit trips in coastal motor boats with RN officers eager to impress.

Disciplinary penalties for being absent without leave or losing a railway warrant, for example, were restricted to stopping leave and deducting pay. To avoid the rumours that had sullied the reputation of the Waacs, Dame Katharine determined to recruit only the most respectable 'steady' girls, whom some people nicknamed 'Prigs and Prudes'. The rules could seem senselessly rigid. Mary Batterbury lived with her brother, a naval assistant paymaster. They walked a few yards together before going their separate ways to work and she was fined *10s* (50p), as ratings were not allowed to socialize with officers.

Uniform

Civilian women are not known to have worn uniform, although Dover net-mine workers were allowed a navy blue overall and black oilskin hat.

WRNS officers wore a dark-navy double-breasted suit, white shirt, black tie, tricorne hat and brown leather gloves. The distinctive black velour tricorne hat was edged in black braid with a naval badge embroidered in blue. This hat felt rather over-ostentatious for some – one officer tried sidling past the sentry hoping not to be noticed, only to hear the loud comment 'Look at the Lady Admiral!'

The Treasury forbade gold lace, so royal blue was chosen (with a diamond, instead of the curl). Up to August 1918, only ranks of deputy assistant director and above had a diamond. Lower ranks had only stripes: three for a principal, two for a deputy principal, one for an assistant principal and quarters' supervisor (who also had three keys). After that date, all principal ranks were apparently granted the diamond.

Ratings wore long, navy blue serge shirt-waisters (similar to WAAC coatfrocks), with a version of the naval ratings' collar (smaller and initially without the three white stripes), thick, black lisle stockings and heavy, black shoes or boots. Many ratings hated looking so frumpy when officers looked so smart. The rough serge chafed their skin, although some felt it was daringly short, the hem a full 8in from the ground. The small collars were not popular and they sometimes borrowed real sailor collars from their boyfriends. The tendency was to undo the top button and turn the edges in to form a more attractive V-neck. The black caps with soft pleated crown and round brim were similarly steamed and pulled into a more flattering shape.

WRNS clerical (note crossed quills on the sleeve) and household (note the shell on the sleeve) category ratings. (Peter White collection)

Some categories wore an 'indoor cap', consisting of a dark-blue cotton triangle worn like a headscarf, knotted at the back of the neck. Despatch riders on duty wore tunic and breeches; motor drivers wore coat, skirt and blue shirt. Some depth-charge workers, who had to climb ladders, were supplied with sou'westers and trouser-overalls.

Category badges were worn on the upper right sleeve. A (clerical) had crossed quills; B (household) had shells; C (drivers and garage workers), a wheel; D (general unskilled) had crossed keys; E (postal workers) had an envelope; F (miscellaneous) had a star; G (technical), crossed hammers; H (signal), arrows and lightning.

Officers' tropical kit for the Mediterranean was white, with white stockings and shoes and sola topi for the hottest part of the day, with panama hats at other times. Mediterranean ratings' kit comprised white cotton drill coatfrock with blue sailor collar, blue belt, a white cap cover, white shoes and stockings. CSLs and SLs wore a dark or white jacket with white skirt. Collars and ties had to be worn, despite the heat.

Recognition of Service

The only WRNS honours list of the war was published in the *LG* of 9 May 1919 – seventy-one WRNS officers and ratings (plus naval nurses and VADs attached to naval units) 'brought to notice for valuable services in connection with the war' and awarded military CBEs, OBEs, MEBs and Medals of the British Empire Order. Amy Helen Jenner, a driver, received an MBE for saving a fellow driver who had accidentally set light to her clothing.

Casualties

On 16 October 1918, the mail steamer *Leinster* on its way from Kingstown to Holyhead was torpedoed near Dublin Bay. Josephine Carr, a newly enrolled rating en route for England, became the first Wren to lose her life due to enemy action.

A total of twenty-five Wrens including one officer, Evelyn Mackintosh, are officially recorded as having died, most during the influenza epidemic. A coder at Malta who lost her sight became the only Wren to enter St Dunstan's rehabilitation centre for blind ex-servicemen.

Researching First World War WRNS

The National Archives

Official service records of over 7,400 First World War WRNS – officers (series ADM 318) and ratings (series ADM 336) – are available to search and download via DocumentsOnline.

WRNS officers' appointment registers (ADM 321/1-2) and an official roll of Wrens who qualified for British War Medals (ADM 171/133) are held on microfilm.

ADM 171/174, an original document, is a register of WRNS applications for Silver War Badges.

The *Navy List* includes WRNS officers by rank and order of seniority, with place of posting.

WRNS officers' files, from divisional directors to assistant principals, are arguably the most extensive individual women's service records to have been preserved. Their contents do vary but are likely to contain enrolment details, personal and service details, references, confidential reports, and miscellaneous official memoranda and correspondence. This list cannot possibly convey the vivid picture they paint.

ADM 318 does not include service records for senior WRNS officers (above the rank of divisional director). Some information (dates of service, rank and where served) may be gleaned from their entries in ADM 321/1-2, the WRNS officers' appointments registers. WRNS medical officers, for example, appear in ADM 321, as do Katharine Furse, her deputy and assistant directors (as well as WRNS officers below that rank). The remarks column, normally confined to pay and allowances, may include some further detail on posting.

Some WRNS officers were promoted from the ranks, and may therefore have both a ratings' register entry and an officers' service record.

The WRNS SWB register (ADM 171/174) includes Vera Laughton.

Frederica Frances Gilpin has two service records, having joined as a rating, then become an officer. She enrolled aged 27 in February 1918 as an immobile shorthand typist, serving at *Crescent*, a depot ship at Scapa Flow. Promoted to CSL in May, she leapfrogged to deputy principal in September (*LG*, 27 September 1918). This rapid promotion is possibly explained in the glowing six-monthly report given on her by Edith May.

Surviving WRNS ratings' service records consist of manually entered registers, two entries per page. These give full name, service number, date of enrolment, age, whether mobile or immobile, work category and brief service details including establishment at which served, with dates of service, reason for discharge and in some cases where discharged. The columns for 'Character' and 'Ability' are not always entered, but may typically state 'VG' or 'sat' (satisfactory).

Each entry will normally give a stamped service number (prefixed with G), full name (including sometimes married/single surname, although only one may appear in the online index), age at enrolment and date of enrolment, whether mobile or immobile (some changed their status in this respect during their service) and a number of columns with the headings: ship or establishment (where served), rating (work category and rank), period of service and if discharged, whither and for what cause. This was usually demobilization, but could also include promotion to officer, DD (Discharged Died) or Discharged Urgency and Consideration (compassionate reasons).

Sometimes this column records transfer to the WRAF. A search of WRAF online records in such a case may only offer a discharge certificate, but this may supply more information than the WRNS record. Lilian Gertrude Schroder, for example, enrolled aged 19 as a photographer in the WRNS in July 1918, and was sent to RAF Calshot. Her WRAF certificate of discharge on demobilization gives her enrolment in July (i.e., including WRNS service) at Southampton and her discharge on 26 October 1919 at Photo Park Farnborough. Her height, build, colour of eyes and hair are included, her work was satisfactory and her character good.

The 'Ship or Establishment' column may contain a name – for example, *Cormorant*, *President II* or RAF Great Yarmouth. *Shore Establishments of the Royal Navy* may be helpful in identifying where a shore establishment was, although it does not cover all the establishments where WRNS were stationed. More information on shore establishments may be found in the *WW&S* database at the IWM. If the rating is shown as 'immobile', next-of-

Net-mine worker Annie McCullock's entry in the WRNS ratings' register. (TNA ADM 336/24)

kin address will usually indicate where the establishment was. Ratings' records are frustratingly brief, but it may be possible to complement them from other sources.

The abbreviation SNLR appears on many WRNS ratings' service register entries, standing for 'Services No Longer Required'. Likewise, 'Lady Qr [Quarter] Ledger' in the remarks column refers to an accounting period. (The navy made payments according to the church/agricultural calendar.)

Some WRNS ratings records offer tantalizing hints – one is asterisked in the remarks column with the note 'see correspondence 946' with reason for discharge as 'urgency and consideration'. (TNA ADM 116/1917-1918 may possibly hold the answer.) The story comes to light, however, in *WW&S*, where this rating is described as angling to be discharged.

Shore Stations

Names like *Pactolus*, *President III* or *Victory VI* may be mentioned in WRNS officers' service records, or the 'Ship or Establishment' columns of entries in the ratings registers. These sound like, but are not, ships.

WRNS were employed at RN and RNAS shore stations which were often

given the names of ships and referred to as 'stone frigates'. Some had orig-
inated as moored unseaworthy hulks used as training bases or stores.
Before 1959, the Naval Discipline Act only applied to men on the books of
a ship of war, so those not serving aboard ship were nominally allocated
to a ship. Roman numerals were given to satellite stations. HMS *President*
existed during the First World War as an accounting base with six different
departments named *President I* to *President VI*.

These can be quite confusing: HMS *Pembroke II* was apparently a RNAS
air station at Eastchurch, *Pembroke VI* an accounting base at Chatham,
Pembroke VII a depot ship for auxiliary patrols at Grimsby.

Naval histories naturally focus on the drama of the conflict at sea, with
very little written about shore-based establishments. Aside from Warlow's
book, information on some shore establishments may be found on
Wikipedia, from local record offices or local history groups.

WW&S offers a glimpse into the workings of some shore-based naval
establishments, through WRNS inspection reports and administrative
correspondence (WRNS 8.2). *Pactolus* is described as a ship lying alongside
the quay at Ardrossan, with part of the main deck enclosed as an office for
WRNS decoders. (Internet sources add that *Pactolus* was converted before
the First World War to a submarine depot ship and served the 9th
Submarine Flotilla.) Codebooks could not be moved from the ship, so
decoding was done on board. The ledger clerks served ashore, however,
in a grand municipal library.

Researching WRNS Casualties

'DD' on a rating's service record stands for 'Discharged Dead', i.e., having
died while serving. Josephine Carr is the only Wren in the GRO index to
Naval War Deaths 1914–1921. Other deaths appear in the civil death registers, although names and some details have been included in 'Naval
Casualties 1914–1919', see www.findmypast.co.uk. This gives full name,
category, birth date and place, service number, date of death, cause (may
only state 'from disease'), location of grave and details of relatives notified.

ADM 171/174, WRNS Silver War Badge applications from 1919,
includes typed lists of *c.* 150 WRNS officers and ratings discharged on
medical grounds, arranged by letter of the alphabet. The listings are brief,
giving name, initials, rating and service number where appropriate.

Imperial War Museum

WW&S has extensive material on the WRNS in the First World War,
including photographs of senior WRNS officers, as well as reports on
WRNS work in the various divisions and copies of correspondence with
references to individuals and lists of personnel. A group of feisty Wrens
signed a letter offering their services for mine-sweeping duties after the

Armistice, after hearing of a shortage of male volunteers. (The offer was politely declined.)

Reports (WRNS 9/6B) compiled to support the argument for continuing the existence of the WRNS give much detail on the work of the different WRNS categories.

A Wren mentioned only by surname and service number may be identifiable by cross-checking the online service records. Many items are faded, some copies illegible and surnames are sometimes misspelled – it is worth searching under place name or division where known, as a name may be found misspelled within a report on their station. Reports in WRNS 8.2 include lists of WRNS officers by surname and initial.

WW&S contains a copy of *The Wrens: Being the Story of their Beginnings and Doings in Various Parts*, which describes each division's development and work.

The IWM holds a typescript entitled *W.R.N.S. a brief record of the Royal Naval Base, Lerwick 1914–1919*.

The IWM also holds the *Wren*, the magazine of the Association of Wrens, from its first issue in February 1921 onwards. It exudes warmth and fellow feeling, nostalgia for the camaraderie of the service, and contains columns of news of ex-Wrens with their former rank and place of service as well as how their lives developed between the wars. There are lists of subscribers, marriage and birth announcements, articles on visits to old service haunts and memories of service. Many names are included (sometimes misspelled).

Wrens who enjoyed their time in the service, those who emigrated and officers are more likely to figure in these pages, although ratings appear also. Names are not indexed, but often appear in bold type. These magazines convey a strong sense of how it felt to have served as a Wren, and how ex-Wrens struggled to make a living after the war, while others still worked as civilians for the navy.

'Mrs Jackson' contributed news from Portsmouth, where over a dozen ex-Wrens were still working at the barracks. In a later issue, Mrs Jackson identified herself as E K Jenkins, former deputy principal, Portsmouth (revealed in DocumentsOnline as Ethel Kellett Jenkins) and gives more news of ex-Wrens, with their surname and trade. McCulloch, a CSL tracer (identifiable as draughtswoman Emily Dorothy Winifred) was still working in her old job in 1923. By 1931 she was married with two small daughters, while others were still working on valve testing.

Isobel Crowdy contributed a detailed description of a journey to Canada in July 1921 escorting ex-servicewomen on free emigration passages. Kathleen Ussher wrote from Sydney, Australia in the spring of 1921 that fifty former servicewomen were arriving each month.

Other Research Sources

RNM holds original ratings' enrolment papers, bound in registers, as well as the WRNS Collection, including photographs, documents, uniform, paintings and drawings relating to the WRNS in the First World War and microfilmed copies of WRNS officers' records (TNA ADM 318).

The Liddle Collection holds contributions from First World War Wrens including Kathleen Ussher.

The National Maritime Museum holds material on First World War WRNS in the collection entitled 'HMS *Dauntless*' (a post-Second World War WRNS shore establishment). The collection relating to the WRNS mostly concerns the setting up and administration of the WRNS. This collection also holds a bound copy of *The WRNS at Lerwick with a brief history of Lerwick Naval Base 1914–1919*, together with correspondence (ref. DAU/124). A bound volume 'Divisional Records 1918–19' (DAU/88) covers the activities of the Portsmouth division.

The Women's Library holds a scrapbook of press cuttings (ref. 10/49) on the WRNS in the First World War.

Online Sources

WRNS officers' appointments appeared in the *LG* in May and July 1918 and March 1919.

Printed Sources

Vera Laughton Mathews, *Blue Tapestry* (1948)
John D Drummond, *Blue for a Girl, the story of the WRNS* (1960)
M H Fletcher, *The Wrens, a history of the Women's Royal Naval Service* (1989)
Dame Katharine Furse, *Hearts and Pomegranates: the story of forty-five years 1875–1920* (1940)
Ursula Mason, *The Wrens 1917–77: a history of the Women's Royal Naval Service* (1977)
Lieutenant Commander B Warlow, *Shore Establishments of the Royal Navy* (1992 and 2000).

A few naval histories convey the atmosphere of places where WRNS were stationed:
Tito Benady, *The Royal Navy at Gibraltar*, for example, contains a description of HMS *Cormorant*, the depot ship at which WRNS were based at Gibraltar
Roy Humphreys, *The Dover Patrol 1914–1918* gives a vivid account of the dramatic backdrop against which WRNS net-mine workers, clerks, cooks and stewards worked.

Chapter 16

WOMEN'S ROYAL AIR FORCE

The first WRAF lasted exactly two years, from April 1918 to April 1920, when it was disbanded in favour of a boy apprentice scheme. Set up concurrently with the Royal Air Force, its early history was troubled and chaotic.

Origins

For most of the First World War, the army and navy had their own flying sections, the Royal Flying Corps and the Royal Naval Air Service. On 1 April 1918, these were amalgamated to form the Royal Air Force. This independent new armed service reflected the growing significance of aerial warfare. As well as RFC and RNAS squadrons, a wide range of storage parks, repair depots, schools, balloon units, and experimental establishments came under Air Ministry control, some of which employed civilian women, Waacs and more recently Wrens, in domestic, clerical, driving and semi-skilled technical work. A large WAAC contingent worked in France at the RFC reinforcement park at Pont de l'Arche.

The WRAF was officially born on the same day as its brother service. Several thousand QMAAC and WRNS members were to be absorbed and new recruits enrolled. An attempt was made to call them 'Penguins', since they did not fly. This nickname did not catch on, and they became known simply as 'Wrafs'.

Early History

The WRAF did not enjoy the measured beginning of the WAAC or the felicitous start of the WRNS. There was no mutually supportive team to see it through the early stages, no real authority for its senior officer, nor even, while former army and navy factions in the new flying service jockeyed for power, a solid, well-oiled administrative machine to slot into.

The WRAF's first chief superintendent recognized she was simply a figurehead and hastily resigned. Her successor, WRAF Commandant Violet Douglas-Pennant, appointed May 1918, had a more impressive title, but without status or authority. Her civilian women assistants resented her for not automatically making them WRAF officers and all her requests and instructions had to pass via the male officer she had effectively replaced. She found it difficult even to order a car.

Waacs and Wrens on air stations were to be given the option either of transfer into the new service or re-posting elsewhere, with a month to make up their minds. This at least was the theory.

Nearly 7,000 Waacs were rubberstamped as transferred en masse on 1 April. But no arrangements had been made to pay them, nor had the RAF decided on their uniform. The WRNS decided to delay transferring the Wrens and continued recruiting personnel for air stations. Most Wrens on air stations were not transferred to the WRAF until November 1918.

About 3,000 Wrens finally transferred, together with nearly 500 WL motor drivers, unhappy at being demoted from lady drivers to mere airwomen, but warned they would be replaced by Wrafs if they did not join.

At the start, many WRAF units had no officers. Appeals were made in the press for applicants aged 25–45 as WRAF hostel administrators, quartermistresses and technical superintendents. Many started work with no initial training, giving a poor impression.

WRAF did not take part in the June 1918 Royal Silver Wedding anniversary procession of all the women's services, because their uniforms had not arrived. Another problem arose in July, when the woman MO who had previously attended the QMAAC hostel at Handsworth pointed out that she had no authority to treat them now they were members of the WRAF.

By August 1918, about 5,000 new recruits had been enrolled but the administrative difficulties, lack of training and team spirit led to discontent. They had been promised smart uniforms but were drilling and doing dirty jobs in their own clothes and overalls. Their accommodation was cramped, draughty, dirty and damp.

Douglas-Pennant persevered, having been persuaded not to resign, but was then suddenly dismissed. Helen Gwynne-Vaughan, QMAAC Chief Controller in France was summoned and effectively ordered to run the WRAF. Her appointment in September 1918 rapidly boosted morale. She combined warmth and efficiency. Senior officers were appointed to each are; officers were posted to all camps with airwomen, their work and position clearly defined; inspections were held.

Organization

The WRAF was organized into areas, each with a depot for reception, kitting and unit training, commanded by a WRAF officer. The first had opened at Handsworth College, Birmingham. Others opened in Glasgow, Hampstead and at Flowerdown Camp, Winchester.

WRAF officer ranks comprised: commandant (equivalent to RAF air commodore, with the same rank badge); deputy commandant (equivalent to group captain) in charge of inspections and attached to the staff of the

RAF inspector general, and four assistant commandants I (equivalent to wing commander) at the Air Ministry.

Each area HQ had an assistant commandant II (equivalent to squadron leader), aided by a deputy assistant commandant. A deputy assistant commandant served at each Group HQ. Units usually had a WRAF administrator (equivalent to a flight lieutenant), deputy administrators and assistant administrators.

WRAF officers were all mobiles and (bar a few instructors, and some on secret wireless experimental work) mostly administrative, responsible for the discipline and welfare of the women in their unit.

Subordinate officers comprised senior leader (equivalent to warrant officer), chief section leader (equivalent to flight sergeant) section leader (equivalent to corporal) and sub leader. Other ranks were called members or airwomen.

WRAF were ultimately employed in over fifty trades. On joining, they were assigned to one of four trade categories: clerical and storewomen, household workers, technical and non-technical.

Sick airwomen could be treated by male or female doctors but medicals, monthly inspections and hygiene lectures were usually given by female doctors. The Area Depot Sick Quarters at Hampstead was converted into a WRAF hospital. Wards for WRAF were also opened at Halton, Cranwell and Blandford.

The service was beginning to establish itself when the war ended. After the Armistice, in response to public clamour to release servicemen as soon as possible, demand increased for WRAF shorthand typists, clerks, cooks, mess orderlies (waitresses), orderlies and laundresses, motor drivers and motorcyclists.

From March 1919, a WRAF recruiting officer at each large RAF reception depot interviewed applicants and arranged medical boards. New recruits spent a few days being drilled, kitted out and learning service routine. Each area depot had a drafting officer who arranged postings, made out railway warrants and occasionally accompanied a group to see them safely across London.

Training

Officers were trained at Southwood Hostels, Eltham and Hackney College, Hampstead. WRAF motor drivers were trained at 1 Mechanical Transport (MT) Depot, School of Instruction, Hurst Park. The course was sufficient for those with some experience, but not long enough to produce competent drivers from novices.

In October 1918, Berridge House Hampstead (later renamed the WRAF School of Instruction) opened for training in trades, starting courses for cooks, mess orderlies and general domestics and later also trained CSLs and junior officers.

First World War Trades and Categories

Most WRAF were clerical and domestic workers, but they also worked in many technical trades, including mending balloon silk and oxyacetylene welding. In most units, women worked alongside men.

Service life involved endless form-filling and the Clerical branch comprised almost half the total strength. WRAF clerks worked in unit pay offices, clothing and equipment stores, and for senior officers. Dorothy Howe, a shorthand typist at 2 Fighting School, RAF Marske (where pilots trained for aerial combat), recalled having to stand to attention when she took dictation from the CO. Copy typists copied incoming correspondence (no photocopiers then).

Over a thousand women worked as stores clerks in 3 Stores Depot, Milton, Berkshire. Many RAF switchboards were run by WRAF, and there were some WRAF telegraphists. The Wireless Experimental Station, Biggin Hill employed several WRAF officers.

WRAF Records Office at Blandford kept record cards for every Wraf, recording all postings, arrivals, admissions to hospital, promotion, leave and fines, which were sent daily from every station employing WRAF. In October 1918, when Administrator Corbett took over from the RAF officer in charge, she found a 2ft stack of unprocessed transfers in a cupboard. Then demobilization started, and thousands of women's documents arrived, piling up in large huts. During the final 6 weeks, 15,000 women were demobilized. The records office finally caught up and closed down in March 1920.

The Household branch was the next largest group, among the poorest paid, working the longest shifts. They included cooks, kitchen assistants, mess orderlies and general domestics and worked in WRAF and RAF messes and cookhouses, usually under their own WRAF subordinate officer. Many mess orderlies had been waitresses in civilian life. Some larger units, like the Armament School, Uxbridge, with over 1,200 men and women, employed WRAF laundresses.

Technical branch WRAF worked on all parts of aircraft construction as carpenters, sailmakers, dopers and painters, riggers and as salvage workers. Aeroplanes had a canvas-covered, wooden frameworks and WRAF helped assemble these in carpenters' shops. RAF riggers (who tensioned rigging wires that ran between the wings) taught WRAF riggers who worked under supervision.

WRAF fabric workers in the sailmakers' shop cut, stitched, machined and eyeleted the canvas fabric In some stations, they would fit it to the framework and lace up the cords that held it together, before sending it to the dope shop. Most dope shops were entirely manned by WRAF under a CSL. Doping was skilled work. The dope, which tautened and strengthened the canvas, smelled of peardrops and gave off toxic fumes. Dopers were given fresh-air breaks and extra tea and toast. WRAF signwriters often painted the RAF red, white and blue roundels on aircraft, as well as their serial numbers and squadron code letters.

At 1 Scientific Aeronautical Research Depot (SARD) Farnborough, WRAF riggers and sailmakers made fittings for airships. All hands might be called out – including cooks – to help moor an airship in windy weather.

Salvage work was all done by WRAF. Newcomers were put first in the air station salvage section, dismantling crashed planes. The wreckage would be towed into a hangar and cleaned of grass, mud and other more disturbing stains. It would then be stripped and broken up, with the parts sorted into separate bins.

Women with an aptitude for this were moved on to aircraft repair shops (ARS) where planes were rebuilt and new aeroplanes assembled. The supervising RAF officer picked out the more skilful women to train for more specialized work. Some learnt oxyacetylene welding, others became vulcanizers, coppersmiths, tinsmiths, sheet metal workers, electricians, wireless operators and mechanics.

Many WRAF were employed in the larger RAF technical stores, keeping accounts and issuing parts, cleaning materials, etc. Some WRAF engine fitters were employed on servicing engines.

A small number of clerks volunteered for training for the RAF Meteorological Service.

Pigeons were carried on aircraft or airships and released with a message if the plane ditched or crashed. WRAF pigeon women in several coastal units looked after the birds and kept records on them.

21st Aeroplane Repair Section, 42 Training Depot, RAF Hounslow, showing an assortment of QMAAC coatfrocks and hats with WRAF badges, WRAF uniforms and mackintoshes. (Peter White collection)

WRAF (with VAD or other nursing experience) were assigned to nursing duties in hostels and camps. For larger depot hostels, an RAFNS nurse was provided.

WRAF aged over 23 trained as patrols. They carried a whistle and patrolled in public in pairs, preventing WRAF entering public houses, smoking in public or simply hanging about. They also checked passes at WRAF camps or quarters and supervised fatigues (punishments). They might be sent to pick up an airwoman who was AWOL or meet a draft arriving at the station and march them to camp.

Drivers worked long hours in all weathers, washing, cleaning and greasing their cars as well as driving them. They were difficult to discipline, their work often absenting them from drill and unit routines. They might chauffeur VIPs, fetch rations in a van or drive the breakdown tender, going out at dawn to stand by in case of an accident or forced landing. WRAF drivers also taxied relatives of casualties and drove lorries carrying personnel. One driver described having carried 'officers, food, ambulance cases, coffins, messages and pigswill'.

The Non-Technical branch included motorcyclists, telephonists, general labourers, tailors and shoemakers, storewomen working in clothing, furniture and other non-technical stores, packers and armament assistants, for example at Uxbridge, where women at the School of Armament cleaned, greased and tested guns and filled gunbelts. WRAF motorcyclists worked as couriers, or carried RAF officers in sidecars.

At 3 Stores Depot, Milton many WRAF worked in the timber yard. They also stacked and despatched metal, sorted, greased and packed nuts and bolts and received and despatched aeroplane parts for which WRAF carpenters made packing cases.

About seventy WRAF worked at the London Photo Centre processing aerial reconnaissance photographs and film used for training and publicity.

At 1 SARD, Farnborough, WRAF repaired and tested magnetos. They also worked on airship rigging, patching holes in the envelopes or gas-bags and repairing kite balloon silks.

WRAF tracers and colourists made copies of navigational maps and charts. WRAF electricians worked in the Power House at Blandford, which supplied electric power for the camp.

Service Abroad

Plans for WRAF to go to France in December 1918 were cancelled after the Armistice. However, men's demobilization created demand for 1,000 WRAF to substitute for airmen in France and Germany as clerks, cooks, mess orderlies, general domestics, storewomen and fabric workers.

Volunteers signed that they understood they would be subject overseas to the Air Force Act. Officers were asked to recommend the smartest, fittest and best disciplined. The first four drafts, mainly Household branch, were sent from March 1919 to northern France. They arrived at the new WRAF reinforcement park, at Maresquel, near Hesdin, 3 miles from HQ RAF in the Field at St André, where they worked in a hutted camp. Clerks were also drafted to deal with pay, mail-forwarding and a backlog of paperwork.

Maresquel was a busy transit camp with WRAF drafts passing through on their way to other stations in France and Germany. WRAF officers lived in Nissen huts, the airwomen in Adrian huts. These accommodated thirty-five, sleeping on iron bedsteads with army 'biscuits'. The huts had earth floors and windows cut out of tin, with sacking blinds rolled up during the day. They had cold-water washing facilities at one end and a coal-burning stove in the middle, tended by German POWs. Latrines were some distance away.

Camps in the surrounding countryside teemed with bored, restless men. Invitations to concerts, parties, sports days and dances poured in, were occasionally accepted and the women sent chaperoned by patrols.

WRAF were stationed in France at air, supply and repair depots, the Pay Office at Wimereux (later RAF rear HQ) and the port depots at Boulogne (guiding newly arrived drafts to boats and trains); Rouen (processing paperwork for equipment returned to the UK) and Dieppe. About forty WRAF clerks and domestic staff also worked at 91 Wing HQ until it moved to Cologne.

Service with the British Army on the Rhine

On 1 May 1919, the WRAF got their chance to join the Army of Occupation, as the first women ORs to serve in Germany (nursing sisters, VADs and QMAAC intelligence officials were already there). Only women of exemplary record and character were allowed to go. They were given two days to think it over.

They were sent to HQ RAF on the Rhine, Cologne, and to Merheim and Dormagen. In Marienburg, an attractive suburb just south of Cologne, a former beerhouse adjoining RAF HQ became the WRAF mess. Large huts for WRAF were erected in the garden. Eventually, they had to be surrounded by barbed wire. Hostility in Germany often focused on the WRAF, who were not allowed to go out singly.

They worked as clerks, telephonists, general domestics, storewomen, motor drivers, sick quarters' nurses and patrols. For British servicemen, the WRAF brought a cheering breath of home. They were never short of invitations, for dances, plays and trips down the Rhine. They produced their own small unit magazine, titled the *WRAF on the Rhine*. A WRAF jazz band played once a week at the WRAF teashop.

By September 1919, over 1,500 WRAF were serving overseas. This included over 600 in Germany, who had all left by the end of October. Those in France stayed longer. Last to leave, on 12 March 1920, were WRAF at the Port Depot, Boulogne, supervising the final WRAF returning to the UK.

Demobilization

Plans in early 1919 to retain a small permanent service came to nothing. It was decided that female civilians could be obtained if necessary. Permission was, however, given to keep 300 WRAF cooks and clerks until April 1920.

At the end of 1919, immobiles could stay on as mobiles for service in the UK or abroad, but otherwise were demobbed with a week's pay, a certificate and their uniform. Mobiles were given two weeks' pay and a railway warrant home, WRAF officers two months' pay as a demobilization grant. By November 1919, all WRAF quarters had closed down except at Blandford, where final demobilizations were processed. By 1 April 1920, only abandoned cats wandered around silent empty huts.

Nearly 32,000 women had served with the WRAF, including about 6,800 transferred from QMAAC, 2,800 from the WRNS and about 500 from the WL. Over 400 officers were trained; 67 had transferred from QMAAC and 46 from the WRNS.

A WRAF Old Comrades' Association was formed and produced a monthly newsletter. A few WRAF were re-employed as civilians. In late 1920, 20 former Wrafs and Waacs working at one military camp enjoyed whist drives, dances or films every night – and a ratio of 100 soldiers to every woman.

Life in the WRAF

The early administrative problems, lack of uniform and poor accommodation naturally affected morale.

Accommodation in camp usually comprised a fenced compound with huts, including officers' quarters, airwomen's dormitories, cookhouse, stores, mess and recreation huts, and a sick bay. Entry was guarded. Most nights, unless they had a special late pass, WRAF would have to be back in camp for evening roll call at 9pm. Evenings were spent chatting, darning stockings, polishing buttons, dancing to records, reading or writing home. Lights out was at 10pm, except for officers, often catching up on paperwork.

Immobiles and mobiles living outside camp would arrive in transports for daily roll call. Those with untidy hair or shoes not shiny enough might be put on a charge. Although some RAF COs were against it, part of the day was normally devoted to drill and PT, with the drill sergeant bawling at them, but not allowed to use swear words. Miscreants on a charge were marched to the administrator's office, where they might have privileges withdrawn, be given a fine, or fatigues like collecting coal, scrubbing floors or peeling potatoes. Most charges were for wearing a sweetheart brooch, the wrong colour stockings or altering your uniform neckline.

Uniform

Photographs of First World War WRAF often show a variety of uniforms, reflecting the supply difficulties as well as changes of colour and style during the WRAF's short life.

Many women serving on air stations continued to wear QMAAC or WRNS uniform after April 1918, partly because no WRAF uniforms were initially available and also because the Wrens had not formally transferred. Early new recruits often had to wear their own clothes. Topsy Austen thought she was joining the WRNS but was posted to an air station at Lee-on-Solent and given a khaki WAAC coatfrock and some time later wings to sew on the shoulders and the felt hat.

WRAF Assistant Administrator Mary Lyndon Cuming wearing RAF officer's badge on QMAAC-style felt hat. (Peter White collection)

173

WRAF officers' uniform finally appeared in August 1918. The khaki tunic without shoulder straps resembled that of RAF officers, but had small buttons below narrow braid on the cuffs, to indicate rank. It was worn with black lace-up shoes and a khaki soft-peaked cap (soon replaced by a stiff-peaked one) with the same cap badge as RAF officers. The illustration of an RAF medical unit (see p. 98) shows two women officers, one wearing WRAF uniform with stiff-peaked cap and the other in WRNS uniform.

In September 1918, pale-blue uniform of the same pattern was authorized. In October, the rank buttons (regarded by WRAF officers as rather ridiculous) were replaced by gold braid as for corresponding RAF ranks, and the 'bird and crown'. WRAF officers now crowed over their WRNS counterparts, who only wore blue braid. Alice Chauncey was so proud of her new tunic cuffs that, regardless of the cold, she couldn't bring herself to wear her greatcoat and cover them up!

Airwomen's uniform, up to October 1918, comprised QMAAC-pattern khaki coatfrocks. After October 1918, a khaki tunic and skirt was introduced, with black stockings and black lace-up shoes. Wings were sewn on the tunic and greatcoat sleeves, and a black-and-white cloth RAF badge was worn on the cap. Immobiles had the letter 'I' on their tunic sleeve.

CSLs at first wore a sleeve badge comprising a laurel wreath

Group photograph in WRAF uniforms. Note centre front row, two wearing new high-buttoned uniform and behind them, CSLs showing off their stripes.

WRAF Chief Section Leader wearing the centre-buttoned uniform with rank chevrons.

WRAF Section Leader in the new uniform, wearing two rank chevrons. CSLs had three chevrons, Sub Leaders, one.

surmounted by a crown, beneath the RAF badge; Section Leaders had the laurel leaves without the crown. In November 1918, these were replaced by RAF-pattern chevrons, of which the women were very proud. WRAF patrols wore a lanyard and a dark-blue armband with 'WRAF Patrol' in red. WRAF on nursing duties wore white aprons. Despatch riders had breeches and boots, with goggles and gauntlet gloves.

Towards the end of November, pale-blue uniform in a new design was issued for ranks below CSL. The tunic buttoned high to the left-hand side and the skirt was daringly short – 12in from the ground. Metal RAF cap badges were now worn.

The smart new uniform was much in demand. Official rationale for continuing to wear QMAAC or WRNS coatdresses was that they should be used with RAF badges until worn out. RAF badges were also worn by those in khaki overalls. Caps were apparently worn all day while on duty, even at meals, except when in overalls.

Those posted abroad were initially issued with khaki uniform (while the

RAF serving abroad were not wearing blue), identity disc, knife, fork and spoon, and a haversack. In spring 1919, WRAF in France were issued cardigans to help keep warm. In August 1919, Winston Churchill reviewed the women's services abroad. Strenuous efforts on the part of WRAF officers ensured that the airwomen were wearing the new high-buttoned uniform.

The pale-blue material proved impractical (and made RAF officers resemble cinema commissionaires). A more serviceable darker blue-grey was introduced in the autumn of 1919, although it is unclear whether the WRAF were issued uniforms in this colour. Accurately identifying different (and faded) shades of khaki or blue in black-and-white photographs, affected by light conditions or type of film used, can be difficult.

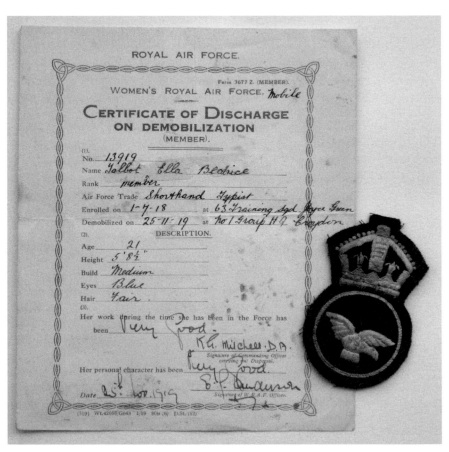

Ella Talbot's certificate of discharge and WRAF cap badge.

WRAF Casualties

About 300 women were employed in Ireland in camps fenced with barbed wire, due to the political situation. A lorryload of WRAF on their way through Dublin was attacked by Sinn Feiners who tried to drag out the RAF driver. The WRAF successfully fought them off. However, eleven WRAF were assaulted and injured in Dublin Peace Night celebrations.

Officially, 108 WRAF are recorded as having died during or as a result of service in the First World War, probably mostly victims of the influenza epidemic.

Recognition of Service

Mrs Marjorie Beryl Brisley was awarded the military division Medal of the British Empire Order (BEM) for rescuing two airmen from a crashed plane at Upton, Chester. WRAF also received 16 MBEs and 127 commendations.

Researching First World War WRAF

The National Archives

WRAF airwomen's service records (series AIR 80) are available at DocumentsOnline. They are brief, often consisting only of the certificate of discharge on demobilization, of which each airwoman was given a copy. This gives service number, name, rank, air-force trade, date and place of enrolment and date and place of demobilization. It should also show age, height, build, eye and hair colour, brief description of quality of work and personal character, signed by a WRAF officer, but sometimes not all parts are filled in. Alice Chauncey admitted dashing off hundreds in a short space of time.

Sometimes the service record comprises an enrolment form and/or a 'statement of the services'. The former gives name, age, home address, marital status, whether mobile or immobile, category and sub-category of work for which selected, and date of enrolment. The form was signed by a woman MO following a medical examination, with a classification, for example, 'Fit for General Service'. Abbreviations were sometimes used – 'Mid Area' stands for Midland Area. Other abbreviations (which may differ from those used in later years) include TS – Training Squadron; AAP – Aircraft Acceptance Park; AD – Air Depot; ARS – Aircraft Repair Shop; SD – Stores Depot; ARD – Aircraft Repair Depot; FS – Fighting School; S of A – School of Aeronautics.

Much is likely to have been omitted – Helen Chappell's service record gives no hint that she served in Germany. The only clue that Florence Maple served in France is her late demobilization from Uxbridge, on 5 December 1919.

The statement of services may disappointingly only carry name and next of kin, with no service details. However, Ivy Partington's WRAF service record includes her WAAC enrolment form and her statement of services. This has her WAAC service number crossed out and WRAF service number substituted, with her posting as category A (clerk) to the Hostel, Folkestone, transfer to the Hostel at Mortimer Street, and official date of transfer to the WRAF, 1 April 1918, endorsed by a special stamp.

Frances May Pontos' WRAF service record includes details of service with the WAAC, and the slip of paper she signed on 26 April 1918, indicating her willingness to transfer to the WRAF. Ivy Lily 'Topsy' Austen's WRNS and WRAF service records reflect her confusion about which service she actually joined, as well as the arrangement whereby transfer of WRNS to WRAF was delayed. Her WRNS service record shows her date of enrolment as 1 May 1918 and date of discharge to WRAF 30 October 1918. Her WRAF certificate of discharge also gives date of enrolment in the WRAF as 1 May 1918, as well as that she was 5ft tall with blue eyes and brown hair.

Some service records include or consist only of army form B103 headed 'Casualty Form – Active Service' used to record postings, promotions, transfers and sickness or injuries during active service. Grace Halcrow's B103 shows that she enrolled for duty as a waitress with 8 School of Aeronautics, RAF Cheltenham and was posted to 9 (Observers) School of Aeronautics.

Trade is not fully specified in what remains of some WRAF service records. Violet Fanny Burkett is described merely as a worker at AS (Air Station) Pulham (Pulham St Mary). She had, however, transferred from the WRNS, and her WRNS service record shows her as a pigeon woman there.

A slightly different certificate of discharge form (RAF Form 3677) was used in instances of unsatisfactory service. One C2D WRAF probation driver enrolled at Farnborough in June 1918 was discharged in November, after having 'received instruction only (not satisfactory)'.

Sadly, WRAF officers' service records do not appear to have survived. However, an extensive list of their appointments with date and rank was published in the *LG* in February 1919, with further shorter lists in May, July and September to November 1919, and a few notices relinquishing appointments in December and February 1920. (A less extensive list appeared in the monthly *Air Force List* between April 1919 and March 1920. TNA and the Royal Air Force Museum (RFM) hold a few of these issues.)

Appointments gazetted in February and May 1919 show previous service with either QMAAC or WRNS, which (in the case of former WRNS officers) should open up opportunities for further information on First World War service. Over 100 former WRNS officers and QMAAC officials appear in lists of WRAF officers gazetted in February, May and July 1919. (While the QMAAC records of many former QMAAC WRAF officers have not survived, a few may still be found, for example, that of M S Frood.) Mrs

B D Beckett, on the other hand, appointed to the WRAF from the WRNS, may not have a WRAF service record, but as Bessie Drummond Beckett her WRNS service record runs to more than 200 pages.

AIR 1/1964/204/263/1 Field Returns from RAF Port Depots at Rouen, Calais and Dieppe, includes lists of 1919 postings and re-engagements of WRAF officers and airwomen, with rank and trade. One list has over forty names of clerks, cooks, domestics, etc., re-engaged until April 1920.

A few campaign medal index cards exist for WRAF, who mistakenly applied or were entitled through earlier service.

Imperial War Museum

WW&S has a section on the WRAF, including detail on uniform and regulations.

The IWM also holds Alice Chauncey's detailed and authoritative account, mentioning individual WRAF officers; papers of Letitia Fairfield, including a notebook recording several WRAF deaths and a list of *c.* 130 pregnant unmarried WRAF, 1918–1919; also WRAF Old Comrades Association monthly newsletters (May 1920 onwards).

The WRAF OCA had 1,300 members, mostly CSL and airwomen, with a few officers. Much slimmer than its QMAAC sister publication, the newsletter includes names with former rank and sometimes former station, with births, marriages, etc., and some branch member lists. An early Birmingham branch list gives name, former rank, address and current occupation.

One contributor bemoaned how old friends from civilian life – 'pre-Wraffealites', she called them – had never seen her with her hair stuffed into her cap; had never blacked her shoes for her; let alone washed her collars, or eaten pudding on the back of her stew plate. Such things, she claimed, including scrubbing out a filthy ablutions hut together, cement real friendship.

Other Sources

RFM holds photographs of WRAF at work, diaries, letters, typed accounts, badges, medals, certificates and other memorabilia relating to First World War WRAF service, including some issues of the WRAF OCA magazine. First World War casualty cards for RAF personnel are held, but are not known to include WRAF.

The Times has items on the setting up of the WRAF and a list on 23 January 1919 including WRAF personnel, mentioned for valuable services in connection with the war.

A WRAF roll of honour is included in the panels at York Minster. Some casualties are included on the Commonwealth War Graves Commission online Debt of Honour database and may give where they were employed, for example: Mabel Dye, 1 Stores Depot, Kidbrook; Grace Zenobia Collins, 39 Squadron.

Printed Sources

Alice Chauncey, *Women of the Royal Air Force* (1922)

Beryl Escott, *Women in Air Force Blue: the story of women in the Royal Air Force from 1918 to the present day* (1989)

Molly Izzard, *A Heroine in her Time: a life of Dame Helen Gwynne-Vaughan 1879–1967* (1969)

Gertrude A George, *Eight Months with the Women's Royal Air Force* (1920)

Andrew Cormack and Peter Cormack, *British Air Forces 1914–1918 (2) Uniforms of the RAF* (2001) for more detail on WRAF uniforms.

Chapter 17

WOMEN'S FORAGE CORPS

Although the army became increasingly motorized during the First World War, thousands of horses were requisitioned for the Western Front, creating enormous demand for feed.

A War Office Forage Committee was formed in November 1915, to organize the supply of forage to the British Army at home and abroad. Forage Department ASC comprised six areas in England, one in Scotland and one in Ireland. Having established they could manage hay baling, civilian women were increasingly employed to release ASC servicemen.

Organization

In March 1917, a special women's branch of the Forage Department called the Women's Forage Corps was formally created, under the Quartermaster General, with a general's daughter, Mrs Athole Stewart, as superintendent of women, responsible for supervision and welfare. Women area administrators and inspectors were appointed. Areas were sub-divided into districts, with district purchasing officers and assistant and deputy assistant superintendents, all classed as first grade officials.

The second grade consisted of forwarding supervisors and their assistants, with section clerks dealing with clerical work for each section. Motor-transport drivers took section transport supervisors on inspection rounds, and quartermistresses distributed rations.

The third grade, manual workers, called industrial members, worked in gangs of six headed by a gang supervisor, promoted from the ranks of ordinary members. Gangs moved from farm to farm, with a steam baler. Baling hands forked hay into the baling machine, tying the bales with wire and checking the weight of each bale, using a large hook and counterbalancing weight mounted on wooden struts. Horse-transport drivers took the hay-bale loads in horse-drawn wagons to the nearest railway station, where forwarding supervisors oversaw loading them into railway trucks to the correct tonnage and sheeting the loads.

Forage work also included chaffing, wire-stretching, mending tarpaulin sheeting (pre-war, this cumbersome task was strictly men's work) and making and mending sacks. Doubts that women would be hardy enough for the strenuous, dusty baling work proved unfounded,

Women's Forage Corps members with ASC NCOs and men. (Peter White collection)

although they were often looked at askance in rural districts when they first appeared.

The transport girls included women from the leisured classes, accustomed to horses, while many industrial members were former domestic servants. No strangers to hard work, they appreciated the open-air life, although after the bustle of towns it could feel very lonely, especially on dark winter evenings.

Large numbers were recruited to work in Norfolk. Some discipline problems apparently occurred, and moving from place to place created accommodation difficulties. Gangs were normally billeted in local cottages, under a deputy assistant supervisor, who controlled two sections of twenty-four girls. WFC members drew army rations and sometimes a gang of six girls was provided with a cook and a caravan as a communal mess.

From October 1917, all women forage workers had to sign on for a year and enrol as members of the Women's Land Army (WLA), interchangeable with other WLA sections. In October 1918, this arrangement ended. The Women's Forage Corps was instead formally constituted as a branch of the ASC, to substitute for soldiers on hay baling and other related work in the UK.

Supervisory officials (previously on yearly agreements) were now required to enrol for the duration of the war. Industrial section workers were required to serve either for one year or the duration of the war, whichever was longer. Gang members received a bonus depending on output and were paid in full during periods of enforced idleness, transfer to another station or temporary shortage of work.

The WFC was very proud of its association with the ASC. By the end of the war it had over 5,000 members. At the end of December 1919, when the WFC disbanded, the QMG praised how, untrumpeted behind the scenes, they had ensured a constant supply of forage in the UK and France.

Casualties

Nineteen WFC members died either during or as a result of war service, mostly from pneumonia. Although entitled to four weeks' sick pay, WFC members had to pay for their own medical treatment.

Uniform

From 1917, WFC members wore clogs, high laced black boots or khaki gaiters, dark-green breeches and jerseys, khaki overalls, overcoats and haversacks, and dark-green brimmed hats. They wore the letters FC in brass on their shoulders straps and hat or cap. They were very proud of their association with the ASC. Other uniform seems to have consisted of a belted khaki coatdress with a necktie and peaked cap.

Baling hands, motor-tractor drivers and horse-transport drivers were issued with greatcoats in place of mackintoshes. Horse transport drivers could wear puttees instead of canvas or leather leggings.

Officials wore a khaki belted tunic and skirt, with rank badges on the shoulder, dark-green hat and bronze badge on their hat and coat collar. These badges had FC enclosed in the ASC eight-pointed star.

Depending on rank, supervisory officials wore gilt or bronze badges, and gold and green or worsted rank badges on each shoulder. Forwarding supervisors and section clerks wore bronze badges and a worsted star on each shoulder; assistant forwarding supervisors a bronze badge on each tunic lapel and one on their hat.

All other grades, from section transport supervisors to baling hands, wore brass FC titles on each shoulder and one on their hat. Section transport supervisors, motor-tractor drivers and horse-transport drivers wore a worsted rank badge (two in the case of ST supervisors) on their right breast. Gang supervisors wore two green chevrons inverted, assistant gang supervisors wore one.

Researching WFC Members

The National Archives

WFC service records are not known to exist, although the *LG* effectively provides a nominal roll of WFC supervisory staff, whose appointments appear (immediately beneath RASC appointments) between March 1917 and December 1918, with relinquished appointments in 1919 and 1920.

A few women applied for service medals and appear among the campaign medal index cards. Mrs L Melhuish, formerly Giles, has two cards, one citing her as a quartermistress in the WFC.

Series T/1 holds two files relating to FC member injury claims and MUN 4/6483 concerns organization and operations of the WO Forage Department and Forage Committee.

Other Sources

The IWM has photographs of WFC at work, and two first-person accounts of WFC service. *WW&S* contains some information on WFC, including brief details of ten who died.

FPD lists names of nineteen WFC members who died.

Chapter 18

WOMEN'S LAND ARMY

E nemy attacks on British merchant shipping in the First World War created food shortages, underlining the UK's dependence on cheap imported foodstuffs. This highlighted the need for increased home production, but thousands of male farm labourers had joined up, and mucky farm labouring was not at first considered suitable work for women.

Origins

In 1915, the Women's Farm and Garden Union (WFGU), an organization which promoted outdoor careers for women, instigated training schemes for women land workers and the Women's Legion started an agricultural section. In January 1916, using several farms as training centres, the WFGU launched the Women's National Land Service Corps (WNLSC), as a mobile force of educated women to help recruit, supervise and organize women land workers, overturn farming community prejudice against women and encourage village women to do their bit.

The Board of Agriculture appointed Meriel Talbot to liaise with recently formed county War Agricultural Committees (WACs) and registers were compiled of village women willing to work on local farms. During 1916, fifty counties set up Women's War Agricultural Committees (WWAC), to focus on recruiting and training of female land workers. The WNLSC, the Women's Legion, the Women's Defence Relief Corps and the National Land Council all dealt with applications from women to work on the land. A few women's co-operative smallholdings were formed.

The WFGU set up 13 training centres and provided over 9,000 women land workers, including temporary seasonal workers, mainly college students and teachers for hop picking, fruit gathering and as flax pullers. Flax, which had to be carefully pulled up by hand, was an essential wartime raw material – used to make the canvas required in aircraft construction.

Hundreds of women had taken short training courses and about 50,000 village women registered for part-time work, but 40,000 more were needed. In December 1916, the WNLSC offered the Board of Agriculture two alternatives: expanding the WNLSC on a much bigger scale, or starting a government-run land army.

In January 1917, the Board of Agriculture accepted the plan for a centralized land army and in March 1917 the Women's Land Army was officially born.

Organization

Fit, active and intelligent women over 18 were invited to enrol in the WLA for the duration of the war, to work wherever they were sent. They were offered a month's free training on special farms, travelling expenses, a free outfit to work in, an allowance during periods of unemployment (farmers paid them direct and much work was seasonal) and eventually a guaranteed minimum wage.

The WNLSC continued supplying trained milkers, stockwomen, carters and ploughwomen. Nearly 100 of its members became WLA gang leaders, group leaders and training centre superintendents.

Group leaders trained and organized local village labour and helped train WLA recruits. Training centres were organized throughout the country, accommodating trainees in hostels or private houses, and training them at local farms, supervised by the farm bailiff and women selected by the WWACs. One farm had wooden cows with rubber udders, then nanny goats to practise on, before women were allowed near the valuable dairy herd. Training was extended to six months, with efficiency tests to assess students' abilities, and an increase in wages if they passed. Each WLA recruit was given a handbook.

Candidates had to pass a medical. By July 1917, although nearly 50,000 women had applied, most were not fit enough and only about 5,000 were at work or in training. Many more were needed, mostly for milking and stock-keeping. WLA members could be drafted to timber-cutting work or sent to work with the Forage Corps or as forage guards.

A Women's Branch was created in the Board of Agriculture's new Food Production Department (FPD), with Meriel Talbot as director, in charge of a staff of women inspectors to foster employment and training of women in each county. In August 1917, this Women's Branch took over administration of the WLA from the Department of National Service and ran it through the county WWACs.

Large numbers of women were, however, employed direct by farmers, by-passing the WLA. By September 1917, this part-time workforce was estimated at 200,000 (mostly on seasonal, part-time harvesting work), compared with 7,000 in the WLA.

More women were still urgently needed. The FPD Women's Branch began promoting Women's Institutes (WI), with a view to encouraging village women to take up agricultural and horticultural work. WI branches increased from 137 to nearly 700.

WLA members put on displays and competitions at agricultural shows, in general labouring, dairy work and tractor ploughing. Recruiting rallies

Land workers, mostly without armbands. The flax clutched by the central figure and the gymslips worn by others suggest they include seasonal workers. (Peter White collection)

were held, stressing that the thousands of acres of extra crops must not be wasted for lack of harvesting labour. A rally was held at Woolwich, to attract girls being laid off at the Royal Arsenal. It was rumoured that soldiers' separation allowances paid to wives were kept low, so they would take up work on the land.

In January 1918, the WLA was re-organized into three sections: Agriculture and Afforestation (tree-planting and wood management) under the Board of Agriculture; Timber cutting, under the Board of Trade Timber Supply Department; Forage Work under the Forage Committee of the War Office. Women were interchangeable between sections and now allowed to enrol for six months (one year for forage work), rather than the duration. In October 1918 this arrangement ended and the WLA included only the first two sections, although WLA members on forage work could choose whether to stay in the WLA, or join the WFC.

By now, local women on the land had increased to nearly 300,000, mostly village women who had previously considered farm work degrading. The WLA had 15,500 members, with a forewoman for every 100 women. The majority were field workers. Over a third worked on milking. Other jobs included ploughwomen, carters, thatchers, shepherds, tractor drivers, market gardeners, threshers and molecatchers. Women only constituted one-third of the workforce for the 1918 harvest, however, which was mostly brought in by German POWs and male volunteers.

In 1919, demand for women on the land increased. More were recruited and trained for the coming season, but in November 1919, the WLA disbanded. The National Association of Landswomen was formed, to encourage women to work in agriculture and horticulture. Many farmers still preferred men to women, but a few women did stay on as permanent workers.

The president of the Board of Agriculture later recalled the growing numbers of women on the land and their increasing expertise, which gradually changed farmers' attitudes. At first any mention of using women had met with silence or disapproving grunts. This gradually changed to discussion for and against, then a smattering of applause and finally genuine expression of gratitude, calling for three cheers for the women.

But there was to be no war gratuity, and no service medals for WLA members.

Agricultural Section

The letters 'L.A.A.S.' on WLA cloth badges stood for 'Land Army Agricultural Section'.

LAAS did all the general farming work, including milking, sowing, hoeing, harvesting, muckspreading, stock and poultry keeping, or market gardening.

Thatching and threshing were added in the summer of 1918, usually with four land girls and a forewoman to each threshing machine, based in one village and working round the neighbourhood.

Land Army
Agricultural
Section badge.
(Peter White
collection)

Several farms were run entirely by women. Women proved useful in dairy work, rearing young animals, mucking out cattle sheds, looking after pigs and poultry, spreading manure, setting and digging up potatoes, hoeing and helping with the harvest work. After special training they also handled horses and machinery, including ploughing with teams of horses. A government motor-tractor training school instructed experienced drivers in ploughing and safe practice – early motor tractors were particularly dangerous.

Forewomen planters for the Women's Forestry Service were trained in the woodmen's school at Lydney, in the Forest of Dean.

Timber-cutting Section

Several hundred women were employed, working in gangs, felling trees and sawing them into lengths for pit props, trench poles, barbed wire poles, railways sleepers, etc.

It's unclear whether they were ever officially called the Women's Forestry Corps, or at what stage they became the Women's Forestry Service.

In some places, the Timber Supply Department employed girls directly, rather than through the WLA, causing concern.

At Wendover, an open-air training camp for measurers, women with a head for figures were trained to girth trees after felling, calculate their cubic contents, mark where they were to be sawn and superintend the stacking of logs and loading by crane onto tractors to take to the station. The only school of its kind, its students included many former schoolteachers.

Life in the WLA

The Land Army was promoted as healthy outdoor exercise. In reality, the work was low paid, often backbreaking and usually monotonous. Long hours – up to twelve-hour days – were spent hoeing, lifting potatoes, muckspreading or mucking out cow byres.

Girls from middle-class homes could find themselves billeted in very primitive conditions. One doctor's daughter breakfasted with a farmer who spat bacon rind to his nine cats sat in a circle round the table. Some farmers expected land girls to scrub floors and babysit.

The LAAS handbook each member received stressed that their work growing food for the whole country was as important as the soldiers and sailors and that 'noisy or ugly behaviour' brought discredit on them all. It was important to keep fit, and aches and pains were best ignored. They were reminded of their promise to have eight hours' rest and avoid any communication with German POWs (30,000 were working on the land).

Talbot worried that a scandal might erupt through lack of supervision. In July 1918, eighty welfare officers were appointed, to visit land workers to boost morale, check on their welfare and arrange sewing classes and evening lectures to keep them out of mischief in their spare time.

Leicestershire WAC proposed fining land girls who went AWOL. Hertfordshire produced a list of rules which included being back in their billets by 9.30pm and banned from public houses, or smoking in uniform.

Uniform

Photographs of First World War women land workers show a wide variety of smocks, overalls, headgear and footwear, as well as necklaces, reflecting the year the photograph was taken and the presence of local workers and temporary seasonal volunteers, as well as WLA members.

Pre-WLA, recommended clothing (which land workers had to buy themselves) consisted of a coat and short skirt or tunic with thick stockings, gaiters and stout boots. In the early days, villagers were shocked by women wearing breeches, so it was advised to wear a smock or overall over them. (Eventually, even village women saw the practical sense of breeches and began wearing them for farm work.)

From February 1916, those who had not previously worked on the land were entitled after thirty days' service to a green baize armband with a red crown.

WACs and district sub-committees had an outfit officer responsible for distributing clothes. Pictures of WNLSC members show smocked overalls with ties and flat-brimmed hats, with WNLSC on the hatband. They appear to have worn a brown canvas armband, with Women's National Land Service Corps embroidered in darker brown capitals.

Early WLA uniform consisted of a belted knee-length overall, breeches, leggings, boots, clogs and a soft-brimmed hat. (Unused to trousers, girls complained that the rough corduroy seams chafed their legs.) From August 1917 the uniform included a mackintosh, and from October, a jersey. Jewellery was discouraged.

A badge was issued after two months' service. Leaders wore green and red shoulder straps. Each section had its own embroidered cloth badge, worn on the left overall lapel, after two months' service.

The Women's Forestry Service had a wide-brimmed brown felt hat with a cloth badge depicting crossed axes and the letters WFS. Otherwise, those working in forestry are variously described with berets or green caps, and cloth sleeve badge of a spruce tree. It's not clear whether these relate to women working in forestry planting or those in timber cutting.

Recognition of Service

From February 1916, all women who started on the land and continued for at least 30 days or 240 hours were given a coloured certificate, embossed with the royal coat of arms.

A green armband with an embroidered crown was given after 30 days' or 240 hours' work and worn on the left sleeve. Every six months' work earned a stripe; four stripes were then exchanged for one diamond, sewn on the armband.

From mid-1918, Good Service Ribbons were issued for six months' satisfactory work and conduct. The WLA Distinguished Service Bar (DSB) was introduced in October 1918, for special deeds of good service and worn attached to the Land Army badge. There appear to have been fifty-five of these awarded. One recipient, Miss L M (Peggy) Fisher, married the cowman she had rescued from a bull.

Casualties

FPD records twelve WLA members as having died during or as a result of wartime service.

Researching First World War WLA

Although WLA numbers reached 23,000, unfortunately very few records of individual WLA service have survived.

The First World War campaign medals index (TNA DocumentsOnline) includes a few cards for WLA members who mistakenly applied for service medals. (The reverse of the original card, held by the IWM, should carry their address.) TNA series T has a few files of individual WLA members' claims. MAF 59/1 has a list of agricultural colleges training women; MAF 59/2 is a copy of the WLA handbook.

Lists of winners may be found in reports of WLA competitions held in many counties. Good Service Ribbon recipients are listed by county in *The Landswoman* (held at the IWM); WLA DSB recipients are also featured with photographs and brief details.

The IWM holds photographs, documents, some uniform items and first-person accounts relating to WFS, WNLSC and WLA service. WW&S includes reports of the work of the WNLSC and of county WWACs. County record offices and local heritage centres are worth investigating for WAC administrative records, WLA memorabilia and local newspaper reports.

Appendix 1

ARCHIVES AND WEBSITES

Archives

Adjutant General's Corps Museum (AGC)
The Guardroom, Peninsular Barracks,
Romsey Road, Winchester SO23 8TS
Tel: 01962 877826
Email: curator@agcmuseum.co.uk

Army Medical Services Museum (AMS)
Keogh Barracks, Ash Vale, Aldershot GU12 5RQ
Tel: 01252 868612
Email: armymedicalmuseum@btinternet.com
Website: www.ams-museum.org.uk

The British Library (BL)
96 Euston Road, London NW1 2DB
Reader enquiries St Pancras tel: 020 7412 7676
Reader Information Newspapers Colindale tel: 020 7412 7353
Reader services enquiries Boston Spa tel: 020 7412 7676
Email: reader-services-enquiries@bl.uk
Asian and African studies enquiries tel: 020 7412 7873
India Office family history website: indiafamily.bl.uk/UI/Home.aspx
Website: www.bl.uk

British Red Cross Museum and Archive
44 Moorfields, London EC2Y 9AL
Tel: 020 7877 7058
Email: enquiry@redcross.org.uk
Website: www.redcross.org.uk

Florence Nightingale Museum
2 Lambeth Palace Road, London SE1 7EW
Tel: 020 7620 0374
Email: info@florence-nightingale.co.uk
Website: www.florence-nightingale.co.uk

Imperial War Museum (IWM)
Lambeth Road, London SE1 6HZ
Tel: 020 7416 5000
Collections enquiry service tel: 020 7416 5342
Email: collections@iwm.org.uk
General enquiries email: mail@iwm.org.uk
Website: collections.iwm.org.uk

Library and Archives Canada
395 Wellington Street, Ottawa, ON K1A 0N4
Website: www.collectionscanada.gc.ca

The Liddle Collection
Special Collections, Leeds University Library,
Woodhouse Lane, Leeds LS2 9JT
Tel: 01133 435518
Email: specialcollections@library.leeds.ac.uk
Website: www.leeds.ac.uk/library/spcoll/liddle

London Metropolitan Archives (LMA)
40 Northampton Road,
Clerkenwell, London EC1R 0HB
Tel: 020 7332 3820
Email: ask.lma@cityoflondon.gov.uk
Website: www.cityoflondon.gov.uk/lma

National Army Museum (NAM)
Royal Hospital Road,
Chelsea, London SW3 4HT
Tel: 020 7730 0717
Email: info@nam.ac.uk
Website: www.nam.ac.uk/research

National Maritime Museum
Caird Library, Park Row,
Greenwich, London SE10 9NF
Tel: 020 8312 6516
Email: library@nmm.ac.uk; manuscripts@nmm.ac.uk
Website: www.nmm.ac.uk

QARNNS Archive
Institute of Naval Medicine Historic Library (INM)
Crescent Road, Alverstoke, Hampshire PO12 2DL
Captain J Massey, QARNNS Rtd

Royal Air Force Museum, London (RFM)
Grahame Park Way, London NW9 5LL
Dept of Research & Information Services, Hendon
Tel: 020 8358 4873
Email: research@rafmuseum.org
Website: www.rafmuseum.org.uk

Royal Naval Museum (RNM)
HM Naval Base (PP66), Portsmouth PO1 3NH
Tel: 023 9272 7562
Email: library@nmrn.org.uk
Website: www.royalnavalmuseum.org
Website: royalnavalmuseum.org/researchonline.htm

The National Archives (TNA)
Kew, Richmond TW9 4DU
Tel: 020 8876 3444
Website: www.nationalarchives.gov.uk

Wellcome Library (WLL)
183 Euston Road, London NW1 2BE
Tel: 020 7611 8722
Archives and manuscripts tel: 020 7611 8899
Email: arch+mss@wellcome.ac.uk
Library enquiries tel: 020 7611 8722
Email: library@wellcome.ac.uk
Website: library.wellcome.ac.uk

The Women's Library (TWL)
London Metropolitan University
25 Old Castle Street, London E1 7NT
Tel: 020 7320 2222
Reading room tel: 020 7320 3515/3516
Email: twlinfodesk@londonmet.ac.uk
Website: www.londonmet.ac.uk/thewomenslibrary

Useful Websites

Access to Archives (A2A)
www.nationalarchives.gov.uk/a2a

Ancestry.co.uk
www.ancestry.co.uk

British Journal of Medicine Archive (*BMJ*)
www.bmj.com/archive

Commonwealth War Graves Commission (CWGC), Debt of Honour register
www.cwgc.org/debt_of_honour.asp

Findmypast.co.uk
www.findmypast.co.uk

Flight Magazine (1909–2005), Flightglobal/Archive
www.flightglobal.com/pdfarchive

Hospital Records Database
www.nationalarchives.gov.uk/hospitalrecords

The *London Gazette* (*LG*)
www.london-gazette.co.uk/search

Royal College of Nursing online archives (*BJN*), historic nursing journals
rcnarchive.rcn.org.uk

Service Personnel and Veterans Agency
www.veterans-uk.info/service_records/service_records.html

Scarletfinders
www.scarletfinders.co.uk

Appendix 2

KEY TO ABBREVIATIONS

Archives and Websites

A2A	Access to Archives
AGC	Adjutant General's Corps Museum
AMS	Army Medical Services Museum
APAC	Asia, Pacific & Africa collections (BL)
BJN	British Journal of Nursing and predecessors, Nursing Record, etc., Royal College of Nursing
BL	British Library
BMJ	*British Medical Journal*
CWGC	Commonwealth War Graves Commission
IWM	Imperial War Museum
LG	*London Gazette*
LMA	London Metropolitan Archives
NAM	National Army Museum
RFM	RAF Museum, London
RNM	Royal Naval Museum
TNA	The National Archives
TWL	The Women's Library
WLL	The Wellcome Library
WW&S	*Women, War & Society 1914–1918*, Women's Work Collection (IWM)

Other Abbreviations

ANS(R)	Army Nursing Service (Reserve)
APD	Army Pay Department
AP(M)MC	Almeric Paget (Military) Massage Corps
APO	army pay office
AS	army schoolmistress(es)
ASC	Army Service Corps
AWOL	absent without leave
BEF	British Expeditionary Force
BRCS	British Red Cross Society
CCS	casualty clearing station(s)

CHR	Civil Hospital Reserve
CO	commanding officer
DGAMS	Director General Army Medical Service
DORA	Defence of the Realm Act
FANY	First Aid Nursing Yeomanry
FPD	*Femina Patriae Defensor*
GH	general hospital(s)
GS VAD	General Service Voluntary Aid Detachment (member)
IANS	Indian Army Nursing Service
IOR	India Office Records
(I)STM	(Incorporated) Society of Trained Masseuses
LAAS	Land Army Agricultural Section
LGH	London General Hospital
MiD	Mention in Despatches
MM	Military Medal
MO	medical officer
MoD	Ministry of Defence
MT	Motor Transport
NCO	non-commissioned officer
(PM)RAFNS	(Princess Mary's) Royal Air Force Nursing Service
QAIMNS(R)	Queen Alexandra's Imperial Military Nursing Service (Reserve)
QAMFNS	Queen Alexandra's Military Families Nursing Service
QAMNSI	Queen Alexandra's Military Nursing Service for India
QARNNS	Queen Alexandra's Royal Naval Nursing Service
QAS	Queen's Army Schoolmistress(es)
QMAAC	Queen Mary's Army Auxiliary Corps
QMG	Quarter Master General
RAF	Royal Air Force
RAMC	Royal Army Medical Corps
RASC	Royal Army Service Corps
RFC	Royal Flying Corps
RNAS	Royal Naval Air Service
RNNS	Royal Naval Nursing Service
RRC	Royal Red Cross
StJJ	St John of Jerusalem Ambulance Association
SARD	Scientific Aeronautical Research Depot
SH	stationary hospital(s)
SMP	Special Military Probationer
SNO	senior naval officer
SWB	Silver War Badge
TFNS	Territorial Force Nursing Service
VAD	Voluntary Aid Detachment (member)
WAAC	Women's Army Auxiliary Corps
WFC	Women's Forage Corps

WHC	Women's Hospital Corps
WI	Women's Institute
WL	Women's Legion
WLA	Women's Land Army
WMO	woman medical officer
WNLSC	Women's National Land Service Corps
WO	War Office
WRAF	Women's Royal Air Force
WRNS	Women's Royal Naval Service
YWCA	Young Women's Christian Association

INDEX